CARE OF PERSONS, CARE OF WORLDS

CARE of PERSONS, CARE of WORLDS

A Psychosystems Approach to
Pastoral Care and Counseling

LARRY KENT GRAHAM

ABINGDON / Nashville

CARE OF PERSONS, CARE OF WORLDS

Copyright © 1992 by Abingdon Press

93 94 95 96 97 98 99 00 01 02 03—10 9 8 7 6 5 4 3 2

This book is printed on acid-free, recycled paper.

Library of Congress Cataloging-in-Publication Data

Graham, Larry Kent.
  Care of persons, care of worlds: a psychosystems approach to pastoral care and counseling/Larry Kent Graham.
    p. cm.
  Included bibliographical references and indexes.
  ISBN 0-687-04675-0 (alk. paper)
  1. Pastoral counseling. 2. Pastoral theology. I. Title.
BV4012.2.G72   1992
253—dc20   92-5132

Cover art by Pablo Picasso. *Three Musicians*, 1921 (summer), Fontainbleau. Oil on canvas, 6' 7" x 7' 3¾" (200.7 x 222.9 cm). Collection, The Museum of Modern Art, New York. Mrs. Simon Guggenheim Fund. Photograph © 1992 The Museum of Modern Art, New York. Used by permission.

Scripture quotations noted NRSV are from the New Revised Standard Version of the Bible, copyright 1989 by the Division of Christian Education of the National Council of the Churches of Christ in the USA. Used by permission.

MANUFACTURED IN THE UNITED STATES OF AMERICA

To the Memory of My Parents,

LEON HOWARD GRAHAM
1915 – 1952

and

KATHLEEN ROBERTA SANDLIN GRAHAM
1917 – 1991

CONTENTS

Contents

PREFACE

This book ventures an approach to the ministry of care that attends simultaneously to the needs of persons and to the environmental realities that make persons what they are. It represents a combination of theoretical and practical considerations. It is based on Seward Hiltner's axiom that "a theory without a practice is irrelevant and a practice without a theory is noncorrectable."

The first part of the book develops a theoretical interpretation of the meaning of care in the context of multiple influences between individuals and their social, cultural, and natural environments. The second part of the book revisits and expands the earlier theoretical part, and applies it to specific situations of care. Both parts of the book combine theory and practice. Theory is more focal in Part I; practice, in Part II. Some readers may want to read from chapter 5 until the end of the book before reading chapters 1 through 3. Others will find it better to read from beginning to end at the outset.

I am deeply indebted to many people who have helped me during this project. The Iliff School of Theology granted me a year's sabbatical to do the initial research and preliminary writing. Dean Jane I. Smith has accommodated my requests for an ongoing reduction of regular duties in order to continue working after the leave ended. The Lilly Foundation provided a grant to study the congregation reported on in chapter 10. The Society of Pastoral Theology provided an occasion to present portions as a "work in progress" at one of its study conferences. The response was supportive and encouraging, even as it was sharply critical and challenging. Individual colleagues in the Society offered regular encouragement to continue.

Many persons allowed their personal situations to be reported in this writing. All pastoral situations are true, though the identities have been thoroughly disguised in this presentation. I deeply appreciate the consent these individuals gave to use their materials. But more, I appreciate the way their efforts to overcome their impairments have inspired me with their courage, and informed my understanding of the intricacies involved in the ministry of care.

I am grateful to many professional colleagues who read earlier sections of the manuscript. Professors Rodney J. Hunter, Carolyn Stahl Bohler, Carroll Saussy, and Delwin Brown provided especially insightful responses. Professors John Spangler and Wallace Clift, colleagues in the joint doctoral program in Religious and Psychological Studies at the University of Denver and Iliff School of Theology, provided ongoing support and incisive questions.

Cynthia Huffaker and Alice Stefaniak were research assistants in the later stage of preparation. Their efforts were essential for bringing the book to completion. Jeff Huber and Lucretia Fehrmann came to my aid at the very end and provided substantial help with the Glossary and Indexes. My secretary, Gene Crytzer, has not only memorized the present version, but all previous versions as well. I cannot thank him enough for his sustained effort and intelligent responsiveness to this project.

My editor at Abingdon Press is Ulrike Guthrie. She has encouraged me from the beginning and has ably combined a supportive attitude with firm guidance about how to make the book readable. She is superb at what she does and I have appreciated the opportunity to collaborate with her in this project.

Finally, I am fully aware that without the support of my family this book would still be a clutter of notes. My children, Renée, Megan, Peter, and Emily, kept me engaged with the "palpable immediacies" of living in spite of my efforts to spin away into professional Never-Never Land. My spouse and colleague, Sheila Greeve Davaney, helped me sustain my efforts during the times when I thought it fruitless to continue. Her precise suggestions on the portions of the manuscript I made available to her, in all cases made the book more valuable.

Had I listened better to all those whose suggestions I solicited, the book would have been better. Nonetheless, I am now happy to turn it over to the reader.

INTRODUCTION

We may indeed envision a world that is being recreated, a personalness that is being recreated, and in fact we may speak of participating in the creation of God.

Harry James Cargas[1]

The task of pastoral theology is to help us recover our heritage and to recover from it.

John Patton[2]

CARE OF PERSONS, CARE OF WORLDS

My college education and my foundational theological studies occurred in the 1960s. This period was filled with enormous intellectual and social ferment. Exciting new possibilities presented themselves for the church's ministry to the community on the one hand, and to persons in individual distress on the other. Clinical pastoral education was highly encouraged. Depth psychology was prestigious, and increasingly integrated into theological literature. New forms of social relationships and religious community were affirmed. The secular order was regarded as a primary arena of God's vitality and the source of transformative knowledge and experience. We seemed to be on the threshold of unprecedented personal freedoms and more radically humane social structures throughout the culture.

It was in this milieu that I decided to pursue doctoral studies in pastoral theology at Princeton Theological Seminary, beginning in 1970. I believed that in the Princeton context I could blend intellectual inquiry with a commitment to minister to suffering persons while simultaneously addressing unjust social structures. A great part of this agenda was indeed fulfilled during this period. I was sensitized to the issues of sexism, racism, and militarism, and worked with others toward social transformation. Receiving psychotherapeutic training from persons based in family systems perspectives aided in expanding my individualistically oriented

11

pastoral care skills. An introduction to process theology provided more adequate theological foundations for linking personal and social care. Learning a pastoral theological method of relating diverse perspectives and experiences from the standpoint of care ensured necessary conceptual tools to fulfill my commitments.

However, as the seventies and eighties progressed, I experienced a widening split between care of persons and care of the larger environments in which persons live. The field of pastoral care and counseling and the psychotherapeutic models upon which it was based, took an increasing turn toward individual fulfillment and other primary interpersonal relationships. I began to realize that I was mistaken to think that pastoral care in the sixties and earlier was oriented to social change as well as to personal healing. In pastoral care and counseling circles, there was little or no attention paid to addressing larger social and political issues. Social critique was minimal in the literature and practice of pastoral care and counseling. Instead, there seemed to be a headlong rush for social acceptance as qualified health care professionals. In spite of a few writings from professors and others in the field, matters of theology, ethics, and social change were seriously marginalized by clinical specialists in pastoral care and counseling.

Simultaneously, however, among theological educators I experienced an escalating assault on the rampant individualism and privatism of our culture. Psychotherapy and pastoral care approaches that focused upon the health and growth of individuals were often criticized for contributing to this individualism and privatism. Some social ethicists and theological educators challenged the notion of "profession" in relation to ministry and the specialized task of pastoral care and counseling. The CPE model of education came to be viewed as increasingly nonintellectual and nontheological, and almost exclusively oriented to subjective and interpersonal dimensions of experience. Chaplains and pastoral counselors appeared to be increasingly out of touch with current cultural and theoretical issues emerging in theological education. Consequently, the psychological paradigm was diminishing in stature in many theological and ecclesiastical circles.

I found myself uncomfortable with this unnecessary polarization, and I rekindled my original concern to find a coherent theory and viable practice to synthesize individual healing with a fuller engagement with the world. Particularly in my clinical work and my teaching of pastoral care in a seminary setting, I found that the increase of sexual and domestic violence among parishioners required a rethinking of our models. To care for persons in situations like these compelled me to address more fully the culture of violence in the structures of our society, which I realized were defining it. It became clear that the psyches of these injured and injuring persons were inextricably linked to the violent cultural patterns of our society. To respond to one required attention to the other.

Upon further reflection, I have found that *all* pastoral situations involve a bewildering set of interconnections between the psyches of persons and the larger forces influencing them. Paul's view that we "are not contending against flesh and blood, but against principalities and powers" has taken on a new depth of meaning for me. Certainly the "forces" against which we are arrayed are carried by human beings, embodied in flesh and blood form. But at the same time it has become clear that they are larger than individual persons and have cultural, ideological, and systemic dimensions, which powerfully shape concrete persons and their options. These larger forces that contribute to the construction of the human personality and its development are not all benign, and they are not easily negated. To treat the individual in isolation from these forces is often to throw a straw into the wind. These very forces need challenge and modification along with the changes necessary in individual persons.

I was not able to find a single theory that helped me transcend the polarities between care of persons and response to the larger social order. Gradually, I began to see the outline of a new theoretical framework, which I subsequently labeled, "psychosystemic." The term, "psychosystemic," refers to the reciprocal interplay between the psyche of individuals and the social, cultural, and natural orders. This interplay is not neutral or static; it is value-laden and teeming with possibilities. The character of persons and their worlds come into being by the mutual influences of each upon the other.

The concept of psychosystems orients pastoral caretakers in particular ways to our past concern for individual healing and offers a promising way of conceiving our future relationship to the multiple environments influencing care. Psychosystemic theory enables us to position the ministry of care more prominently among larger social and political interpretations of the pastoral situation, without losing focus of the healing, sustaining, and guiding needed by individuals, groups, and families. It joins microsystemic with macrosystemic arenas of experience. It attempts to resolve, both conceptually and practically, the ongoing tension between concern for individual psyches and the increasing awareness of the ecological or systemic connection between all living things.

The basic thesis of this book is that to care for persons is to create new worlds; to care for the world is to build a new personhood. The destiny of persons and the character of the world are intertwined. Each is made poorer or richer by the quality of the other and of the forces uniting or dividing them. Thus, the call to care for persons is simultaneously a call to care for the world. A psychosystems approach provides theoretical and practical assistance for persons in the pastoral helping role to understand more fully the character of these forces contending within and for the psyches of persons. And even more, once understanding them, it will help pastoral caretakers and the caretaking community find ways to interrupt, oppose, and channel them toward constructive and transforming ends.

The orientation of this book to the ministry of care sharply distinguishes itself from the current dominant mode of pastoral care and counseling. The current model draws almost exclusively upon a variety of individualistic psychological theories and existentialist-based theologies and philosophies. In theological circles, it is most closely ordered by anthropological considerations. I think of it as an existentialist-anthropological model of care. This model focuses upon intrapsychic dynamics, with autonomy and self-realization as its primary goals. It is assumed that persons and their primary groups may go about the task of fashioning fulfilling lives largely in spite of "external" realities such as culture, society, and nature. These realities are only secondarily regarded as arenas of ethical responsibility requiring strategic intervention and change if care is to be possible for individuals and their families in the first place.

This book proffers a more comprehensive theory of care. It is based in process theology, liberation and feminist theology, family systems thought, and the interactional dimensions of personality theory. Attention to individual personhood is set within a larger theoretical framework, which allows us to stay focused upon the personal and the interpersonal arenas of life while simultaneously connecting to the macrosystemic network. Alongside the theoretical framework are diagnostic criteria and practical guidelines for implementing a ministry of care in concrete situations.

AN ARTISTIC ILLUSTRATION

To begin to grasp the way a psychosystemic orientation perceives the world, in contrast to the dominant individualistic orientations, an artistic illustration may be useful. These distinctions become evident by comparing Albrecht Dürer's *The Knight, Death and the Devil*, with Pablo Picasso's *Three Musicians*.[3] In Dürer's ink drawing the knight is the central figure, and indeed the only human figure in the scene. Accompanied by his horse and his dog, he is riding alone through a forest peopled with gargoyles, devils, and demons. His horse's ears are laid back in fright, and his dog is obviously aware of the surrounding danger: both the animals are eager to be in safer territory. By contrast, the knight is outfitted with protective armor, and seems self-reliant and confident. In the distance, on top of a small mountain, is a beautiful castle. The obvious destination, it represents a heavenly city as well as earthly safety. This Christian "knight of faith" is concentrating on reaching his goal; though his journey is perilous, if he is strong and determined he can assume that he will finally arrive uninjured.

The world is seen as a dangerous place that must be overcome personally with God's help. It must not be observed too closely, or one may be swept away by its destructive powers. The knight travels without human companionship, but is reliant upon himself and God. Insofar as nature plays a beneficent role, it is to provide him animals for protection and companionship. The whole scene depicts enormous tensions and conflicts surrounding and underlying the knight's journey. But, in contrast to his animals who are more attuned to the rhythms of the universe, he seems to be unaware of and unaffected by them. He is clearly in the world, but neither of nor for it. The world is merely a means to an end; he transcends its powers and dynamics on the way to the fulfillment of his own personal destiny. Even more important, Dürer depicts the world itself as a dangerous, uninhabitable place. There is little beauty here, either of culture or nature. There is nothing that would encourage the knight to pause and stay awhile. The world is alien, threatening, external, and incidental to his goals. He is on his way to a better place, confident of his powers to get himself there.

Picasso's *Three Musicians* gives a substantially different view of the human-world relationship. In this picture, three males are simply sitting in a room playing their instruments. However, Picasso paints the picture in such a way that the environment has a dynamic influence upon the picture and the very character of the musicians themselves. The figures of the musicians and of their instruments are distorted and dislocated. Their limbs and lines blend with one another, and with the furniture, walls, and windows of the room. The viewer is struck by the degree of fragmentation and disruption in the picture. This fragmentation and disruption includes both the persons and the environment, and upon closer inspection it becomes clear how intertwined are the environment and persons. In the midst of this disarray, it is also clear that there is considerable harmony. The musicians are together, and they are playing music in spite of their participation in a broken, interconnected world. They are not alone, and they are not without the power or means to accomplish at least some measure of what they value. They are a part of the environment, integrated into its brokenness, but also contributing to its beauty. The broken, fragmented, and distorted environment is also necessary for the musicians to have a central place in the picture. The environment is more than a backdrop or setting to be together playing music. Picasso paints it in such a way that it plays a dominant role in determining their bodily features and relationships to one another.

Picasso captures the systemic relationship between persons and their worlds to a greater degree than Dürer. For Picasso, the persons and environments mutually comprise one another, and only relatively transcend each other. For Dürer, person and world are juxtaposed, having little, if any, internal relationship to one another. Such possible relationships existing between the person and world are negative for Dürer. For Picasso, they are both positive and negative. For Dürer, the knight can exist without the natural world, and is on his way to doing so. For Picasso, persons and environment have no reality without one another, and constitute one another's very being. Dürer's person is without human companionship, moving on alone; Picasso's persons are thoroughly social, staying put and making music together. Dürer's knight makes no contribution to improving this world; he takes what he needs from it as he moves on toward his goal. Picasso's musicians are making their contributions now, blending their harmony to benefit a fragmented, but beautiful world.

A systems view of life underscores the internal relationship between the person and the world. It is the world which has fallen into sin and brokenness, but which is redeemed and in the process of being transformed by God—not cast off or left behind. The mandate to increase the love of God, self, and neighbor, and to promote justice and responsible ecology has consequences for the world as well as for persons. Understanding the interlocking relationship between our brokenness and the brokenness of the world we inhabit may help us come together to make and create beauty in the midst of, and in place of, brokenness. Such is the vision, at least, of a psychosystemic understanding of persons, the world, and their mutual care.

THE NETWORK OF VIOLENCE AND
THE MINISTRY OF CARE

Generally, it is not enough to say that all things are connected for good or ill. It is important to specify how they are connected and how (and why) those connections might be modified by the ministry of care. This book maps and explores many of the connections within and between persons and their primary relationships. However, in all respects, this book will also examine how these microcosmic dynamics are influenced by larger realities. A major theme of this book is that the network of care at the microcosmic level is rendered necessary and organizes itself largely in response to a massive network of oppression and violence at the macrocosmic level. Further, it is assumed that these levels are intimately related, and reinforce one another.

In recent years, sociologists, feminists, and liberation thinkers, along with a host of others,[4] have made it abundantly clear that our personal identities and our social fabric are fundamentally ordered by a variety of oppressive social systems. Whether we are aware of it or not, these systems organize our psyches and our behaviors into patterns of domination and subordination. These systems are pervasive, and mightily influence the definition and practice of care. Pastoral care and counseling often cannot directly affect the larger economic and historic forces giving rise to and sustaining oppressive social orders. But it has become unthinkable that pastoral care and counseling can proceed in its self-understanding without a grasp of the horrible ubiquity and devastating consequences of such patterns as they appear in our ministries.[5]

Dominance refers to the unjust power and value arrangements whereby one or more persons or groups subordinate other persons and groups for the advantage of the dominant group. The unjust differential of power is assumed to be "the way things are meant to be," and persons deviating from or challenging the pattern are regarded as criminal, ill, or immoral. There are many types of dominant-subordinate arrangements. Some are more unjust and more oppressive than others. The dominance-subordination paradigm is apparent in the school-yard pecking order as well as in genocidal policies of nations and races. Most hierarchies are erected on it. Racism and sexism assume it. Relationships among nations and cultures, complicated by racial, gender, and economic factors, are predominantly guided by this paradigm. Aggression and violence, which are normally derived from the dynamics of maintaining or ameliorating one or more systemic structures of domination-subordination, impregnate all dimensions of our careseeking and caregiving.

To be sure, some of the models of personality undergirding pastoral practice have recognized the capacity for aggression at the center of the individual personality. In pastoral care circles we have discovered that our capacity for destructive aggression and violence might even be incorporated positively into our personal and interpersonal relationships. However, we have largely failed to recognize the systemic character of violence in its social and cultural structure of domination and subordination. And, even for pastoral caretakers who have been sensitized to these matters, it has been assumed that it is not necessarily our role to respond as caretakers. We have either assumed that it is our role to strengthen careseekers to deal with these matters according to

17

their own needs or value systems, or we have delegated the task to those taking up the church's social dimensions of ministry.

In contrast, this book embraces the assumption that social and cultural realities are not merely out there, but are in every setting where pastoral careseeking and caregiving take place.[6] It is the caretaker's role to understand this, and to respond accordingly in keeping with the dynamics of the situation. To assist this ministry, the internalized and institutionalized culture of violence will be addressed explicitly throughout the book.[7] Its recognition calls for new categories of analysis, new definitions of ministry, and new theories of the person. It will result in alternate modes of intervention, and a modified language of care. Specifically, it will require a language of care that makes the concepts of power, values, and justice central in our thinking and practice. It will require that feminist and liberation social ethics be allowed greater shaping power in the ministry of care.

BLENDING PASTORAL AND PROPHETIC PERSPECTIVES

In the contemporary North American context, there has been a strong tendency to contrast ministry to individuals with efforts toward social change. Pastoral care and counseling has been assigned the former task; social ethicists and peace and justice programs have been responsible for the latter. One is regarded as pastoral ministry, the other as prophetic. In spite of attempts to modify this false dichotomy, it has persisted and increased.[8] Robert Bellah's work underscores how pastoral counseling, along with the psychotherapeutic industry of which it is a part, has contributed to a diminution of social solidarity and responsibility for the quality of the world we inhabit.[9] The unrestrained philosophy of expressive individualism undergirding the human services industry erodes the theoretical and functional level considerations of an organic connection between personal welfare and public order. The pastoral and the prophetic are fractured into competing claims.

Rethinking pastoral care and counseling along psychosystemic lines both reflects and requires a new constructive relationship between prophetic perspectives and the orientation of contemporary pastoral care. The prophets of ancient Israel provide the model for my thinking. The basic principle that seems to guide their work is that God is present in all historical circumstances. The task of the prophet was to assist God's people to discern God's will for a particular situation, rather than to apply universal principles to the reality at hand. The prophets spoke out of competing theological traditions, and were highly contextual. They were crisis-responsive, and identified themselves with the plight of the nation.

The prophets did not separate the personal from the public. They saw the organic interconnection between the individual and the community. For them, the political and the cultic were joined, and there was no fundamental distinction between the secular and the religious.[10] Their comprehensive vision is epitomized in Micah's concern for a righteousness that combines justice, mercy, and humility in fellowship with God and others (Micah 6:8).[11] As a partial corrective to the individualism of our culture and to the dominance of the existential-anthropological paradigm in pastoral care, this book incorporates neglected resources from the prophets into a specifically pastoral mode of functioning.

There are several interlocking elements characterizing a pastoral perspective.[12] It is person-sensitive and life-span inclusive, empathically focusing upon the dynamics of actual human beings, as invited or welcomed, in all of life's vicissitudes. It is primarily addressed to the subjective and intersubjective spheres of living, proceeding from the particular to the general and from the emotional to the conceptual. It is situation-specific and symptom-responsive, discovering in crises hidden possibilities for growth and transformation. It embraces ambiguity and stands beside victims and perpetrators of evil, as well as by the birth pangs of beauty (recognizing that sometimes these are taking place simultaneously in the same events). It is ethically-oriented and accountability-focused, requiring careseekers to recognize their own contributions to their difficulties and to take appropriate responsibility for the moral consequences of their choices and actions. It is faith-informed and spiritually acute: it asks for God and seeks to discover and enhance the operational belief systems contributing to or ameliorating the distress for which care is sought. It is ministry-grounded and theologically-creative, arising from and on behalf of an identifiable religious community and leading to revised theological understandings. In addition, it is pluralistic and interdisciplinary, welcoming partnership with cognate secular and religious orientations.

When these prophetic and pastoral perspectives are combined, they lead to a revised definition of the ministry of care, and to principles and methodologies to guide it. Care is understood as a subjective and strategic participation in the dynamics within persons and between persons and their world. The nature of the human personality is understood in contextual rather than individualistic terms. Change is extended to include modifying or enhancing the environment as well as tending to the motivational energies and adaptive capacities of the individuals seeking assistance. Diagnostic categories skew toward an interpretation of the situation itself, rather than locating what is wrong "in" the symptomatic players. In addition to empathic, subjective, and intersubjective considerations, intersocial and intersystemic modes of relatedness are identified and developed. Pastoral care becomes characterized by interpathy, or "the intentional cognitive and affective envisioning of another's thoughts and feelings from another culture, world view, epistemology . . . the embracing of the truly other."[13] The classic pastoral care tasks of healing, sustaining, guiding, and reconciling are expanded to include prophetic efforts toward emancipatory liberation, justice-seeking, public advocacy, and ecological partnership.[14] In the model I propose, these dimensions are interconnected conceptually and organically, rather than added linearly or sequentially to a list of tasks.

EXPANDING PASTORAL THEOLOGY

This book is an enterprise of pastoral theology. Pastoral theology is the branch of theology which develops theoretical understandings of and practical guidelines for the ministry of care.[15] Broadly speaking, pastoral theology attempts strategically to relate specific acts of pastoral caretaking to selected aspects of the religious heritage in which the caretaking occurs and to relevant secular theories about the nature and care of persons. The desired outcome of this activity is the creation of new interpretations of the religious heritage, new understandings of human persons, and a clearer grasp of what is required for effective ministry to careseekers. This book corrects the individualistic bias in pastoral theology. It brings the theory and practice of care more fully into relationship with the larger systemic realities impacting the psyches of those providing and receiving care.[16]

There are five major sources of knowledge and experience which I have found essential for the pastoral theological task of creating a psychosystemic theory and developing guidelines for the ministry of care. The first is the actual practice of the ministry of care, especially with victims and perpetrators of sexual and domestic violence. Not only has this been an occasion to become intimately related to a number of complex and fascinating persons, it has also been an occasion to witness directly some of the horrors of evil and human sin, as well as the grandeur of human resiliency and divine generosity. Nearly everything that I hold dear has been challenged, negated, opposed, discovered, and reconstructed in the crucible of ministry to these suffering persons. It was largely in the context of this practice that I realized that I had to expand my theoretical understandings and functional interventions to attend to the interplay between the individual and her or his larger world.

The second source of knowledge necessary for the pastoral theological enterprise is the social and cultural context in which the act of ministry occurs. Nancy Chodorow's *The Reproduction of Mothering* and Joanna

Rogers Macy's *Despair and Personal Power in the Nuclear Age* have made major contributions to my understanding of how our internal lives are structured and limited by the culture in which we live.[17] Feminist theory and therapy clarify how the definitions of illness, norms of health, and methods of healing dominant in therapeutic practice (and mostly taken over wholesale by the pastoral caretaking movement) basically reflect and maintain an oppressive patriarchal culture.

The third resource for pastoral theological work is the living religious tradition contextualizing the ministry of care. There are two interlocking religious dimensions. First, there are formal traditions, embodied in scripture, dogma, doctrine, apology, and critically constructive contemporary theological and ethical analyses. Second, there are operational traditions, embodied in the belief systems, liturgical practices, moral codes, and views of ministry of those seeking and offering care. Pastoral care tends to focus upon the latter; pastoral theology tends to focus upon the interplay between them, and to make conceptual advances in the formal tradition.

Exploring the psychological and behavioral consequences of belief systems in the ministry of care allows pastoral caretakers and theologians to rediscover the power of the tradition, as well as to gain a view of its limitations or irrelevancies. As a result, the pastoral theologian is positioned to re-engage the heritage and reformulate it in the light of the contextual engagement in the ministry of care. Accordingly, the pastoral caretaker is better able to employ religious resources in confronting and changing the painful circumstances of the careseeker. John Patton's statement at the beginning of this Introduction, that pastoral theology is the means by which we recover our heritage and recover from its misuse or misunderstanding, underscores this approach.

In the light of my ministry to sufferers, I have found process theology and liberation theology to be crucial for reinterpreting pastoral theology along prophetic and psychosystemic lines. These orientations have enabled me to recover central elements of my religious heritage, and to recover from some of the negative consequences of a one-sided, individualistic approach.

Process theology provides a much-needed contemporary ontological foundation for pastoral theology and care. It renders meaningful the contention that all things are dynamic and relational. It affirms that the universe is not indifferent to human welfare and that differences between individuals and groups may become the occasion for cooperation and mutual enrichment, rather than necessarily lead to violence and brokenness. It grounds the belief that God is meaningfully related to the world as a whole and to every part comprising it, and that our efforts, or lack thereof, always make a difference, however small. Process theology has provided the foundation for rethinking sin and evil, and for understanding how these are, in fact, neither the will of God nor preventable by God. These insights have enabled me to help suffering persons to interpret and more fully grieve their real losses without making God somehow responsible for them.

In liberation theology I have found an unsettling challenge to individual fulfillment models of theology and ministry, and to the character of much North American church life and theological endeavor. Liberation theology has helped me reaffirm my Protestant conviction that all theology and ministry are to be under the perpetual judgment of the gospel, and that the church is always in reformation and renewal. Specifically, liberation theology requires all theologies, including practical and pastoral theology, to look critically at how their methodologies and conclusions overtly and covertly function to keep persons in untenable personal and social arrangements. Further, liberation theology requires that all communal and institutional expressions of religious life be examined in terms of those who have social and economic power and those who do not.

Liberation theologies have made it easier to see how the theological orientations, personality theories, and psychotherapeutic techniques most directly incorporated into the ministry of care serve to maintain unjust power differentials, and to keep from awareness crucial social and ideological orientations which in themselves promote the suffering we are seeking to ameliorate. Just as family systems therapy has taught us that the presenting issue usually reflects as well as masks serious dysfunction somewhere else in the larger family social system, so also liberation theology is helping us to understand that dysfunctional persons, families, and groups are both reflecting and masking serious dysfunction elsewhere in our social and cultural milieu. These perspectives are essential, I believe, for recovering from individualist models of pastoral theology. They are necessary for the process of recovering and recreating from our neglected religious heritage a pastoral theology that is responsive to the social requirements of ministry.

The fourth source of knowledge for pastoral theology is any "cognate secular knowledge" judged to be relevant for developing appropriate theory and guiding effective practice of caretaking. Normally the cognate secular knowledge judged most appropriate has been the behavioral sciences in general, and personality theory and the psychotherapeutic sciences, in particular. I still draw heavily upon psychodynamic personality theories and object-relations thought in this book. However, it has become clear to me, as indicated above, that these personality theories and the dominant psychotherapeutic theories derived from them are themselves perpetrators and regulators of cultural orientations that limit the fullest development of persons, and neglect important social and ethical dimensions of ministry.[18] Thus, family systems thought and some feminist therapy practices provide important correctives, and are more compatible with my definition of ministry and the theological resources informing it.

The fifth source of knowledge is the personhood of the caretaker and pastoral theologian. Pastoral theology is a lived enterprise as much as an intellectual and academic discipline. Since the pastoral caretaker and theologian is a person who is systemically related to other realities, his or her personality is a central resource for creating new theory and practice for ministry from the interplay of forces operative in the ministry of care. Thus the religious, psychological, social, and cultural heritages of the pastoral theologian play significant roles in the pastoral theological enterprise. In the final analysis, pastoral theology, like all theology, probably reveals more about the beliefs and experiences of the theologian (as these are informed by personality, culture, and experience) than about reality, God, and those groups being spoken about.

But how will these resources for pastoral ministry be related to one another? Which is more important? How does one proceed to connect them, and to critically evaluate their differences? There are many answers to these questions. In my view, praxis drives theory. The practice of the ministry of care must be central in formulating the nature of the problem to be treated, in ordering the resources drawn upon to treat the problem, and in evaluating the nature of the conclusions reached. Like the prophets of ancient Israel and contemporary liberation theologies, pastoral theology arises from and is directed to an analysis of the particular sufferings of particular persons in a particular context.[19] And while it may help us recover from our inheritance from the past, pastoral theology does not merely apply universal religious principles or yesterday's revelation to the situation at hand. At the same time that it critically reappropriates the past, it also boldly constructs new configurations of religious meaning arising from the contemporary crucible of care to suffering persons.

To summarize, pastoral theology is defined as a subsystem within theology in general, and practical theology in particular. Its task is to develop theory and practice for the ministry of care. It draws the resources for its creative work from the setting and acts of ministry, the living tradition, cognate secular knowledge, and the personhood of the one carrying out the act of ministry. Methodologically, these resources are ordered by praxis. This book argues that pastoral theology must expand its theoretical foundations and practical responses in the light of more contextual and systemic resources. Family systems and feminist perspectives from the field of psychology, and process and liberation perspectives from the field of theology, are the major resources drawn upon to delineate the psychosystemic nature of persons and their care. Finally, pastoral theology, like practical theology, contributes not only to the formulation of theory and practice relevant to the ministry of care, but also recovers, corrects, and expands viewpoints in other branches of theology and ministry.

THE PLAN OF THE BOOK

The first four chapters lay out the theoretical foundations of the book. These are amply illustrated by references to the ministry of care. The remaining six chapters expand the central concepts and apply them diagnostically and strategically to specific pastoral situations.

Chapters 1 and 2 describe the view of ministry and care underlying the psychosystemic approach, and introduce the major concepts organizing the remainder of the discussion. A comprehensive psychosystems map is presented in chapter 2. Chapter 3 revisits the concept of the person from a psychosystemic perspective. Chapter 4 theorizes about symptoms and change, and outlines diagnostic criteria. The concepts of strategic love and redemptive justice anchor the discussion of symptoms, diagnosis, and change.

Chapters 5 through 10 connect the psychosystemic concepts to actual pastoral situations. Chapter 5 discusses transactional impasses leading to the need for care. Chapter 6 focuses upon power dynamics, while chapter 7 examines the relation of values to care. Chapter 8 links care to contextual creativity, particularly to liberation from oppression. Chapter 9 links the concept of contextual organization to diagnosis and change. The last chapter draws all of the concepts together through an extended study of care of a congregation recovering from the trauma of its minister's sexual abuse of female parishioners.

The ideas upon which this book is built derive from many sources, as I indicated in the previous section. It is not possible to develop and apply the theory at the same time that I build strong critical support for it. The methodological and critical groundwork will appear mostly in footnotes, or will be omitted altogether. To do otherwise would make the book unreadable, as I have learned from previous drafts. I have therefore assumed the risk of drawing upon a variety of sources and ordering them for my purposes, without always demonstrating critical control of these sources. In all cases, I have consulted with biblical, theological, ethical, medical, and psychotherapeutic authorities to validate my use of materials from these fields. Further, I have provided rather thorough suggestions for additional reading.

I have decided to base the case discussion upon ministry in the sexual arena in general, and with survivors and perpetrators of sexual and domestic violence in particular. Although other examples of ministry situations will be drawn upon, issues of gender, violence, abuse, and sexual orientation have been central in my ministry and teaching for nearly a decade, and have largely influenced the direction of my thinking. It is also clear that these types of cases are calling for more attention from all levels of ministry, and for a greater response from across the theological curriculum and the life of the church. Certainly, a psychosystemic approach is not limited to these kinds of cases, but potentially illumines any type of pastoral care situation, as I shall demonstrate throughout the book.

The case material is presented in three ways. Sometimes related aspects of a case are drawn upon to illustrate a specific concept or intervention. Sometimes a fuller description of the case is given in one place to demonstrate how change may or may not occur. At other times, a case is carried over many chapters to gain a comprehensive overview of how the theory and intervention strategies work together cumulatively. All the elements of the theory and intervention come together in the pastoral situation described in chapter 10. While it has not been possible to provide a discussion of all the pertinent issues in every case presented, taken as a whole, the book illustrates how a psychosystemic approach addresses issues of love, justice, and ecological partnership in responding to suffering persons and destructive situations.

PART I
THEORETICAL FOUNDATIONS

CHAPTER 1

TRANSFORMING CARE: LINKING PSYCHES AND SYSTEMS

*The I is real in virtue of its sharing in
reality. The fuller its sharing the
more real it becomes.*

Martin Buber[1]

FROM PSYCHE TO SYSTEM

This book challenges the reader to visualize ministry to individuals through longer lenses, which bring into focus the impact of society, culture, and nature upon the caretaking enterprise. The challenge to move from psyche to society, without losing either, is neither simple nor direct. It is difficult to let go of old models and to find viable new ones. Yet it is often surprising and exhilarating.

My experience of discovering the challenge of a psychosystems approach and its enormous dimensions can be illustrated by my recent experience of reading an article about a sailboat crossing of the Pacific Ocean. To follow the text, I opened an atlas to find a map of the Pacific Ocean. To my surprise and astonishment, I discovered a spectacular map of the *floor* of the Pacific Ocean! This map revealed a complex of previously unrecognized geographical structures and relationships that have a significant influence upon water conditions, marine life, surface geography, and the like. I was fascinated by the beauty and power of this schematic drawing, and found the ocean to be at once more challenging and complex than I had previously supposed. My pleasure of reading the account of the crossing was greatly enhanced by simultaneously attending to the underlying trenches, ridges, fractures, zones, and shelves that stood in hidden but powerful relationships to the currents, the weather, the moon and stars, the boat, and the experiences of the human beings who were steering toward their goal.

Likewise, my experience of overcoming an individual bias in providing pastoral care and counseling has not proved to be as straightforward as I had originally supposed. My background as a North American white

29

male, along with much of my education and training, led me to believe that the environment was basically objective and subject to manipulation. What we made of it had more to do with our own resources and imagination than with its energies and influences. After all, I was taught that the self is transcendent over history and nature, and is more or less free to find its home in God and in its own power for actualization.[2] Growth, healing, and development were not regarded as easy tasks or assumed accomplishments, but they were largely understood to be individual achievements relatively independent of, and sometimes in spite of, our social and natural environments. It has been both sobering and exhilarating to discover how irrevocably the conditions for self-fulfillment are linked to the often unrecognized configurations of our environments. Moving into this viewpoint has been like an ocean crossing for me and, once on the other side, I still marvel at how complex it all is, and how much there is yet to discover.

The complexity of the interplay between the individual psyche and the various worlds of the person is well illustrated in a verbatim presented by a member of a class on lay caregiving that I conducted in a local congregation. A person, whom I shall call Jean, volunteered to work in a women's shelter. She shared a conversation with a woman, whom I shall call Patricia, who was a survivor of physical battering by her husband. Patricia said that she had first gone to her minister for help. He reportedly told her that if she prayed harder and tried to be a more patient and understanding wife, the husband would probably stop beating her. Patricia reported to Jean that she had followed this advice, but that the beatings had continued. She decided to leave when her husband threatened to beat their three-year-old son. Patricia asked Jean, "Was I wrong to leave my husband? Is God angry at me for this? I don't know what to do or think, but I just know that I could not let Frank beat up on Freddie."

It was obvious that Patricia was in deep conflict about this dilemma, and was asking for religious guidance about how to handle it. Jean reassured her that she had shown love for her son to protect him from injury, and that it was not her fault that her husband beat her. Jean remarked that though God's love expressed itself in forgiveness, it did not condone such acts of violence. Jean said, "I do not believe that God is angry at you for leaving." From the verbatim, it was clear that Patricia was relieved to hear this interpretation, but was not yet ready to internalize and work with it. Jean informed us that Patricia soon went back to her husband and that the cycle of violence continued.

The members of the class were very angry with Patricia for going back to Frank. They thought she did not really want to change her situation or she would not put herself at risk. They considered that her faith in God was not very strong if she could not trust God to help her move on. A few members of the class felt that the suffering would strengthen her faith and make her a better Christian, and perhaps even be a Christlike witness to her husband and son. They agreed that she should have removed herself from immediate danger, but also that she should not leave him or try to retaliate for his violence. Nearly all members of the class wondered if Patricia wasn't somehow egging on her husband and deserved his attacks.

What struck me about the discussion was how focused they were upon Patricia! It was as though she were totally responsible for what had happened and how to deal with it. They did not recognize Frank's responsibility for the violence. There was little awareness that Patricia, Frank, Freddie, and Jean are entangled in a web of dynamic interrelationships, many of which are hidden from view, but all of which make their lives extremely difficult. Guidelines for responding are conflicting; the pastor seems to reinforce attitudes that contribute to her victimization, while Jean wants to release her to more autonomy. Patricia seemed unable to act on her own behalf, but was acting to protect her son from injury. Focusing upon Patricia alone grossly oversimplified the realities of the situation, and, paradoxically, put her and her son at greater risk, while leaving her husband unaccountable.

There are many more levels to this crisis than simply Patricia's motivations and behaviors. They all contribute to maintaining the crisis, with some offering a way forward. Psychologically, members of the family are depressed, angry, frightened, and trapped. The developmental tasks of each family member are arrested or impeded. The marriage and family structures are in serious trouble and need focused therapeutic attention. Sociologically, we might infer that Frank feels burdened with the responsibility of being an economic success, or otherwise to be more competent than he currently is as a male. He may want to control Patricia and keep her in line. Patricia probably remains financially dependent upon him for lack of marketable skills. She may fear injury or death if she leaves him. Theologically, for Patricia at least, there is a crisis of moral values and religious belief systems about God, love, justice, forgiveness and reconciliation, and marriage and divorce. This crisis reflects cultural attitudes concerning the acceptability of violence in human relationships, and reflects the dominant-subordinate character of the power arrangements between males and females, and parents and children in our society. There are crucial legal and medical dimensions involved. Frank is committing a crime and faces prosecution.

All of these interacting systemic elements are not mere abstractions. They constitute virulent forces contributing to deep suffering on the part of very real human beings. These forces come together in the psyches of Patricia, Frank, Freddie, Jean, and Patricia's minister. They clash together, creating a psychological and systemic vortex of incredible complexity and power. Tending to them with awareness and skill becomes a central pastoral challenge. They cannot be minimized, bracketed, or excluded from concern, since they themselves directly contribute to the nature of the pastoral situation. In this case, those providing assistance were in disagreement with one another, and there was little if any systemic awareness of the problem. The prevailing winds determined the course of events, and this family headed farther into dangerous waters. Jean and the women's shelter did their best to modify the conditions that kept the family at risk, but these conditions were too powerful, and not malleable under the circumstances. As far as we know, Patricia struggled unsuccessfully against multiple pressures and remains in a vulnerable position. Frank continued to avoid genuine responsibility for his violence.[3]

Difficult situations like Patricia's and her family's call for a broader interpretation of the person-world relationship than those operating in the dominant culture of care. They require a broader understanding of the role of the caretaker and the caretaking community in the lives of persons, and in relation to the legal, social, and economic order. To move from psyche to system requires a capacity to evaluate our extant models and practices of care, and to become more visible in the public domain than our recent history has encouraged.

THE EXISTENTIAL-ANTHROPOLOGICAL MODEL OF CARE

To be more precise about the uniqueness of a psychosystemic approach to the ministry of care, it is useful to compare its differences and to identify its continuities with the dominant orientation toward caretaking in the North American context.

The existentialist-anthropological model puts the health and fulfillment of individual persons on center stage. It is essentially individualistic. There is an emphasis on helping individuals identify what they think and feel, and to encourage them to behave more autonomously according to their heightened awareness of their own needs and aspirations. The concepts of self-realization, fulfillment, and growth provide the organizing center and the desired outcomes of this type of pastoral care. Its ethical underpinnings are expressive individualism, or individual egoism, which understand good and evil in terms of the degree to which something enhances or impedes the needs of the self.[4]

I have called this an existential-anthropological model because its professional home is found in existentialist philosophy and theology, as well as in psychologies that emphasize the autonomy of personality and selfhood. It orders its perceptions and interpretations through these lenses, rather than through other more social and communal viewpoints. It largely neglects explicit attention to broader questions about the nature of reality (ontology and metaphysics) and social ethics, though it operates on the basis of implicit assumptions about these areas. It holds up for suspicion sources of knowledge and wisdom based on tradition, and erodes the psychological and philosophical foundations necessary for human solidarity. The existentialist-anthropological approach to care certainly recognizes our finitude and contextuality; it recognizes the contribution of the world to human distress. But ultimately, the existential-anthropological model underscores our relative capacity to transcend these pressures and to order them for higher individual purposes.

It neglects our moral obligation to take account of how our individuality and participation in social and cultural realities impact the lives of others. In this model, values such as choice, freedom, responsibility, awareness, growth, health, and intimacy underscore the qualities of being or the primary needs of individuals. Values such as justice, love, mutuality, ecological partnership, and liberation are either neglected altogether, or they are psychologized and limited to the horizon of personal and interpersonal relationships. And while some psychosocial, self-psychologies, and family systems thinkers appreciate the shaping power of context, individual needs and family health are seen as prior to contextual responsibilities. Context is background; personhood foreground. Contextual realities are measured in terms of their consequences for persons; individuality is seen as prior to relationality, at least in mature functioning.[5]

Derald Sue, a theorist in cross-cultural counseling, provides a useful way to illustrate the predominance and limitations of the existentialist-anthropological model in North America.[6] His overall argument is that "the lack of a theory on cultural oppression and its relationship to the development of world views continues to foster cultural blindness within the counseling profession."[7] To make his case, he contends that there are a variety of world views possible, but only one of them is given normative status in the dominant white, middle-class culture of North America. Using the concepts of locus of control and locus of responsibility, he identifies four possible types of world views and relates them to one another in terms of their impact on counseling and therapy.

The first type, which is another way of describing what I mean by the existentialist-anthropological model, is characterized by internalized locus of control and responsibility. Persons with internalized locus of control believe that individuals shape their own fate and that their actions will be rewarded. Persons with internalized locus of responsibility believe that the individual, rather than the system, is blamed when things do not work out. Thus, the first type of world view posits individual responsibility and control over personal destiny. It underscores independence, uniqueness, and individual-centeredness. "A high value is placed on personal resources for solving all problems; self-reliance; pragmatism; individualism; status achievement through one's own effort; and power or control over others, things, animals, and forces of nature."[8] This world view is the basis for Western orientations to counseling that dominate our culture. "Most counselors are of the opinion that people must take major responsibility for their own actions and can improve their lot in life through their own efforts."[9] The major responsibility for what occurs in counseling and in the counselee's life is the responsibility of the person. Sue points out that this approach can be punitive and oppressive for those in society who have less power for self-realization, and in fact can readily lead to blaming them for their disadvantaged situation. Further, the development of self-assertive traits can function deviantly in the context of the values of some ethnic communities, contributing to further distress and dysfunction.

The second type of world view is characterized by external locus of control and internal locus of responsibility. Individuals and groups with this world view believe that they are essentially responsible for their own situations, even though they have no control over them. In spite of adverse environmental conditions, they believe that persons who are disadvantaged are this way because of their own laziness or stupidity. They reject their own cultural heritage and overaccommodate the behavioral prescriptions of the dominant culture. These values and prescriptions for success have been internalized without having the social foundations to fulfill them. Persons with this world view are trapped in a subordinated and marginalized situation, and personally blamed by themselves and others for it.

The third type of world view is characterized by a conviction of external control and external responsibility, as one would find in slavery and other blatant subjugations. Persons and groups with this world view may develop a sense of helplessness and futility at achieving personal goals. They may appear to the counselor as lacking strong egos, as overly passive and dependent, and being devoid of courage or autonomy. While these traits may in fact be evident, they may also belie disguised inner strength and a defiance of imposed authority and norms.

Finally, Sue describes the orientation characterized by external locus of responsibility and internalized locus of control. These persons do not believe that the current state of affairs is due to their deficiencies, but that they have some capacity "to shape events in their own life if given a chance."[10] This orientation characterizes racial and ethnic minorities who are becoming more aware of their cultural heritage and of their current social location. These persons, unlike those in the dominant pattern, do not see the problem as residing in the individual, but as external to the individual. They will recognize the need for more activist approaches to change, and will more naturally seek collective rather than individualistic means of change. They will be suspicious of modes of counseling requiring self-disclosure of feelings to a typical counselor, and they will prefer more directive than reflective counselor responses.

There can be little doubt that Sue is correct in identifying and expanding the main features of the dominant model of caretaking in our society. He also delineates its negative impact and functional alternatives. In addition, numerous studies have confirmed and criticized the dominant individualistic bias in North American care and counseling.[11]

A more difficult question is whether pastoral care and counseling is also captured by the existentialist-anthropological model and its unrelieved individualism. E. Brooks Holifield argues that until about 1960 the major writers in pastoral care, under the influence of Rogers, Freud, and Fromm in particular, emphasized the conflict between individual self-realization and the moralizing and collectivizing functions of society.[12] While they recognized the importance of the ecclesiastical and moral context, these writers were more concerned to free the creative powers of the personality from largely restrictive social influences. This did not mean that their anthropologies were exclusively individualistic, or that their view of self-realization did not require a social and moral context for coherence. It did mean that the directionality, under the influences of existentialist theologies and individualistic personality theories, was from the individual to the context rather than conversely. Further, during this period, there was little if any attempt to conceptually articulate the constructive relationship between the individual and the environment.

Since 1960 a number of authors writing about pastoral care and counseling have contended that the field reflects the dominant individualistic model of care in the culture. Don Browning has argued this point consistently.[13] Gaylord Noyce has wondered if the psycho-therapeutic underpinnings in pastoral counseling have cut the nerve of ministry.[14] Many have attempted to provide constructive alternatives. Gordon Jackson has drawn upon process theology to reconstruct personhood along social lines, and to reincorporate the doctrine of God into pastoral counseling. But he pays little or no attention to social and contextual matters in his theory of care.[15] James Lapsley has also used process theology and ego psychology to develop a view of personhood that emphasizes community and participation as developmental characteristics of the self, and he has valued the interpersonal dimensions of Kohut's view of selfhood.[16] But he has not fully explored the relational character of selfhood, nor has he constructed a theory that consistently appreciates the constitutive interconnection of the self and its larger worlds.

John Patton and Brian Childs have developed a model of care that grounds personhood in a transgenerational concept of relatedness.[17] However, they fail to tend to relatedness beyond the kinship structure. Charles Gerkin has made ambitious and fruitful attempts to "widen the horizons" of care to incorporate the congregational, social, cultural, and historical networks that constitute persons and contextualize the nature of their symptoms and their need for care. His is the most theoretically advanced approach to this subject. Drawing upon Moltmann's theology of hope, Gadamer's hermeneutical theory of interpretation, narrative theology and a variety of psychodynamic self-psychologies, Gerkin maintains that the self is constituted by its interpreted narrative in relationship to its life in society, time, and history, under God.[18] I find this to be a promising approach, and one that clearly moves beyond the existentialist and anthropological orientation. Yet I am haunted by Gerkin's central emphasis upon selfhood, and his view that the self is an interpreter rather than a lover, justice-maker, and partner with nature. The moral dimensions of his model still seem to be ordered by a concern for individual self-realization and fulfillment of primary relationships. While the impact of contextual realities on individuals is highly emphasized in Gerkin's work, the reciprocal influence and social responsibility of individuals to their context is not developed.

Archie Smith has written a helpful book that combines pastoral care, liberation theology, and the black church experience to develop a relational model of selfhood and a theory of change that addresses the simultaneous need for personal and social transformation.[19] I have especially valued his discussion of Paradigms in pastoral care. He argues that Paradigm I is limited because it falsely thinks that social change results from changing individuals alone. He rejects Paradigm II because he thinks it wrongly concludes that social change alone will result in transformed individuals. Paradigm III is his own model, which links emancipatory struggle in the social order to transformation of consciousness in the personal and interpersonal arenas, and vice versa. While this is a very important book (now sadly out of print), it is unfortunate that Smith did not carry his theory forward to interpret the implications for pastoral care practice in specific terms, or to include specific psychotherapeutic resources.

Howard Clinebell, of all writers in the field, has given the most sustained attention to combining care for persons and care for environments. Along with occasional writings, he has provided a theoretical model and functional guidelines. I have been inspired and informed by Clinebell. His charge to pastoral counselors at the Nashville convention still rings in my ears:

> An important expression of the systemic orientation in psychotherapy is the growing awareness of the complex interdependence of individual healing and growth with the wider social context. Behind every personal problem is a cluster of societal problems. Including these issues explicitly in our counseling goals is the most difficult challenge we face in moving toward more holistic, socially responsible pastoral counseling. Reclaiming our prophetic heritage in pastoral care by developing ways of integrating personal and social healing is critical if our field is to be the power-for-transformation which it can be in a world drowning in injustice and social oppression.
>
> To respond effectively to this challenge, we must rethink the interdependence of power and love, theologically and psychologically, and make *empowerment* (not adjustment) a central goal in all our counseling, therapy, and growth work. Liberation theology should become a major conceptual resource in both our theory and practice. Hyperindividualistic, privatized pastoral care can cut the nerve of prophetic awareness and motivation to action. For persons who are economically exploited, and persons oppressed by the social malignancies of racism, sexism, ageism, classism, materialism, speciesism, militarism, and tribal nationalism, such pastoral care can be misused as a therapeutic tranquilizer. The recovery of sight by the blind must never be separated from releasing the captives and enabling the broken victims of societal pathology to go free through counseling. Since sound pastoral counseling must include consciousness raising, we need to incorporate more insight and methods from the radical therapies, including feminist therapy, in our work. Pastoral counseling must become much more countercultural than it has been in the past. We should learn to use our clinical skills to do pastoral care *of* institutions (to make them more wholeness-nurturing) and pastoral care *through* social action. The goals of counseling should include enabling persons to claim their inner power and to use it in cooperation with others to liberate themselves and others from the systemic roots of diminished wholeness.[20]

I fully affirm Clinebell's agenda. This book builds a theory from the bottom up based on it. Clinebell himself has incorporated many of these elements into his revision of his classic and influential text in pastoral counseling.[21] However, there are several ways that Clinebell's perspective is still fundamentally ordered by the existential-anthropological model, and its underlying ethical egoism. His central goal in caring is to facilitate "the maximum development of a person's potentialities, at each life stage, in ways that contribute to the growth of others as well as to the development of a society in which all persons will have an opportunity to use their full potentialities."[22] Though he has a clear element of care for others and the larger social order in his central commitment to growth, the criterion and goal of this care is the opportunity for individuals "to use their full potentialities." While this is an expanded ethical egoism, it continues to be organized around the goal of self-realized and fulfilled individuals. Further, the psychological foundations of his theory remain largely humanistic psychology. The liberation theology upon which he draws is nonspecific, and does not address in social, political, and economic terms the conditions of oppression and the new consciousness and tools that are needed to address them. Clinebell seems to assume that whole persons will automatically contribute to whole societies, without recognizing that his definitions of wholeness participate in an individualism that is at the root of many of our difficulties.

Clinebell's passion for wholeness in mind, spirit, body, relationships, institutions, and the biosphere is to be fully affirmed. To tie personality fulfillment to caring social involvement is a major gain for the field. But conceptual coherence and effective realization of these dimensions of wholeness require that they are grounded more centrally in social and systemic viewpoints and treated organically rather than sequentially and linearly.

THE MEANING OF SYSTEMIC THINKING

My search for more adequate resources has led me to embrace a variety of "systemic" theories to articulate the complex interplay between individual psyches and the environments that create and are created by them. To be sure, all pastoral care theories that are based on modern studies of the person have some way of understanding the relationship between the individual and the environment. As I have indicated, I have worked with some of them and found many helpful. However, I have found that a systems view of life can affirm many of the central concerns of other theories while making a creative advance upon them. It is therefore important to gain a basic understanding of what is meant by systemic thinking, and what is meant by joining the concepts of psyche and system.

The meaning of the terms "systemic" or "systems thought" is neither easy to grasp nor to convey. The term "systemic" is in itself often a barrier to communication. Its meaning is not self-evident; formal definitions are often obfuscating; its usage jargonistic, and sometimes elitist. However, it is my belief that the fundamental basis for communication problems about the term "systemic," is that it refers to a foreign way of thinking. In our culture, we basically do not live our lives with a systemic consciousness. A systemic perspective emphasizes togetherness; our way of life emphasizes separateness. Systemic refers to ongoing processes and transactions; we emphasize causes, effects, and outcomes. A systemic orientation affirms both/and; we assume life requires choices between either/or alternatives. A systemic view emphasizes cooperation and reciprocal influence; our way of life emphasizes competition and coercive influence. A systemic view affirms that creative advances include what has gone before; our way of life is built upon the negation of earlier values. Systems analysis underscores the individual's ongoing relationship to society, culture, and nature; our way of thinking underscores the individual's opposition to society, culture, and nature. Systems thought concerns itself with holism; our way of thinking focuses upon the autonomy of the parts in themselves.

The list could go on, and in subsequent chapters I will expand on the character of a systemic view of reality. For now, it is important to begin to clarify the meaning of a systemic perspective in order to overcome the difficulties inherent in appropriating its meaning for ourselves.

The first characteristic of systemic thinking is its affirmation that all elements of the universe are interconnected, standing in an ongoing reciprocal relationship to one another. This reciprocal relationship is not always immediate or direct. Neither is it always discernible. But the interconnections exist and their influences make life what it is, and shape what it will become. The systems view of life emphasizes that this relational interconnection is not an optional matter. We do not have a choice about whether or not to be related; we *are* related and continue to be so. We do have some degree of choice about how we will or will not be related, but this choice itself results from systemically-derived options. Systemic pastoral care therefore affirms the interconnection between all things, and responds to persons accordingly.

A second dimension of systemic thinking is its affirmation that reality is organized. The universe is an organized totality whose elements are interrelated. As an interrelated organized totality it is viewed as a system, comprised of subsystems. Each subsystem is a whole in relation to the parts making it up, and a part in relation to the larger whole. Thus, the circulatory system of the blood is a subsystem of the person. The person, which is a whole in relation to his or her circulatory system, is a part, or a subsystem, in relation to his or her family. Thus, the organization of a system occurs differentially with relative degrees of power, accountability, and influence.[23] The parts differ from the whole in which they participate, and there are greater and lesser levels of power and complexity between the elements constituting the system. Pastoral care from a systems perspective is therefore concerned with the structured organization of persons and of the nature of the power relationship between persons and their environments.

A third characteristic of systems thinking is its emphasis upon homeostasis, or balance and self-maintenance. Balance is maintained by transactional processes such as communication, negotiation, and boundary management. To maintain stability and continuation of the system, these transactions are reciprocal rather than unilateral. That is, they move back and forth in two directions, rather than only from one to another. As in the case of Patricia's family, the violence in the family was sustained by a number of reciprocally connected elements that were not at the time subject to modification by other internal or external influences.[24] Pastoral care from a systemic perspective attempts to identify, stabilize, and modify the reciprocal transactions at work within individuals, and those that operate between individuals and their environments.

A fourth characteristic of a systems view is its emphasis upon creativity in context, or finite freedom. Though systems are self-maintaining, they are also self-transcending. They change their structural character as a result of internal and external pressures. There is patterned indeterminateness in systems. Each part or subsystem stands both in support of and in opposition to every other part, resulting in a certain inherent instability. The character of the parts, and of the whole, have only relative autonomy in relation to one another. Their identities and functions are always subject to change, within limits. When any part of the system changes, the whole system also changes, however minimally. Change in the whole affects the character of the parts; change in the parts affects the character of the whole. For example, when children are born to parents, there are dramatic shifts within the family system, and the family's relationship to the social order is modified in a variety of ways. Systemic pastoral care recognizes that change is inherent in the nature of things and attempts to influence change in such a way that environments as well as individuals are enhanced.

To summarize, systemic thinking is a view about the universe, or a picture of reality, that affirms that everything that exists is in an ongoing mutual relationship with every other reality. The universe is organized differentially into subsystems of relatively autonomous units, so that the relationship between the parts is not always direct or immediate. There are exchanges of energy and influence between these units in their struggle both to maintain and to modify their relationships to one another. Systems are therefore more or less stable, and more or less open to change. Change at one level affects what happens at other levels.

Systems thinking is not without historical and religious roots. It is not the purpose of this book to trace those roots. It may be helpful to note, however, that the apostle Paul's view of the universe having unity and coherence in Jesus Christ, its creative agent, is akin to the systems affirmation that reality is purposefully interconnected. For Paul, as for systems thinking, the universe is a stable entity that is also moving creatively toward transformation and new form. Change is inherent in the nature of things; the old is taken into and transformed by the new (Romans 8:18-21).

Paul's analogy of the church as the body of Christ, in which each part serves the whole and in turn derives its identity and value from the whole, also parallels systems thinking (1 Corinthians 12). Just as a system is characterized by differential structure, functional accountability, tension between balance and change, and mutual influence, so Paul characterizes the body of Christ. Not all have the same function, but all are necessary for the church, and all are called upon to bear one another's burdens. He recognized the systemic reality that when one suffers, all suffer; when one is joyful, all rejoice. Much of Paul's writings can be interpreted as attempts to maintain the systemic balance and creativity of the church, attempting to clarify its internal and external boundaries, modify the quality of its internal interactions, and facilitate the achievement of its purposes. Even though we live in a culture that is adverse to "the system," and especially to systems of "organized religion," it is simply a fact that we are inherent parts of multiple systems. As Paul realized in terms of the Christian church, one's relationship to these systems—as well as their relationship to us—is the source of both tremendous joy and overwhelming pain.

THE MEANING OF THE PSYCHE, OR SOUL

This book is subtitled "a psychosystems approach" to pastoral care and counseling. I have introduced the reader to a general understanding of the term, "systemic." The other half of the subtitle concerns itself with the psyche, or soul, which is descriptive of persons rather than environments. The burden of this book is to demonstrate the ongoing, permanent, and reciprocal interaction between the psyches of persons and the larger environments that are bringing psyches into being and influencing their nature. It is my conviction that psyches create systems and systems create psyches. The relationship between them is synaptic, or spiritual, characterized by mutual reception, rejection, struggle, and creative accomplishment.

I shall use the terms *psyche* and *soul* interchangeably throughout this book, recognizing that some imprecision will exist as a consequence. I am using the concept of psyche or soul to refer to the synthesizing and creative center of the human personality. The preferred term will be *psyche* because of its more common acceptance in contemporary pastoral care and counseling. However, I want to retain the use of the term *soul,* owing to the religious concerns that motivate this writing. Ministry has always concerned itself with the care, cure, or salvation of souls, however souls have been understood. The historical concept of soul has been discarded by many in the contemporary religious world largely because of its dualistic, spiritualistic, privatistic, and essentialist overtones. However, I believe that rather than simply discarding or replacing the term, our ministry is advanced if the concept of the soul is reinterpreted in holistic, social, and developmental terms. Such a reinterpretation will contribute to re-establishing vital links between spiritual formation and pastoral care, body and soul, personal salvation and social justice, and the sacred and secular dimensions of experience. By reclaiming and reconstructing the language of our heritage in contemporary terms, pastoral caretakers will be in a better position to explore both their continuities with and differences from the other helping professions.

When applied to the human personality or psyche, the concepts of systemic thinking reveal the human self as a relatively open system rather than as autonomous and nonsocial. The soul is both the *activity* of synthesizing and creating experience, and the *outcome* of the process of synthesis and creation. As an activity, the psyche or soul is the process by which the person receives influences from the multiple systems in which it participates, and by which the person offers creative influences back to those systems. As an outcome, or accomplishment, the soul is that which results from the synthesizing and creative process. The psyche, therefore, is an ongoing relationship between activity and achievement, and the modifications of each upon the other. What is received and transformed by the soul depends largely upon environmental influences; how these are synthesized and transformed by the psyche or soul depends upon its own contribution and prior accomplishments. The outcome may be more or less valuable. Not all accomplishments of the psyche are of equal worth. As Jesus said, "Of what value is it if you gain the whole world, and lose your soul?" The capacity of the soul to receive and transform experience in this case has resulted in a negative outcome for the soul, including, presumably, its loss of capacity to function at all.

If the soul is both an activity and a qualitative achievement, which comes into being through dynamic systemic interactions, it follows that it is not a fully formed "thing" planted inside persons from all time, and potentially uninfluenced by the world in which it exists. The soul must rather be thought of as a social reality that is always coming into being at new levels of organization, function, and value. It is ultimately never completed. It is a capacity, an achievement, and a discovery. And though it has continuity and identifiable parameters, these remain modifiable to some extent. It is a systemic reality that constitutes a whole in relation to the subsystems comprising the person, and a part in relation to the macrosystems in which the person resides. The psyche derives its identity, function, and value from its participation in these systems and subsystems, even as they derive their identities, functions, and values from the power of the souls or psyches comprising them.

The soul or psyche is both conscious and unconscious. Its subsystems are the body and the structures of the personality that it unifies. Its macrosystems are nature, culture, society, religion, and family. The nature of the exchanges between these systemic dimensions creates the soul and creates the world that will in turn create new souls. Thus, in its task of curing, caring for, and saving souls, the pastoral caretaker is also about the business of modifying the larger structures of the world and creating a new heaven and earth. Pastoral care and counseling is therefore by nature psychosystemic.

THE PSYCHOSYSTEMIC NATURE OF CARE

What interpretation of ministry drives our theory of care and guides its practice? Can we find—or can we fashion—a view of ministry that lends itself to a psychosystemic approach to the ministry of care? Since the ministry of care is a subsystem of the larger religious community, it is imperative to relate our view of care to the nature of the ministry of the community on whose behalf care is offered.[25]

For the purposes of this book, religious ministry is understood as the totality of strategic activities engaged in by the religious community and its individual members to increase the love of self, God, and neighbor, and to promote a just social order and a livable environment. This is a hybrid definition, expanding upon H. Richard Niebuhr's classic view of the purpose of the ministry as increasing the love of God and neighbor.[26] The practice of pastoral caretaking itself has contributed to expanding Niebuhr's interpretation to include an increase of proper self-love as a goal of ministry. The ecumenical and ecological movements, along with the threat of a global nuclear winter, have contributed to the expansion of the definition of ministry to include explicit concern for a just social order and a livable environment.[27]

Ministry is one of the vehicles by which God's love is affirmed and shared. For Christians, God's being is defined by love, God's activity is characterized by love, and God's destiny is love. To be a believer in God, and a part of the fellowship of God's people, is to be called forth by God's love, and to be its receiver and agent. This love has two dimensions: the first dimension is love's unitive energy in which love seeks to restore that which is estranged to new harmony and cooperation.[28] The second dimension is love's transformative energy, in which love seeks to promote "new beings" in a "new creation" whose fecundity is novel and unprescribable.[29] Love, as I am using it here, is the generous embodied giving and receiving on behalf of the welfare of individual persons and the larger social communities comprising them. It extends to include a benevolent reciprocal engagement with nature. Love is increased when persons move from estrangement and disharmony with themselves, one another, and nature, to an expanding and open communion and creativity within and among themselves.

Justice is a corollary of love, inasmuch as it is principally directed to right relationships between persons and the various components of their worlds. Justice further specifies the quality of embodied love in both personal relationships and in the more impersonal dimensions of organized social life. Justice seeks mutuality and reciprocity rather than dominance and subordination in social relationships.[30] Specifically, justice underlies the search for a social order characterized by shared power, shared opportunity, and shared rewards. It is the basis for true peace in domestic as well as public arenas.[31]

Another goal of ministry is the promotion of an ecological partnership, or efforts to enhance "the integrity of creation."[32] Feminists and Native Americans, among others, have raised consciousness about the interconnection between justice in human relationships and care for the earth.[33] Personal life-styles and national and international policies have reciprocal ecosystemic impact. To refuse care for the earth is to deprive ourselves and our offspring of the life support systems necessary for our health and welfare. It is to further fracture our relationship with the God who participates in creating and enhancing the world. The enhancement of ecological partnership is the dimension of ministry that seeks to foster personal life-styles and public social policies that enhance the capacity of nature to renew its bounty. Such a ministry will require, among other things, that we replace our current philosophies of domination of nature with ecosystemic philosophies of partnership and bondedness with nature.[34]

A ministry whose defining purpose is the increase of love, justice, and ecological partnership lends itself to a systemic interpretation. It combines the pastoral and the prophetic. It places the quality of relatedness at the center of its mission. It transcends, without negating, an individualistic orientation to ministry. It connects love, justice, and ecological responsibility. A proper love of self is foundationally related to the increase of the love of God and neighbor, and to the ability to work for justice and the creation of a livable environment. Proper self-affirmation and self-love enables me to share my being and resources with others, to seek their welfare, and to welcome their efforts on my behalf. If I love my neighbor, I will work to alleviate her or his suffering from an unjust social order and to ensure the conditions necessary for her or his physical survival.

In turn, love of God and self are fundamentally made possible by being the recipient of neighbor-love. We love self and others because we are first loved; we introject and project that which comes to us from our worlds. My capacities for love are thereby enhanced by neighbors who demonstrate their love by working for a just order in which I might live. Their love for themselves and for me is demonstrated concretely in the reduction of activities which may eventuate in my destruction by war. They seek to preserve my life and the life of the human race by refraining from irresponsible and dangerous ecological practices. When these efforts are appreciatively received and genuinely reciprocated, we move closer to the fulfillment of a psychosystemic ministry in which love, justice, and ecological partnership are increased.

How then might this general view of ministry apply to a psychosystemic theory of pastoral care?[35] Subsequent chapters will discuss in more detail how particular aspects of care relate to these general purposes of ministry. For now it is important to underscore that pastoral caretaking is the primary setting in which these goals of ministry are related to the specific circumstances of persons in crisis. Pastoral caretaking is the primary focused context in ministry where the casualties and perpetrators of injustice, lovelessness, and ecological disarray seek assistance. Congruent with the general purpose of ministry, it is the task of the ministry of care, individually and corporately, to offer a presence and to develop strategies that will reverse the consequences of lovelessness, injustice, and ecological disarray in the psyches and behaviors of careseekers. Simultaneously, it is the task of pastoral caretaking to increase the capacities for the love of self, God, and neighbor, and the abilities to work for a just social order and a livable environment on the part of careseekers. As we saw earlier in the case of Patricia, it is no simple task to combine so many goals in particular acts of ministry. To do so requires attention to many factors not generally regarded as within the purview of the ministry of care.

PRINCIPLES OF PSYCHOSYSTEMIC CAREGIVING

Psychosystemic pastoral caregiving provides assistance to casualties and perpetrators of various forms of lovelessness, injustice, and environmental disorder. It combines restoration and transformation of persons and their contexts. There are five identifiable principles that identify the nature of psychosystemic caregiving, and that may be drawn upon to guide its practice.

First, there is the principle of *organicity*. The principle of organicity may be stated as follows: To assist symptomatic persons, the pastoral caretaker must discern and respond to the patterns of interconnectedness accounting for the pastoral situation. The interconnections extend backwards in family and culture, as well as outward to the multiple influences in one's contemporary world. This principle rests on the assumption that all reality is embodied and socially located in a pattern of reciprocal influence. Symptoms function to stabilize and destabilize; they reveal the beneficiaries and losers in current organic patterns, and point out the direction of transformative change. For example, an acting-out child almost always reveals a rift in the parental and marital relationship, which in turn usually uncovers problems in the relationships parents have with their own parents and with their social situation. In addition, there inevitably are social pressures from the school and peer group acting upon the child that diminish his or her capacity to respond more freely. For change to occur, the pastoral caretaker must become an organic part of this situation and help persons recognize that more than individual symptoms are determinative.

Second, there is the principle of *simultaneity*. The principle of simultaneity may be stated as follows: In order to promote change, the pastoral caretaker must recognize and strategically respond to the intersystemic consequences of and resistances to his or her efforts. This principle rests on the assumption that changes in either the parts or the whole of a system, or between interlocking systems, affect one another. Psychosystemic pastoral caretaking responds to the organic relationship between persons and their worlds simultaneously. Though all interventions are technically sequential or linear "punctuations," they are viewed in terms of their simultaneous impact on other components of the system. In spite of whoever is in the room, the pastoral caretaker continually keeps in mind that there is an ongoing interplay between those persons and the larger world. Thus, a parish minister who counsels full acceptance of homosexuality and encourages a parishioner to come out of the closet will simultaneously be faced with (and face the parishioner with) familial, congregational, occupational, legal, and other social challenges. Any responsible strategy of care must intersect these realities as well as the concrete dynamics of the person in the pastor's office.

Third, there is the principle of *conscientization*.[36] The principle of conscientization may be stated as follows: In order for pastoral caretakers to transform symptomatic situations, they must help careseekers combine an awareness of the impact of the social order upon their personal difficulties, and assist them to fashion strategic actions to neutralize, change, or transform the destructive elements in the social order. This principle rests on the assumption that therapeutic insight and awareness must be expanded to include social analysis and political action for change to be in keeping with the goals of ministry. It is an action-reflection mode of ministry that involves both the caregiver and the careseeker in such action and reflection in relation to the larger systemic environment. It looks particularly at the structure of domination and subordination, with an eye to who benefits and who suffers from the intact power arrangements. It uncovers collusion and internalization of oppression, and seeks to empower persons to strategic, accountable action. It is one of the conceptual and pragmatic means by which prophetic concern for justice and ecological responsibility may become focal in the ministry of care. Specifically, the principle of conscientization enables the pastoral caretaker to address matters such as racism, ageism, sexism, heterosexism, and life-style concerns, as issues of care as well as issues of social justice.

Fourth, there is the principle of *advocacy*. The principle of advocacy is stated as follows: To transform symptomatic behaviors the pastoral caretaker lends his or her voice, and the voice of the caretaking community, to shaping public policies that promote a positive environment for the careseeker. This principle rests on the assumption that justice requires publicly accountable contention, and that persons who have little power in the social order need assistance in contending for justice. Pastoral caretakers "hear into speech" those who are victimized by lovelessness, injustice, and environmental rapaciousness; they provide a voice and help them find a voice. The role of advocacy requires that pastoral caregivers challenge their religious communities and their societies to develop policies and procedures that serve rather than impair human welfare. The pastoral caregiver, as advocate, uses his or her power position to share the risks of changing the social order, and lends voice to the directions of necessary change.

Finally, there is the principle of *adventure*. The principle of adventure may be stated this way: To help symptomatic situations change, the pastoral caretaker assists persons to recognize that God is present as an ally on the side of transformation and liberative change, and that such change is an expected but unpredictable gift of grace and fruit of hope. The concept of adventure grows out of process theology, and refers to the capacity for surprise and novelty that is built into the universe at every level.[37] It operates to remind the caregiver that our conceptual models and our technical strategies point to dynamic realities beyond themselves. This principle underscores the creativity and "messiness" which in fact exist in the world and in the process of caregiving, and demonstrates that our achievements are never simple cause-effect outcomes. As adventurers of the spirit, and as participants in the creation of new worlds, we are discoverers more than architects, and witnesses more than contractors.

SUMMARY AND CONCLUSION

The ministry of care is a subsystem of the ministry of a larger religious community. As such, it both derives its function from and contributes to the definition of ministry of the community to which it is related. For the purposes of this book, the ministry of care is the strategic response of love to the crises of careseekers, whether these are individuals, couples, families, or groups of persons. The general purposes of a ministry of care are to increase the love of self, God, and neighbor, and to enable careseekers to develop the capacity to work for a just social order and to engage in partnership with the natural order. Specifically, then, the ministry of care provides a context in which persons who are victims and perpetrators of lovelessness, injustice, and environmental disorder may engage the destructive forces in their lives so that both they and those forces may simultaneously be healed, sustained, guided, and liberated.

CHAPTER 2

A PSYCHOSYSTEMIC VIEW
OF THE WORLD

Relations here are not external but internal so that we are our
relations and cannot be selves save as we are members of each other.
When there is strife in this community there is strife and pain in us
and when it is at peace we have peace in ourselves.

H. Richard Niebuhr[1]

INFLUENCES FROM PROCESS THEOLOGY

This chapter maps the major elements of the systemic interplay of person and world. Additional attention is given in subsequent chapters to those factors that are most central for the ministry of care.

Process theology provides the theological center for my systemic view of reality. Process theology is a general term given to a number of theological orientations that have emerged in the modern period. I am using it here to refer to the theological contributions resulting from the work of Alfred North Whitehead, as interpreted through John Cobb and David Ray Griffin. The basic affirmation of process thought that is relevant for the present discussion is that of the "kinship" of all things. Each moment of experience draws its content from its environment, and the environment is in turn shaped by what has contributed to bringing it forth.[2] This interdependence is as true for the most fundamental unit of experience as for more complex syntheses of experience such as human beings. In this view, "we influence each other by entering in to each other."[3] Like Picasso's musicians, persons and their world are in mutual interaction, for better and for worse. This situation is not one of optional choice, but it is the way things are. That is, we have no choice about whether or not to relate interdependently; we only have relative choice about how we will relate to our world.

Process theology is a philosophical interpretation of the way things are in the universe. It is an ontology and a cosmology. For the most part, pastoral theology has used more functional and person-centered philosophies for its foundations. It is my belief that pastoral theology requires theological foundations that begin with the "way things are" in a metaphysical sense before moving to more particular concerns. It is crucial that we establish that the basic structures of reality support and further our central assumptions about the capacity for love to increase, justice to emerge, and ecological responsibility to occur. If the universe is viewed as impersonal and deterministic, then it is difficult to argue that our efforts on behalf of love, justice, and preservation make much difference. Likewise, if aggression or "survival of the fittest" are regarded as the laws of life, then values such as love, cooperation, forgiveness, and reconciliation are essentially foolhardy. Or, if the universe is regarded as either hostile and threatening, or as a resource for our achievements, as in the Dürer drawing, it is difficult to see it as a loving creation of God in its own right.

Process theology builds its claims regarding the interconnection of life upon an analysis of the concrescence process of the smallest unit of experience, called actual entities or actual occasions of experience. For Whitehead, reality consists ultimately of these discrete and individual subjects of experience. These are the basic "units of process," or the smallest "droplets" of experience. They coalesce to form the universe in all its variety, novelty, and possibility. In Whitehead's own terms, "the subjectivist principle is that the whole universe consists of elements disclosed in the analysis of the experience of subjects."[4] While Whitehead is here speaking of the most fundamental or basic elements of the universe, his analysis of this basic level provides a model of understanding the processes by which more complex entities such as humans come into being. The basic point is that whatever is metaphysically true at one level in the universe, is also true for all other realities in the universe.

The process of becoming, or the concrescence process, is of vital importance in this orientation. Everything that exists in the universe has come into being as a result of an interacting process. An experiencing subject—whether this subject is an actual occasion of experience, a human person, or God—comes into being through a series of transactions with the environment. Since the environment is made up of the entities that have already come into being, it also can be regarded as the past. Thus, the past, which constitutes the environment of the subject that is coming into being, has a real influence on what the subject can and will become. Like the environment in the *Three Musicians,* the past shapes, orders, and becomes inherent in whatever emerges in the universe.

But the past is not necessarily simply repeated, nor is the environment merely cloned in the concrescence process. There are two other influences shaping the outcome. There is the activity of God and the intentionality, or aiming, of the emerging subject. So, the fundamental metaphysical situation of the emerging subject consists of a given "moment" in which all of the past occasions are immediately present offering massive influence. God is also present envisaging all possibilities for what the emerging subject will become, and selecting for the moment the most optimal opportunity. From the interplay of God and the past, an opportunity for something novel to occur is coming into being. In its own freedom, the emerging subject struggles to combine the powerful influence of the past with God's aim and with its own aim. In this struggle, the emerging subject chooses what it will become. Once it has chosen, it has come into being as a new object in the universe. Now, as a given element of reality, it becomes a part of the environment that is present to the becoming of new experiencing subjects, contributing to what they may or may not become. This concrescence process operates continually at a rapid rate. It is at a submicroscopic level of experience, and most of it is not conscious. In more complex structures such as persons, it is relatively more conscious, though not entirely so.

For the purpose of this book, a couple of things should be underscored. First, this view of reality has close affinity to modern quantum physics, which regards the fundamental units of reality to be indeterminate electrical patterns rather than small particles of matter. In contrast to the mechanistic, materialistic, and deterministic view of Cartesian-Newtonian physics, process philosophy and quantum physics recognize that there is room for novelty and mutual influence in the universe. This is important for the ministry of care. It bases our efforts to promote change on reality itself, and provides metaphysical support for our view that love, justice, and ecological stewardship are genuine rather than foolhardy possibilities for this world.

Another important implication of this view of reality is that it enables us to restore value issues to the center of our thinking and practice. Everything that comes into being does so in relation to a number of contending options. The past, God, and the subject itself supply value-laden options to be concretely realized. Values are not abstractions, but actualized accomplishments of real entities. They become a part of the environment and contend for loyalty and influence. Not all values are the same, and they are not all compatible. The struggle for actualizing values becomes a crucial struggle in determining what the world will actually become.

A third important implication of this view is that the concept of power becomes central. Power is the capacity to influence and be influenced by the world. Since all experience and all actual entities in the universe are the result of being influenced by interacting objects and subject, power is an essential component for understanding the world. When the concepts of change and values are put together with that of power, this view of reality affirms that the world consists of power struggles between competing values. The resolution of these power struggles will determine the very makeup of the universe, and hence the quality of its life. This view argues for a pluralistic view of the universe, but recognizes that some values become dominant in actual experience. It also appears from this view that changing values will also require changing power arrangements existing in the environment. Since the past has massive influence, such change is difficult—though always possible, and perhaps inevitable over the long term.

In the fourth place, this view underscores the capacity for self-determination, in the context of multiple influences. Although the experiencing subject must take into account its surrounding world—and the past world influencing the present—history and the environment do not completely determine the present. Rather, individual subjects have creative agency that to a large, but not exclusive, measure determines how the environment will be appropriated and how it and the individual will be shaped. This shaping is a dimension of "contextual creativity"[5] and is always an element in living beings, no matter how dominant the past and how limiting the environment. Thus, human beings neither finally transcend their communities, nor are controlled by them. They exist by the establishment of "relative independence" in community.[6] The more the person interacts with others in community, the more individual the person becomes. The more individual the person becomes, the greater one's participation in community. Persons and contexts create, reflect, and transcend one another. The experiencing subject is viewed as both determined and free, limited and creatively transforming.

Finally, because of the multiple realities contending for influence in the universe, it is recognized that nothing comes into being without struggle, conflict, and loss. There is great risk that choices will be made for the worse rather than for the better. Because there is great diversity among living things—and because it cannot be predetermined which choices will be made—the exact form of the future can neither be predicted nor controlled. No one perspective can claim final dominance; no one pattern can ultimately prevail; no one person or social structure has the power to finally determine the outcome of the form of human existence and the content of human consciousness. The world shared by living creatures who are in the process of coming into being will be transformed and recreated by whatever else comes into being.

THE ORGANIZATION OF THE PSYCHOSYSTEMIC WORLD

How is the world organized? What are the major realities influencing persons and their relationships? This study identifies six major components. I shall discuss these beginning with the smallest and moving to the largest unit. The reader should bear in mind, however, that the transactions and influences between the interacting units making up the world are multi-directional—each plays many particular roles in the makeup of the other. Neither is the reader to understand the relationship between these components in terms of a value hierarchy. The best way to image the relationship between them is in terms of concentric circles, with the most inclusive element at the outside. The interplay between these components will become more clear in the next section where I more fully delineate the mechanisms by which they are connected. The chart on the following page provides a graphic overview of the concepts developed in this chapter.

The first, and most basic systemic structure is the actual occasion of experience, or *actual entity*.[7] As indicated in the previous section, the actual occasion is the most fundamental, microscopic "building block" of reality. Everything that exists is constituted by a combination of actual occasions. These occasions are systemic entities in themselves, inasmuch as they come into being through the interplay of the past, or the environment, with God's initial aim and with their own aim. Once they come into being, they become subsystemic elements of what follows from them. Though the actual occasion has a measure of intentionality, this intentionality is not conscious. The intentionality may be either totally or partially fulfilled, and it may or may not be in accordance with God's intentionality.

Whatever accrues in the universe from the coming into being of actual occasions of experience has systemic or influencing relationship to whatever follows from it. If that influence is positive, the world is enriched. If negative, the world is impoverished. In process thought, beauty is the term that describes a positive outcome of the concrescence process. Beauty consists of the richest possible combination of intensity and harmony of experience. Intensity refers to novelty and creativity; harmony refers to balance and synergy among elements. Thus, an artistic production such as Picasso's *Three Musicians* is an example of beauty because it harmoniously combines the intense brokenness of line, color, and the human person with the intense commitment to music and human solidarity.

By contrast, evil may also accrue as a result of the coming into being of actual entities. In process terms, evil is the opposite of beauty. If beauty is the optimal combination of intensity and harmony of experience, evil consists of a malevolent combination of triviality and discord. Triviality refers to an occasion or entity being less than it could otherwise be. It is harmony without intensity. Discord is intensity without the balance of harmony. Picasso's *Guernica* is an excellent picture of evil insofar as the intensity of experience resulting from the saturation bombing is not

APPENDIX

A Psychosystem Map

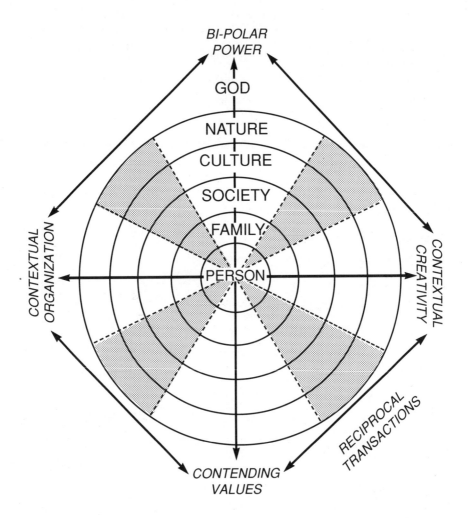

Shaded areas designate unconscious dimensions.

modified by a harmonious balance of care, nurture, and human cooperation. It is a picture of unmitigated discord, resulting in the triviality of experience on the part of the victims. Since they are the victims of the intense experience of discord, their experience and its value makes the world a poorer place than it otherwise would have been. This is characterized as genuine evil, understood as triviality and discord.

From this analysis, it follows that part of the systemic structure of reality consists of good and evil, since good and evil, or some combination, result from the concrescence process. Good and evil are not abstractions, but are inherent parts of the systemic realities contending for influence upon what comes into being next. As we shall see, the goals of increasing love of God, self, and neighbor, working for a just order, and promoting an ecological partnership are understood as morally good. They create the conditions for the most optimal combination of intense and harmonious experience. In contrast, lovelessness, injustice, and environmental rapaciousness are expressions of evil. Though they may be examples of certain forms of intensity, they result in such discord that individuals, groups, and the natural order are rendered less than they would otherwise be. Their experience and potentials are trivialized, resulting in the increase of genuine evil.

The *person* is the second structural component of this psychosystemic model. Because of the centrality of a view of persons for the ministry of care and pastoral theology, the following chapter will elaborate a psychosystemic understanding of the person. For now, it is important to recognize that the person is a synthesizing and creating center of experience, who both reflects and at least partially reshapes the other systems in which he or she is embedded. This receiving, synthesizing, and reconfiguring parallels the concrescence process of actual occasions of experience, but is relatively more conscious. Insofar as the psyche or soul is the master integrating system in the human person, it is a synthesis of many other syntheses among the physical, psychological, neurological, endoctrinal, and other subsystems comprising the person. These subsystems are in turn larger syntheses of cellular, molecular, and quantum subsystems. And these subsystems are larger syntheses of even more fundamental occasions of experiences. The person is a creative and novel synthesis of the microsystemic elements of its own being.

In addition, the human psyche or soul receives, synthesizes, and creates new forms from the macrosystems comprising its world. These influences are not always directly felt by the soul, but mediated through their impact upon other substructures of the person. For example, because of a natural defect resulting in childhood diabetes, a set of experiences is set in motion that will link the person with his or her body and environment in very particular ways. As a consequence, the soul must receive these influences, synthesize them, and create something from them. The creation will be good or evil, or some combination, and will feed back accordingly into the other systems and subsystems.

The *family* is the third component in this psychosystemic model. The family is the structured ongoing kinship system, which consists of two or more persons who by blood, choice, and/or law are bound together in a primary lifelong relationship with one another, and with those to whom each is also similarly related. The family is both nuclear and extended. The nuclear family may be of one party, but it usually consists of parents and minor children, centering in the household of the parents. The extended family includes all of those in the kinship system to whom the members of the nuclear family are related in lifelong fashion by blood, choice, and/or law. While the nuclear family is a one-generational enterprise, the extended family includes all prior and subsequent kinship arrangements in the family.

For the purpose of this book, the family is defined in the broadest possible terms. It is inclusive rather than exclusive. This definition includes single, dual, or multiple parent families. It embraces homosexual, bisexual, and heterosexual families and parentage. It embraces tribal communal arrangements, as well as rather isolated contemporary expressions. The central defining characteristics are the lifelong commitment to be identified as kin, and to retain this kinship by choice and/or by law. This view of kinship assumes, but does not necessarily require, relative degrees of participation in the roles, rules, and rituals of the nuclear and extended family, and a commitment to building viable primary relationships in the kinship structure.

The family fulfills several psychosystemic functions. It provides a context of belonging by which its individual members are protected, nourished, and accepted. In it we develop the capacity for loving and being loved and for balancing emotional closeness and distance. The family also socializes us and influences the values, roles, and rules by which we live. It provides our names and our fundamental social definition. In the family we learn to be separate individuals who are bonded together with others in cooperative social enterprises. We learn conflict management, communication skills, and how to work within limitations. Families also are agents of enculturation. The family is the primary context in which we first learn language, sex roles, religious perspectives and loyalty to race, tribe, and nation. Families provide our basic biological endowments, and instill within us basic attitudes toward work and the natural order. To the extent that our basic needs are met in the family, the world is viewed as a safe place in which we might be at home. To the extent that they are not, the world is experienced and viewed as threatening and destructive to our personality and our dreams.[8]

One of the more striking examples of the interaction between individuality, family, and environment is found in studies relating family and work. An examination of the allocation of work responsibilities in the family illustrates how families reflect and mediate larger social patterns concerning the roles of males and females. Studies have repeatedly indicated that women do more housework and spend more time caring for children than men, even those women who work as many hours outside the home as men.[9] The family is the primary environment where women and girls develop the culturally-expected capacity to be more relational and to be in charge of the details of the "private" world. The male is reinforced in the cultural expectation that he is the representative of the family to the "public" world, from which he derives his status. His home is his "castle" where he is served by women, and relatively free to follow his own pursuits. The family is the context that to a large degree carries the responsibility for reproducing the cultural exploitation of female labor, and the cultural expectations concerning what our boys and girls and men and women will be like. And though the family has some degree of autonomy and creativity, it is not so much "a haven in a heartless world," as the anvil upon which the patterns of the larger world are forged.[10]

The fourth systemic component is *society*. Society is the structured public organization of collective human experience. It refers to the institutional, political, racial, ethnic, and economic embeddedness of persons and families. It incorporates local, regional, and national laws, mores, and customs.

Society is enormously complex, and has pervasive influence on the character of persons and families.[11] The ways we think, feel, and act are inherently shaped by the interaction of persons with their social context. One's world views and sense of well-being are shaped by the larger social groups and institutions to which one belongs, and by the relationships between them. The values one holds, the power and opportunity one is given, the accomplishments one realizes, and the problems one has to surmount, are largely the result of one's skin color, economic status, and sexual identification.

It takes little thought to discern how careseekers are brought to care by the negative consequences of the social order in which they live. They are anxious about employment, and wonder how to provide the basic necessities of life to their families. They struggle to understand and locate themselves in a world of changing sex roles. They are frightened, fragmented, and furious about sexual harassment, exploitation, and violence. They fear losing loved ones to war, and still wrestle with the consequences of current and past wars on their personal and family lives. They are paralyzed with anxiety about losing their farm to larger impersonal market forces, or agonize over the struggle to adapt to diminished living for having lost their family farm. They are terrified of vilification and rejection for their homosexuality. They are angry and defeated in their attempts to gain an equal place in society for their race, and to be respected and valued as a racially different individual. They are terrified and enraged that they are left with no husband, no money, and little or no means of earning a fair wage in the job market. They are mistrustful of adults who do not believe that they are being physically and sexually abused by family members, and caught in a desperate struggle between protest, loyalty, and self-blame. They are uncompensated victims of crime, bureaucratic unresponsiveness, political ineptitude, high taxes, and inadequate restitution by the courts. They are depressed because society has set them aside because of their age or a handicapping condition.

These examples of presenting problems in the caretaking enterprise illustrate how the larger, more impersonal, structures of society may enter with devastating effect into the psyches of individuals and into the dynamics of our families. There are of course also positive contributions made by society upon persons and families. A systemically oriented theory of caretaking recognizes that to increase the love of self, God, and neighbor, we must also work for a just and humane social order. Niebuhr is correct, "When there is strife in . . . [our] community there is strife and pain in us and when it is at peace we have peace in ourselves."[12]

The fifth component of the systemic world is *culture*. Culture is the means by which humans collectively receive, synthesize,[13] and transform the influences of their world upon them. Culture is to the world as the soul is to the individual. Like the soul, culture is more than an activity or capacity for action. It is also the embodied representation and preserver of the outcomes of the interactions between humans and their multivalent world. The medium and embodiment of culture is language and literature. It is conveyed through art, literature, and music. Philosophy and science, as well as religion and moral codes, are expressions and purveyors of culture. Together these expressions of culture coalesce to form civilizations that are geographically defined and racially transmitted. Culture and civilization transcend, but greatly influence, social institutions, families, and individuals. They also mediate nature.

Historicism, materialism, and privatism are three particular cultural forces greatly influencing contemporary pastoral theology and care. Understanding and paying attention to these cultural realities is necessary for the caretaking process, and for modifying the conditions that contribute to distress.

Historicism refers to a broad intellectual movement that seeks to understand individual and collective human experience in terms of their historical function and development. Truth is understood as a particular and unique picture of reality held by a specific group or individual. Because all truth is historically conditioned, it is highly questionable whether there can be cross-cultural, universal truths that apply to all times and places. When linked with pragmatism, historicism evaluates patterns of living in terms of the quality of life they make possible, rather than in terms of pre-established norms.

On the positive side, historicism has liberated the human mind from an uncritical reliance upon external authority and tradition, and individuals from the tyranny of communities. It has enabled us to appreciate the rich diversity of human life, both personally and socially, and to think in terms of collaboration rather than competition. It has led to a greater awareness of the formative powers of our communities in shaping world views and providing a context for belonging, healing, and fulfillment. It has underscored the necessity for individual and communal responsibility in our choices of life-style and behavior.

On the more negative side, historicism has severed individuals and communities from their roots. It has made belief in God extremely problematic, and has raised serious difficulty for retaining loyalty to our religious, political, and cultural traditions. It has contributed to anxiety and anomie and a host of other problems. The result is a lack of a consensual basis for establishing a coherent public order and solidarity across a variety of social and cultural lines.

A culturally sensitive ministry of care recognizes that persons are adrift, without moorings, and that the communities which nurtured their visions of reality often no longer sustain or support them. It is sensitive to the conflicting pulls upon individuals and communities from a radically pluralistic world order. It seeks to reconnect persons and communities with their traditions, while at the same time assisting with the construction of new traditions that are responsive to the personal needs and historical realities of our own time.

A second cultural influence is materialism. I am using this term to designate a number of perspectives that define reality in terms of material forces contending for power and influence. Modern science and technology, and the economic philosophies of capitalism and Marxism, are the dominant cultural expressions of materialism. They have each resulted in major social and cultural revolutions. They have increased longevity and eased the burdens of life for some, and added burdens for others as well. They have been contributors to war, poverty, racism, and to a sense of meaningless dislocation. They have eventuated in environmental exploitation, especially when tied to industrial and technological advance. By reducing life to an attempt to control natural and economic forces, there has been little cultural basis for constructing a meaningful belief in God and for developing positive views of a just social order and responsible stewardship of the natural environment.

The most malevolent legacy of material consciousness is the culture of violence to which it contributes and makes technologically possible. Our century might best be characterized as an age of hostility and violence, made possible by the partnership of science and technology with conflicting economic, social, and political agendas. Accordingly, much of the violence in the modern world derives from an unjust distribution of the world's material resources, and from the capacity of those who have amassed more economic and technological power to control the destinies of those with less. When linked with other cultural realities such as sexism and racism, this form of domination has eventuated in numerous virulent and interlocking oppressions.

Pastoral caretaking works with victims and perpetrators of our violent culture. Unfortunately, it is the victim rather than the perpetrator who most often seeks our counsel. Pastoral caretaking is responsive to many types of victims of violence: those who have been maimed or bereaved by war; survivors of incest, rape, and battering; the unemployed, the underemployed, and the marginalized. However, we are also beginning to discover that our unconscious makeup is affected by our culture of violence. There is a generalized despair resulting from an impotent rage and terror at the possibility of a nuclear holocaust, and the pervasiveness of conventional warfare and terrorism. Many first-world persons experience survivor guilt with respect to our high standard of living at the expense of others. There is a growing sense of hopelessness that the nations of the world will not be able to overcome these coercive and destructive patterns of acquisition and greed.[14]

It remains to be seen whether or not these growing awarenesses will lead to further isolation, privatization, and competition, or whether they will eventuate in a transforming cultural revolution. Whatever the outcome, it seems that these issues are present in full force in the pastoral caretaking enterprise. And just as psychoanalysis provided a major alternative to the culture of sexual repression dominant in its day, so it is my hope that pastoral caretaking informed by prophetic principles might provide a major alternative to the culture of violence of our day.

Privatism is the third cultural factor that must be taken into account by pastoral theology and the ministry of care. Privatism is characterized by focused interest upon the intrapsychic and interpersonal dynamics of persons apart from attention to the larger public social order. It is akin to the existentialist-anthropological model of personal life discussed in the previous chapter.[15] This attention to the interior lives of individuals, and to their primary relationships, is made possible in part because of the extent to which historicism has severed the individual from the community, thereby allowing the concept of selfhood to emerge more predominantly in modern thought. It is also an expectable reaction to the manner in which materialism has removed individuals from center stage by regarding the more impersonal natural and economic forces as determinative of personal experience and behavioral options. As work and home have been more fully separated, individuals have been thrown more directly back onto themselves and to their inner and private worlds.

The positive side has been the opportunity to discover the rich inner world of persons and human relationships. The negative side is that the culture has continued to separate the personal and the private, leaving the public order increasingly in the hands of fewer and fewer people with greater and greater power. Drawing upon the benefits of the larger public order while removing oneself from committed responsibility for its limitations and abuses, ultimately leaves those influenced by the privatistic subculture more vulnerable to those larger systemic forces, and leaves those forces unmodified by other human vitalities. A more or less conscious sense of anomie, anxiety, despair, impotence, rage, and guilt is perpetuated rather than mitigated by focusing upon the psychological dynamics of individuals apart from their relationship to the cultural system that largely generates and perpetuates these emotions. A systemically sensitive pastoral theology and ministry of care will help persons explore the impact of their culture upon their souls and life-styles, and work to modify the culture itself, as well as their reactions to it.

The sixth component of reality is *nature*. Nature refers to all the entities making up the universe that are capable of endurance, generativity, and change apart from human influence. It includes the smallest unit of experience, as well as complex macrosystems such as planets, solar systems, and galaxies. Human life, society, and culture cannot function without nature. These entities are shaped in relation to the possibilities and limitations of the natural world. Nature provides the pervasive context for our greatest achievements as human beings, as well as the greatest threat. We are born as a result of the interaction of social and natural processes. The threat to our existence as represented most ultimately in death itself, is fundamentally an inevitable natural process, however affected by human social experience.[16]

Despite the relative independence of nature from human beings, society, and culture, the relationship between humanity and the natural world must be understood in terms of mutual, rather than linear or causal influence. If nature has given rise to human beings and shaped their social and cultural life, so has human social and cultural life shaped and defined nature. Current ecological awareness makes it clear that human beings have extracted great resources from nature, and have inflicted great harm upon nature in the process.[17] Many species have become extinct due to human activity. Our biochemical explorations may lead to the development of disturbing new forms of life whose existence may be incompatible with our own and with other living species.

The ministry of care exists at the interface between the various components comprising the individual's world. If a person is a victim of a natural disaster, the impact extends throughout her or his family, as well as into the social and cultural context in which she or he lives. Whether recognized or not, a pastoral response to any crisis usually requires attention to the interplay of personal, social, cultural, and natural forces. In the following section, I will explore the mechanisms by which such an interplay is made possible, and by which it may begin to be interpreted.

THE PSYCHOSYSTEMIC CONNECTORS

Process theology, which undergirds the formulations of this book, affirms that all reality, at all times, is dynamic, relational, and processive. There are inherent connections between entities, and entities participate in each other's coming into being. What factors allow us to account for this continuity and change, for the capacity to be influenced by and to influence the actual coming into being of the psychosystemic components of the world? I have identified five elements that account for the connections and transformations in a dynamic, relational, and processive universe. All of these presuppose one another, and must be actualized for anything to exist and for there to be any kind of relationship or novelty. These five elements are contextual organization, contextual creativity, bi-polar power, contending values, and reciprocal transactions.

Contextual organization refers to the identifiable continuity of the system as a whole, and of each subsystem or entity comprising the system. It can be thought of as massiveness, the past, or the givenness of things. Personal identity in individuals is an example of contextual organization in persons. The body is another. In the family, contextual organization is defined by who is in charge, and by the presence of boundaries operating between members of the family and between the family and the external world. Society is organized by laws, mores, political parties, and the like. Culture is organized by religion, art, and language.

Contextual organization represents the enduring power arrangements in a system or subsystem. It also identifies and preserves the creative accomplishments and value orientations of the system or subsystem. It binds and channels the transactional processes within the system, making them more or less predictable and enduring. Contextual organization represents actualized coalescence in the system, rather than what is merely potential and chaotic. Persons in families often seek pastoral assistance because they are disorganized and fear further impairment of their integrity.

Contextual creativity is a term I have adapted from Professor Delwin Brown[18] to refer to the capacity for novelty and creative advance that exists within every subsystem, and within the system as a whole. It is the polar opposite of contextual organization. If an entity has too much structure and organization it would lead to stagnation, or triviality, as discussed earlier. Creativity alone would lead to chaos and disintegration of the system. Contextual creativity is the dimension of the system that connects present structures to new possibilities. It optimally combines the elements of harmony and intensity, in process theology terms. It is the impulse to reform and revolution, in social and cultural terms. It is the impulse to growth, self-transcendence, and structural change in personal and family terms. Contextual creativity is the locus of the appetitive and intentional dimensions of life; it is the "energy" one identifies and joins to promote change. Systemic creativity is contextual inasmuch as it takes into account the enduring influence of the massive realities impinging upon the present moment. Systemic creativity is novel inasmuch as it contributes to the reconfiguration of the power arrangements, value orientations, and transactional patterns dominating the present moment. Persons seeking care are looking in part for assistance in restructuring their contexts in more creative or novel fashion.

Each component of the systemic world is characterized by the interplay of organization and creativity. Each component has within it the capacity for continuity and change, however developed or limited these may be. Since each component is also connected with every other structure, the character of the relationship between continuity and change at one level has potential ramifications for the character of organization and change at another level.

Bi-polar power refers to the capacity of each element within the system and the system as a whole to receive and to provide influence. In a systemically organized universe, there are exchanges of influence, or power, by which stability is maintained and change effected. Power is bi-polar inasmuch as it combines agency and receptivity. All entities must have the power of agency, or the ability to endure and to shape their environment and their own becoming, if they and the world are to be enriched. Agential power is the energy by which creativity reaches its goals, and which complements the capacity of organized structures to be receptive. Likewise, all entities must have the power or ability to be influenced by their environments in order to be enriched by the fullest set of possibilities for their own growth and becoming. Receptive power is the means by which creativity is sensitive to the resources and limitations of the structured context, and which enables the organized structures of the system to change.[19]

Our culture does not regard agential and receptive power as complementary. We are obsessed with agential power on its own terms. Cut off from receptive power, agential power takes the form of controlling, exploiting, and oppressing others for our own ends, without regard for their agency or for what they might have to contribute to our welfare. Receptive power is regarded as weak, vulnerable, or sick. Agential power is identified with stereotypical masculine values, receptive power with feminine.[20]

The analysis of power is central in this theory of pastoral caretaking. Feminist thinkers and third-world liberation theologians have made it extremely clear that the power arrangements of a society, and the ideologies undergirding them, must be analyzed in terms of who benefits and who suffers. Once analyzed, these power arrangements must be modified or replaced so that there are more equitable and just arrangements. Family systems therapy, and especially the structural therapists, emphasize that the power hierarchy in families must be clear and intact for the members of the family to function in a healthy manner.[21] Intrapsychic pathology can also be interpreted as the result of an imbalance in the power arrangements in the psychic structure of persons. Thus, for example, anxiety can be interpreted as insufficient agential power of the ego in relation to the overwhelming agential power of the id, superego, and/or environment. The anxiety is a signal that the ego must mobilize a greater degree of agential power so that it does not become merely a helpless receptor of impinging forces from elsewhere in the system. Persons seeking care are enmeshed in destructive power arrangements and seek to gain power to maintain their integrity and to creatively change their contextual situation.

Contending values refers to the dynamic interplay between the quality of the achievements and creative potentials of the entities comprising the system, and the system as a whole. In terms of process theology, all reality comes into being as a result of choices between contending values. Things could have been otherwise, but once they come into actualization they are characterized in terms of beauty or evil, or some combination. Once into being, they make a qualitative contribution to that which follows from them. What comes to be is therefore qualitatively connected to what already exists. However, there is also some degree of novelty or creativity, rooted in the agential and receptive power of each entity, which adds its own value to the value that already exists. God is also a persuasive influence, adding new possibilities for beauty rather than evil. Hence, there is a contending for influence among competing values. The outcome of this contention contributes to how power will be arranged, or structured organizationally, and which creative options will and will not be actualized in the structures of reality.

In psychosystemic care, love, justice, and ecological responsibility provide the foundational value orientations by which the power arrangements between the personal, social, and natural orders might be most creatively organized and structured. Persons who seek care, like Patricia and her family referred to in chapter 1, are those who are in some form or another victims and perpetrators of lovelessness, injustice, and ecological irresponsibility. Lovelessness, injustice, and environmental disorder are embodied in and perpetrated by inadequate contextual organization, disadvantageous power arrangements, limited creative options, and ongoing negative valuation of individuals, families, and groups. Symptomatic persons reveal symptomatic value systems; repair and transformation of the one in principle may contribute similarly to the other.

Reciprocal transactions are the processes by which influence is exchanged, creativity channeled, power distributed, value communicated, and the system organized. Reciprocal transactions can be mapped and modified, since they are contextually organized as well as creatively responsive to the dynamics at work in the system.

In human individuals, cognition, perception, and behavior are examples of reciprocal transactions with the environment. These transactions are organized structurally. They are characterized by coherence and endurance. They reveal some of the value orientations contending for influence or consideration. They suggest potentially creative alternatives to the dominant power arrangements at work in the person and between the person and his or her world.

In families, reciprocal transactions are organized by roles, rules, and rituals, as well as by dynamic processes such as collusion and triangulation. An examination of the transactions at work in the food chain demonstrates the reciprocal interconnections throughout the psychosystemically connected world. Human beings, it has been said, "are what we eat."[22] Thus, our practice of using petrochemicals in farming, and numerous additives in our food processing procedures, has perhaps been economically and politically advantageous to some. But for most it has increased the risk of disease and cancer, it has made us overdependent upon large food conglomerations—thus separating us from nature and perhaps one another—and it is poisoning the land and the water supply, and the wildlife they support. Likewise, those who have no food to eat, are largely victims of breakdowns along the food chain, which includes political and cultural along with natural and personal factors.

A PSYCHOSYSTEMIC MAP

A psychosystemic picture of the universe emphasizes the dynamic interconnections between all of the components of the universe. The components range from the microcosmic world of actual entities to include the world of persons, families, society, culture, and nature. The elements by which these are connected, maintained, and changed are contextual organization, contextual creativity, bi-polar power, contending values, and reciprocal transactions. My psychosystemic model is diagrammed in the chart on page 54.

The broken lines in the model point to the quality of the boundaries between components. The broken line indicates openness to influence and exchange of energy between intact subsystems. The boundaries between fused subsystems would be indicated by dots; rigidly disengaged substructures by solid lines.

The shaded areas indicate unconscious dimensions of the psychosystem. Unconscious life pertains most clearly to human persons, though there are elements in each substructure that are cut off from awareness. For example, families "forget" certain parts of their histories and are not aware of certain dynamics. Society, culture, and nature likewise neglect or overlook certain operative factors, which remain as hidden potential influences on the dominant conscious pattern. The boundaries between conscious and unconscious dynamics are variable. Unconscious forces, like other dimensions of reality, consist of contextually organized value possibilities, power arrangements, creative options, and reciprocal transactions. These unconscious forces stand in a systemic, reciprocal relationship to one another and to the external world.

The psychosystemic map of reality consists of expanding, more inclusive, circles. One must read this map in terms of interpenetrating influence rather than as a status or value hierarchy. Particularity and universality are not mutually opposed, but assume and require one another. Individuals gain their particularity by the character of their participation in their larger internal and external worlds. The larger systemic world is the structured organization of innumerable transactions, power arrangements, creative potentials, and contending values operating at more particular points in the system.

In such a view, the locus of power and responsibility is quite diffuse. Though human individuals constitute the most clear center of power, individuals are not fully autonomous. Their values and creative options reflect their structured location in families, societies, cultures, and nature, each of which partially defines, limits, and expands the agency of the individual. Personal values and qualities appropriate for one level of the system may be in conflict with personal qualities and values at another.

For example, a parent needs the qualities of tenderness, longsuffering, and patience, while a soldier needs to be adept at killing as efficiently as possible when ordered to do so. A minister may be in conflict between the religious injunction of loving one's enemies and supporting defense policies designed to kill one's enemies. In all cases, responsibility for choice and action normally resides with the individual, or with individuals acting in concert. However, this action is severely influenced by pressures from the psychosystemic world in which the individual resides, and to which he or she is always related.

Finally, because of the inherently dynamic character of reality, it is impossible to claim ultimate superiority for any existing configuration of values, structure, power arrangements, transactional patterns, and creative accomplishments. The psychosystemic world is finally one of pluralism, risk, and change. In keeping with historical consciousness of the modern period, all human accomplishments and claims to understanding are relative to the historical conditions in which they have emerged. They differ for individuals, families, societies, and cultures. It is not possible to identify a priori universal standards by which the various configurations can be evaluated. However, the configurations most in keeping with the goals of Christian ministry are those which promote an increase of the love of God, self, and neighbor, expand justice, and result in ecological fecundity. In terms of process theology, the configurations that are most prized are those which increase harmony and intensity, and reduce discord and triviality. In liberation theology, those which produce personal and social liberation and reflect the most humane configurations are valued.

GOD AND THE PSYCHOSYSTEMIC UNIVERSE

In the light of process theology, as interpreted through systems theory, I believe that God's reality must be reconceived in terms of a systemic and contextual coming-into-being rather than as an eternally completed being. In this view, whether recognized or not, God is present in every context influencing, but not determining, what is coming into being. As we have seen, there can be no reality without the activity and receptivity of God. God offers to each emerging entity the most optimal possibility for its becoming. Further, God receives into God's being whatever comes into existence, and continues to provide the most optimal set of new possibilities to every level of reality. Just as humans are constituted by their interactions with their systemic environment, so the being of God is constituted by the very elements that constitute and connect the psychosystemic world.

In this view, God's being itself is fundamentally contextual. It contributes to and is in turn shaped by the character of every contextual reality in the universe. The aim of God is to promote harmony and intensity of experience, rather than discord and triviality, between every level of reality. Since everything having existence has a measure of organization, power, and creativity—and contributes to the quality of the world through its reciprocal interactions—God cannot ultimately control or determine the final configuration of the world. Each outcome reflects a partial fulfillment of God's intention, and provides the basis for subsequent fulfillments.

To affirm that we can only know God in relation to our own contextual experience, and that each experience of God is valid, is not to say that each experience of God is equal in scope or consequence. Since contexts differ and are sometimes incompatible, so might authentic experiences and views of God differ and be incompatible. Difference in viewpoint does not, however, necessarily mean superiority or inferiority of viewpoint. Neither does a current understanding guarantee permanent understanding. God's reality, as well as the psychosystemic character of the universe, ensures that there will be creative new configurations that will eventuate in novel experiences and transformed understandings of the truths we now hold. These truths and transformed understandings do not already exist in God's being, awaiting discovery or disclosure in some context-free environments. Rather, they will only emerge as possibilities for the creation of a new world when God and the world together bring about the context in which they can be generated.

The radical contextuality of God means that the ministry of care is open to expectation, and is grounded in God's pervasive and providential presence. It looks for the most optimal combinations of intense and harmonious relationships between all the components of the psychosystemic universe. It looks to God as an ally, recognizing its own partiality and unique standpoint. It proceeds with a tentative confidence that God is an unceasing working partner in the caretaking enterprise.[23]

SUMMARY AND CONCLUSION

The universe consists of an interacting systemic whole, organized from smallest to largest units, or components. These components are actual occasions of experience, persons, families, societies, culture, and nature. They are linked by five interrelated connecting elements. Contextual organization refers to the identity and continuity of a component or entity. Contextual creativity points to the capacity for intentionality and change. Bi-polar power describes the inherent capacity for an entity to be influenced by and to influence others. Contending values delineate the qualitative dimension of an entity's becoming and influence upon others. Reciprocal transactions account for the mutual exchanges of power, creativity, and values in and between organized and changing entities.

A psychosystemic map accounts in principle for the interrelationship of all elements in the universe, and provides the basis for understanding God's presence and action. God is systemically related to the world inasmuch as God's presence stimulates the most optimal possibility for each unit of reality, and God's being is influenced by what actually comes into being. God's intentionality is to bring about greater combinations of intensity and harmony of experience on the part of each unit of experience, and between all elements in the world. Increasing the love of self, God and neighbor, increasing justice, and promoting environmental partnership are viewed as expressions of optimal intensity and harmony. Lovelessness, violence, injustice, and environmental rapaciousness are viewed as examples of triviality and discord—or genuine evil—inasmuch as they eventuate in the world becoming in actuality a poorer place than it might otherwise be. Psychosystemic pastoral caretaking seeks to be an ally of God in generating greater harmony and intensity, and in transforming the quality of persons and their worlds. We turn now to a fuller discussion of the relevance of this pyschosystemic orientation to a concept of persons, the primary focus of response in much pastoral caretaking.

CHAPTER 3

THE INDIVIDUAL IN CARE: A PSYCHOSYSTEMIC PROFILE OF PERSONHOOD

I am as Thou art.
Karl Barth[1]

I was going through the hardest thing, also the greatest thing, for any human being to do; to accept that which is already within you, and around you.

Malcolm X[2]

T he ministry of care requires a theory of personhood if it is to effectively increase the welfare of individuals and their communities. Indeed, it is difficult to expand love of self if one does not have some idea what the self is and how it is shaped.[3] Drawing upon philosophical concepts based in process theology, a psychosystemically oriented pastoral theology interprets the human individual as a network of relationships. As the network of relationships expands, the self is enriched and increases its ability to contribute to its own life as well as to the life of the world.

INDIVIDUALISM AND INDIVIDUALITY

In chapter 1, I discussed the existential-anthropological model of personality, which is dominant in the field of pastoral care and counseling today. This approach is largely individualistic, and tends to minimize the connective relationships between persons and their world. In addition, it tends to devalue the impact of family, society, and culture upon individuals, leading persons to believe that they can ultimately be fulfilled apart from a meaningful connection to their multiple environments.

One influential exemplar of this approach is Sigmund Freud. It is commonly known that his personality theory posited an unbridgeable gulf between primary individual vitalities and the need for social order and safety. In order to accommodate this gap, a variety of maneuvers are necessary from both sides. Symptoms emerge when it is not possible for individuals to balance their vitalities with social expectations. Culture in turn is asked to be more tolerant of human vitalities and to find fitting social channels for them. One of Freud's classic formulations of the inherent conflict between the person and the world is found in *Group Psychology and Analysis of the Ego*. Here Freud argues that our belonging to transient social organizations, and to more permanent larger groupings such as class, race, creed, and nationalities diminishes our individuality and forces us to operate at a more primitive psychological level.[4] He admits that this loss of individuality is more or less temporary, and that there remains an opportunity to raise oneself "above them to the extent of having a [remaining] scrap of independence and originality."[5]

Reinhold Niebuhr provides a theological exemplar for an excessive individualism that posits an unresolvable conflict between persons and society. The social order was regarded by him as essentially negative, operating by collective self-interest and power politics. In *Moral Man and Immoral Society*, Niebuhr states explicitly that the morality of groups is inferior to that of individuals, in part because there is less basis for cohesion in society than in individuals and in part because society gives collective expression to the egoistic impulses of individuals in a manner that defies rational control by those same individuals.[6]

Further, Niebuhr's concept of self-transcendence understood the human spirit to be influenced by, but ultimately free of, history and nature. Individuals do not find their ultimate care or cure within history, but in the relationship their self-transcendent spirit establishes with the free spirit of God.[7] Social ethics are employed to counter excessive collective self-interest and the abuse of power in the social arena. But there is little sense that the social order is transformed and that the person-world relationship is mutually positive. Niebuhr believed that while nature and culture were necessary for individuality to be possible, the individual was ultimately morally superior to, and finally found fulfillment apart from, his or her relationship to the environment.

There are three notions central to Freud and Niebuhr relevant to this discussion. First, they believe that the individual and the social order are in essential conflict, with the social order having ultimately a negative impact upon individual welfare. Second, they believe that the self is essentially separative rather than connective. That is, while society, culture, nature, and history may be a primary condition for individuals to come into being, their fulfillment and destiny ultimately results from autonomous rather than interconnected functioning.[8] Finally, they believe that the individual is ultimately self-interested rather than altruistic.

This motif of separative and autonomous selfhood underlies much of the current theological and psychological interpretations informing contemporary pastoral care and counseling. It is also dominant in contemporary North American psychotherapeutic circles. Robert Bellah and his associates have contended that this model of personhood is essentially individualistic. They affirm the many gains that have been made through this approach—heightened self-awareness, better interpersonal relationships, greater congruence between thinking, feeling, and acting. But they argue that this individualistic orientation essentially undermines a basis for conceiving an organic relationship between selfhood and society. Bellah states that

> anxiety and uncertainty about more important and enduring relationships are increasing rather than decreasing. Therapists have grown increasingly concerned about the lack of "community" in modern life. . . . Yet . . . the very language of therapeutic relationship seems to undercut the possibility of other than self-interested relationships. . . . The only morality that is acceptable is the purely contractual agreement of the parties: whatever they agree to is right. . . .[9]

For Bellah, the result of this individual egoism is moral impoverishment, empty relationships, and an empty self, unconnected to time, place, and others. For him, the most serious consequence is the undermining of any positive basis for fashioning a consensual public morality and coherent social order.[10]

It is against this backdrop that a psychosystemic view of the connective and emergent self has particular clarifying and corrective power. I agree with Bellah that the notion of a separative self ultimately leads to an empty and non-social self. Any individuality that comes out of such a notion of the self is truncated, impaired, and ultimately meaningless. It has limited capacity either to receive the richness from its culture or to contribute to a qualitatively positive world. By contrast, a psychosystemic interpretation of the self leads to an individuality that is richly textured and lives in an ongoing, mutually enhancing relationship with society, culture, and nature.

Thus, human beings neither fully transcend their communities, nor are controlled by them, but exist by the establishment of "relative independence" in community.[11] The more the person interacts with others and community, the more individual the person becomes; the more individual the person becomes, the greater one's participation in community. Thus, it is the contention of this chapter that individualism, apart from multiple connections with a richly textured community, ultimately works against a rich individuality. By contrast, a richly textured individuality emerges in the interplay between persons and their context in the mutual creation, reflection, and transcendence of one by the other.

THE CONNECTIVE PERSON

1. The body is the primary basis for connecting with our worlds and for generating our sense of selfhood. There would be no ability for us to connect with our sense of self as individual without the body and its processes. Our organic structures and our five senses interact with the brain to enable us to know ourselves as persons in time and space. The body is the expression for our connections to self and others.

When we meet a person, we respond to him or her primarily in bodily terms. We do not forget what sex a person is. We remember their skin color. Sometimes we are aware of our own bodily reactions to persons, such as tension or attraction. These responses illustrate how the body is the organic foundation and the locating center of the person. Age, color, and gender are dimensions of bodily life that define the person temporally and socially, marking the individual as a subsystem in relation to other systems. The body constitutes both the boundary and the connection between the human being and the other units of experience to which he or she is related. Further, the body is the means by which the world has access to the psyche.

As the organic foundation of the person, the body is also the source of energy for all of the activities of the psyche and the means by which they are carried out. For example, the musculoskeletal system provides the organic structural basis for accomplishing desired behaviors. The neurological system, along with the various sense organs, provides the organic basis for the psyche's work of receiving, synthesizing, and transforming experience. In turn, the condition of the body—in pain and pleasure—contributes in its own way to what the psyche itself becomes. A positive sense of self has its origin in a primal experience of physical well-being. Those whose bodies are abused early in childhood often develop truncated personalities and painfully dysfunctional orientations to their larger world.

As a consequence of these dynamics, the body becomes the repository of the psyche or the self, as well as its organic foundation and generating source. Wilhelm Reich, an early dissenter from psychoanalytic orthodoxy, recognized that the body had psychological vitality.[12] It provided a "character armor" by which the human being was able to preserve or store its most intimate psychological material and protect it from assault by the threatening environment. A number of modern studies have elaborated this insight. Massage and bioenergetic therapies probably provide the most dramatic examples of how the psyche of persons can be accessed directly through the body. Attention to "body language" reveals the extent to which the body expresses the self, here understood as the quality and intentionality of the psyche. Further, the reaction of the environment to the size, shape, and color of one's body has grave consequences for one's relation to the world in which he or she lives, and for the character of the self that emerges in the psyche. The ministry of care is often challenged to respond to the spiritual and emotional dilemmas encountered by persons whose bodies are in demise by illness, accident, or assault. The loss of the integrity and continuity of bodily life constitutes one of the most profound needs for care and empowerment, as Ernst Becker and others have demonstrated.[13]

A concrete example of the interplay between psyche, body, and environment is taken from Salvador Minuchin, a family therapist who has greatly informed my thinking.[14] Minuchin reports experiments with families who have a diabetic child. The child was placed in one room, the parents in another. The child could watch the parents through a one-way mirror, but the parents could not see their child. Blood-drawing needles were placed into the arms of each family member to measure the degree of free fatty acid—a substance in the bloodstream that is a precursor to the onset of a diabetic reaction—present in each person.

The parents were instructed to discuss their problems with one another, with the child watching. As they discussed their problems, conflict escalated between them. There was a simultaneous increase of free fatty acids in the bloodstream of each family member, but the degree of increase was within normal limits and not alarming. The child was then asked to enter the room with the parents. The parents were asked to continue their conversation. After a short period of time, they stopped discussing their conflicts with each other and began focusing upon the child's difficulties. This detoured the parental conflict and gave the child the decisive power balance in the family system. Consequently, the free fatty acids in the bloodstream of the parents diminished radically, while it increased to alarming proportions in the child. It remained higher than normal after the experiment ended without resolution of the earlier parental conflict.

This experiment clearly illustrates that the physiological processes of each member of the family are connected to emotional and relational transactions within the family system. The sense of individual well-being instantly shifts when relational dynamics are altered in the system. The quality of individual well-being reflects the quality of the dynamic connections between the players making up the interactional field.

In psychosystemic perspective, the body and the psyche form an interacting unity. Each contributes to the welfare and character of the other. They are not connected dualistically. Situational dualisms may emerge if the boundaries between the psyche and the body become too rigid or are shattered altogether in a given individual, but functionally the psyche and body are irrevocably linked with each other and their environments. The relationship between psyche and body is not mechanistic and reductionistic, as in the modern western world view, but characterized by a patterned indeterminateness. Patterns and continuities are statistical probabilities rather than fixed, permanent conditions. They are constituted by mutually reinforcing patterns, and subject to modification, however slightly, by environmental influences, including human observation.

2. The reciprocal, transactional interplay between a healthy or ill body, a positive or negative self-concept, and a supportive or malignant social and cultural context thoroughly challenges the individualism dominant in our milieu. Pilisuk and Parks[15] cite impressive evidence linking physical and emotional well-being to the quality of the social environment. They demonstrate that persons living in social circumstances that promoted loneliness and high levels of stress showed lower levels of antibodies necessary to fight a well-known virus.[16] This research is particularly noteworthy inasmuch as it demonstrates that the body's immune system and physiological processes are directly related to "psycho-social influences." That is to say, dualistic interpretations that separate health care needs from physiological and social processes are severely questionable. The connections between them are much more organic and irrevocable.

In addition, Pilisuk and Parks provide other evidence demonstrating that the quality of the self-concept is an important variable in relation to the presence or absence of physical health. Persons with a more positive self-concept seem to have psychological resources which, in effect, support the immune system. Those with a poor self-concept are more susceptible to a variety of health problems. Pilisuk and Parks demonstrate that the quality of the self-concept is not merely an individual achievement, operating independently of the social environment. In fact, they demonstrate that the quality of the self-concept is shown to be greatly influenced by the presence or absence of meaningful social support. Moreover, opportunities for qualitative social support are related to the socioeconomic context in which support is sought.[17] People who are stuck in poverty and who are victims of racism and other situations of social inequality are faced with less opportunity for meaningful social support and the positive self-concept that it generates. This in turn makes them more susceptible to a variety of emotional and physical difficulties. Thus, the self is meaningfully connected to its body and environment, even as these are connected to the self. There is ongoing reciprocal interplay, with positive and negative consequences being possible depending on the specific situations.

3. The structure of consciousness richly connects persons and their worlds. As we have seen, the human individual is multiply conjoined[18] in

body, environment, and psyche. In addition, the connections between persons and their worlds are mediated by a variety of levels of consciousness. Consciousness is defined here as the combination of accountable intentionality and knowledgeable awareness. Consciousness is another mode of linking at multiple levels to the environments in which the self is a player. The larger social system and the subsystems of psyche and body, which together structurally organize the human person, have conscious and unconscious dimensions. That is, some of the processes of the psyche, environment, and the body are present to knowledgeable awareness and accountable intentionality, and others are not. Both conscious and unconscious materials comprise a subsystem that influences what does or does not occur in the interplay between persons and their worlds.

The contents of conscious and unconscious materials are each influenced by one another, as well as by the relationship of the person to her or his multiple environments. Influences from the many contexts interacting with the person are powerful determinants of which materials will be allowed and which disallowed access to consciousness. Repression and suppression are the central mechanisms in determining which materials will be conscious or unconscious. Selective attention is another common example of keeping material unconscious.

Once certain materials become unconscious, they exert a pressure upon the self and the system. A structural boundary between conscious and unconscious materials comes into being and plays an ongoing part in the person's relationship to himself or herself and to the environment. Like all boundaries, the boundary between conscious and unconscious materials may be closed, porous, or fluid. In any case, there is a dynamic interplay between consciousness and unconsciousness, with each having a potentially creative relationship to the other. For example, a psycho-cybernetic view of the mind suggests that the unconscious functions to bring to accomplishment the goals and intentions of the conscious mind, once these are made available to the unconscious.[19] Conversely, the work of Jung and others shows how the unconscious offers correctives and alternatives to the contents of the conscious mind which, if incorporated into awareness, have revolutionary consequences for persons and the world in which they live.[20]

In addition to being fashioned by materials that are repressed in the psychosocial history and multiple contexts of the individual, it would appear that Jung is correct that the unconscious possesses collective dimensions. The collective unconscious is constituted by the memories, images, and accomplishments of the human race as a whole, and probably transmitted genetically.[21] Modern holographic studies of the brain demonstrate its capacity to store a massive amount of data in the same space.[22] It would appear that this material is available, though unconscious or out of awareness. As we learn consciously to access and receive it, we will be able to synthesize and transform it for creative purposes of personal and communal living. As a totality, therefore, the unconscious represents the massive internalized past, which must be taken into account in determining what will emerge in the present moment of experience. As psychocybernetics demonstrates, whatever is consciously desired influences which resources from the personal and collective unconscious will be efficacious in the present moment. This discovery parallels the contention of process metaphysics that the intentionality of the actual entity plays a major role in determining what will be appropriated from the past in determining the present and shaping the future.

A more direct social example of the impact of unconscious or hidden material is illustrated in the phenomenon of family secrets. A family secret is one or more events that affect the family, including the psychological status of individuals of the family, without acknowledgment or accountability. While the intent of the family secret is to protect others and to enhance their lives, it most often functions to create secret loyalties and isolation, and can lead to depression or anxiety for members of the family.[23] Thus, I recall a colleague who became quite depressed and acted out in delinquent fashion in seventh and eighth grades. He sought individual treatment for these problems, which were a mystery to him and to his family. It was only as an adult that he discovered that, at the same time he was going through this difficult period, his father had secretly begun an affair with a work associate. Thus, this family's out-of-awareness material had a tremendous negative influence on the personal life and family environment in which it occurred.

On a larger scale, individuals and cultures are diminished when the connections between their social, mythological, and racial experiences are kept out of awarenesss by not being fully thematized in literature, art, and history. My colleague, George Tinker, is a Native American who argues that distorted or neglected stories from both the Euro-American and Native American past obscure the collective and personal damage done by the conquest of the North American continent by European peoples.[24] For Tinker, our inability to be fully aware of the past means that, while North Americans celebrate the gains made since Columbus' "discovery" of the continent, indigenous peoples must continue to grieve the beginning and endure the ongoing effects of genocide upon them as a group. Tinker believes that the increasing depression, suicide, alcoholism, and unemployment characteristic of so many Native American individuals is inherently related to the denied connections that our culture makes between the situation of these people and our own advances.

To conclude, an analysis of the relation of the body, psyche, and environment demonstrates that persons and their worlds are multiply conjoined. Connection is a fact of life. And, while it is possible to think in terms of separation and dualism, these appear to be distorted forms of existence that do not recognize our essential connectedness, or that occur when the connections are negative rather than positive. Further, an analysis of the structure of consciousness reveals that we are multiply conjoined at various levels of awareness that operate as powerfully influential components of experience. Dürer's "knight of faith" may express the way persons choose to organize a relationship to their environment. However, such an individualism leads to an isolated and truncated individuality. It neglects to explore the vast array of interconnections which in fact do exist, and to see the multiplicity of positive constellations of experience that might emerge as a result of such connections.

THE EMERGENT SELF

As we have seen, the self is not an autonomous entity to which things may happen, but which is ultimately separate from its multiple environments. The self is variously connected and comprises a rich array of multiple influences. However, the self is not only a network of connections, it is an *emerging* reality eventuating from these ongoing connections. By definition, the self is the qualitative and unique expression of the psyche, which emerges from reciprocal transactional processes within individuals and between individuals and their environments. To understand the self as essentially connective and emergent, it is necessary to find a conceptual framework that will consider the relational patterns accounting for its emergence.[25]

1. Reciprocal transactions in becoming a self. Though the human person appears to be a relatively stable and organized unit of body and mind, it is clear from many contemporary views of the personality that the human person is constantly coming into being and changing. This is an extremely complicated process, with many conflicting interpretations. However, in order to illustrate and expand my psychosystemic approach, I would like to highlight some of the major reciprocal processes occurring in the development of the self and in the development of gender identity.[26]

When the infant is born there is very little psychic differentiation or autonomy from the mother or caretaking person. The conscious experience of the self is a later development, which results from the conscious incorporation of background experiences, or "forerunners" to a sense of a self as *myself*. The personal sense of oneself is based upon environmental experiences that were created by parents and others, making one's personal history distinctive in shaping the unique character of one's sense of self.

There are several background, preconscious factors that are foundational to the quality of selfhood that finally emerge in conscious experience. For a positive, well-differentiated and full self-experience to emerge, the infant must have a sense of continuity of being, based upon parental protection from excessive internal and external stimuli. There must be a range of bodily and relational stimuli that evoke quiet satisfaction as well as joy in the infant. The child must experience a growing sense of himself or herself as an actor or agent, whose efforts at mastery are praised and positively attested by the significant others in her or his world. Finally, there must be an embryonic sense of well-being and worthwhileness that flows from the positive experience of these elements taken together. Without such conditions, which are essentially transactional processes between the developing person and her or his familial world, the sense of self is forever diminished and impaired.

Pine cites a study by Brazelton that clearly demonstrates the powerful effect of nonconfirming parental responses on the sense of self and behavioral responsiveness of a child as young as six months:

> In the film, we see an infant at about six months propped in a chair as his parent walks in. The infant's face breaks into a gleeful smile, his arms flap excitedly, and his eyes follow the movements of the approaching parent. But the parent, on instruction, keeps a poker face and sits watching the infant, completely immobile. Within a few seconds, the infant's behavior begins to deteriorate. First he shows seeming puzzlement and he pauses; the exhilaration disappears and active behavior comes to a standstill; and very soon body tone collapses, the infant slumps and sags, and appears to be, for all we can tell, in a depressed state. The effect on the observer is powerful, affectively and conceptually, the latter because it leaves no doubt that infant development takes place in a reciprocal interactive system.[27]

In the second year of life, these background experiences begin to crystallize into a coherent sense of self. This process is characterized by ownership of experience and a growing self-awareness attended by separation and loss of symbiosis with the primary nurturing parents. In this period, it is essential for the child to receive confirming and mirroring responses to his or her developmental differentiation, or, again, the sense of self is impaired or diminished.

As the self continues to crystallize, it incorporates as its own these positive and negative background experiences. The way these things occurred outside of conscious awareness, become the way "I am" consciously at a later time. Even though each human being's developmental experience is unique and could have occurred other than the way it did, it is experienced by the person as the "natural order," and as "the way I am and the world is." As the child continues to develop, the quality of the environment's support remains in a crucial position vis-à-vis the self. As the child seeks to incorporate impulses from his or her primal energies, it is essential that there be a supportive relationship that will help him or her master and own these forces, as well as help to link his or her developing interests and agency to appropriate environmental outlets.

These exchanges between the social world and the emerging self continue throughout the life cycle, though they are most formative in childhood. At each stage of development, earlier resolutions are either solidified or modified, and new accomplishments in the development of the self are achieved. The onset of adolescence and commitment to work, marriage, and parenting are particularly formative of the sense of self. The reciprocal interactions by which personhood comes into being are examples of the receiving, synthesizing, and creating activities of the psyche. They illustrate how external influences become internal constituents of the human being and affect how the self is a creative emergent from its interactions with its world.

2. *Reciprocal transactions in gender development.* Nancy Chodorow offers a profound analysis of the reciprocal transactions involved in becoming male or female in our culture.[28] Drawing upon feminist theory and psychoanalytic object relations thought, she illuminates the interplay of family, society, and culture in the development of the gender dimensions of selfhood. Her basic argument is that women are inducted into the roles of mothers, and men have little to do with parenting, for a combination of mutually reinforcing psychodynamic and socioeconomic reasons. Chodorow acknowledges that biological factors play an important part in the determination that females conceive, bear, and give birth to children. However, she argues, the subsequent process of mothering is not based upon biology, or upon a simple, clear-cut appeal to nature, but upon unconscious psychosocial processes that are culturally generated and supported as normative or "natural."

Chodorow demonstrates that the developmental process differs for boys and girls, leading to different structures of selfhood, at least with respect to gender. In their development, boys emotionally separate from mothers at an earlier age than girls. Further, they separate more dramatically and decisively. Through repression, they repudiate their affiliation and attachment needs—especially those involving dependency and vulnerability. Through identification, they incorporate male models of experience, which emphasize autonomy, self-reliance, and competent mastery over themselves and their environments. This process, according to Chodorow, leads males to have a largely one-sided and negative identity. They gain their identity as males by thinking of themselves as "not female." When boys become adolescents and young adults, they search out a female with whom they can maintain their autonomy, but also with whom they feel free to release a measure of their repressed needs for dependency, nurture, and affection. These needs stand in some conflict with their self-understanding as autonomous. This ambivalence between autonomy and dependency is largely unconscious, and in our culture the independent function has dominance and greater value. It is also rewarded by potentially high status career achievements and the financial success accompanying them.

Girls and women, by contrast, never fully repress their attachments to their mothers, nor do they fully identify with the personal style and psychosocial situation of their fathers. The relative absence and autonomous strivings of the father and brother, coupled with the isolated mother's needs for attachment, function to keep girls more symbiotically related to their mothers. The dependency needs of girls are not as fully repressed as in the case for boys, nor is there adequate social and cultural support for their aspirations toward autonomy. They meet greater resistance than males when they function independently and autonomously. They are less likely than males either to have access to gratifying opportunity or to receive adequate rewards for their labor in the larger social context.

Thus, for Chodorow, to be female is to come to think of oneself as inherently relational, which is acted out with the mother who thinks of herself the same way, rather than to think of oneself as an autonomously functioning person who is also relational. Whereas male identity consists largely in the repudiation of femaleness and inherent relationship, female identity is positively identified and socially reinforced as being for and with others. As a woman grows older, men seek her out to meet their previously repressed relational needs, which further inhibits individuation on the part of women. When women become mothers of their husband's children, the process reproduces itself.

It must be remembered that the transactional processes that become synthesized into a unified experience or identity as male and female are largely unconscious and are sanctioned or approved by the dominant culture in which they take place. As a result, to think of oneself as autonomous male or as relational female has the sense of "naturalness" and "rightness." It is hard to overcome the belief that one is inherently more valuable than the other. Anne Wilson Schaef makes it clear that the "white male system" insists that its definition of reality is correct, thereby making it enormously difficult for both males and females to change their self-understanding without threat to and opposition from the existing order.[29] However, it should be clear that the way we think of ourselves as men and women is in fact based upon transactions between the individual and the larger systemic world, which could be different, though at the cost of some personal anxiety and social dislocation. In subsequent chapters we shall explore how reciprocal transactions might be modified, with an attendant change in the structures of selfhood and gender identification.

THE PERSON AS CENTER OF POWER

The self comes into being through the interplay of multiple influences. These influences are received, organized, and creatively transformed into a coherent structure, which in turn influences its environment and its own becoming. Implied in this view of contextual interaction is the concept of power. In order to have existence, each entity, including persons, must have some degree of power, or the capacity for being influenced by the environment and for acting noticeably upon it. The term for this double influence is bi-polar power. Bi-polar power is the energy by which transactions are made possible, values actualized, and structures organized, maintained, and creatively transformed.

1. *Power as the shaper of personhood.* The idea of power has long been central in personality theory. The psychoanalytic concepts of libido, psychodynamics, and defense mechanisms imply and require a concept of power for understanding what takes place in the development of human beings and in their relationships with their environments. The psychoanalytic tradition used the concept of libido to designate the underlying power of individuals to influence their worlds. The concepts of psychodynamics and character formation were developed to delineate the variety of power arrangements and exchanges of psychic energy, or power, within the person and between the person and the world. The Freudian branch of the psychoanalytic tradition emphasizes the agential side of power, however, and essentially views the human situation as a clash of agencies.[30] This branch of psychoanalysis neglects or denigrates the positive dimensions of receptivity in the human personality and its relationship to society and nature. But, in spite of its almost exclusive emphasis upon the covert, conflictual, and agential dimensions of power, the Freudian orientation clearly recognizes the centrality of dynamic power configurations in the formation of both symptomatic and healthy human persons.

In contrast, a number of persons and schools of thought within personality theory offer major correctives to Freud's one-sided view of power in the human personality and between persons and the world. Jung's ideas about the receptive qualities of the anima and the agential qualities of the animus point to a bi-polar understanding of primary psychological power. He understood the individual as both a receptor of primal libidinal power and of collective social power, as well as an individuating creative integrator and transformer of these energies and influences. Object relations theorists, the ego and self-psychologies, and the psychosocial theorists have delineated the significant interplay between the person and the environment in the process of becoming an individual. All of these approaches emphasize the potentially positive dimensions of the mutual influence of persons and the environments in which they reside, and provide important foundations for my work. They emphasize the creative rather than the stabilizing and conflicting dimensions of power. The capacity to receive as well as to influence is regarded by these theories as normative for healthy human functioning. Pathology and symptomatology, as well as optimal growth and development, are therefore integrally related to the nature and quality of intrapsychic, interpersonal, and systemic power arrangements.

Our discussion of Chodorow's analysis of the development of gender identity underscores some of the dimensions of power that are at work in the transactions between the environment and the developing human personality. However, in addition to influencing gender identity, parents, siblings, and families have power to frustrate aspirations, define roles, and shape a variety of behaviors and attitudes that are desirable to them. The developing child is a receptor of these influences, and is shaped by them, both at the conscious and unconscious level. The kind of agent the human being becomes is largely determined by the character of the agential power of others, which he or she receives throughout his or her life.[31]

2. *Persons as agents of power.* The person is not merely a receptor of the agential power of others. The person is an agent as well. She or he has the capacity, or power, to creatively appropriate these influences and to fashion something new in the world, however minimally. In the very least, the person's own vitalities create a demand upon the larger system, and call for a response. This demand eventuates, often, in a struggle of receptivity and agency between the person and other elements in the system. The outcome will inevitably result in some degree of change on the part of each party, though the quality of the change is unpredictable, and sometimes negligible.

Impaired power arrangements underlie personal distress and developmental difficulty in persons. When persons seek care, they often feel powerless or helpless. They are overwhelmed receptors of the agential power of the surrounding world. They are cut off from their own power to relate creatively to the structures in which they live, including the depths of their own being, and to actualize effectively the power to live their lives according to their needs and values.[32]

The task of care, in these situations, is to help persons find a better relationship to their own power, and to that of others. As we shall see in chapters 4 and 5, often this means activating the individual's own agential power, and making individuals less receptive to the agency of others. In addition, it means changing the quality of power in the environment, so that it is more receptive to other less coercive and intrusive forms of influence and value.[33] The personal and systemic dynamics of power will be more fully explored in subsequent chapters; for now it is crucial to recognize that individual persons may be agents as well as receptors of unjust social power arrangements, and that an understanding of the person requires some theoretical accounting of this situation.[34]

Power is not only capable of problematic or destructive outcomes. It may be organized synergistically and constructively. Synergy refers to a noncoercive and nonexploitive positive interplay between the entities making up the system. Synergy is marked by cooperation, creativity, and novel accomplishment. It represents the most optimal arrangement of agential and receptive dimensions of power. When synergy exists, the transactional patterns of power are balanced and reciprocal, rather than oppressive and unilateral; they are accountable and overt, capable of modification and experimentation. When applied to the dynamics of personal bi-polar power, synergy refers to the optimal combination of receptivity and agency between all the elements of the personality, and between the person and his or her environment. The results of synergy are an increase in the valuation of self and other, more humane structures, creative accomplishments, and life-enhancing interactions. In religious terms, synergistic arrangements of power result in the increase of the love of God, self, and neighbor, a more just society, and responsible ecological practices.

THE SELF AS A SYNTHESIS OF VALUES

The human self arises in its individual particularity from the multiple connections it sustains within itself and between itself and its world. Its growing capacity to be a receptor and agent of power mediates the processes involved in its own becoming. Because the influences that interact in forming the human self are diverse and sometimes contradictory, the human being must synthesize the multiple contending values of its world into a meaningful fabric. Human personhood, and especially the character of the self that emerges from these dynamics, is largely a reflection of how individuals creatively appropriate, maintain, and coherently transform the contrasting value options available to them. In process theology, the greatest value outcome is characterized as beauty. In Robert Mesle's terms

> Beauty is a structure of relationships in which the contrasting parts of a whole mutually support and enrich each other so that each part contributes to the value and richness of the whole while the whole enhances the individual strength and value of each of the parts.[35]

When choices are made that increase beauty—which is the optimal combination of harmony and intensity of experience—the human self has greater texture and value.

1. The self as a value outcome. The idea of contending values undergirds most theories of personality. The psychoanalytic tradition recognized, but did not always appreciate, the extent to which contending values were operative in the vicissitudes of growth from psychological immaturity to maturity, and from pathology to health. Freud postulated an essentially conflictual relationship between the motivating values of the id and those of the ego, superego, and culture. The way these values, and the conflicts between them, are creatively appropriated and synthesized determines the character structure and behaviors of individual persons. Freud's concept of repression points out that many crucial values, or qualitative dimensions of experience, may be lost or indirectly expressed in the process of personality development. For Freud, the mature and healthy personality—in my terms, that personality which is characterized by the most optimal combination of intensity and harmony of experience—expresses itself in the capacity to love and work. Psychoanalysis may therefore in part be regarded as one means of recognizing and recovering lost or neglected values central to the capacity for love and work, and for achieving the greatest degree of beauty of personhood.[36] Liberation theologies and feminist analyses have further demonstrated how the structures of society and culture express power arrangements that value some persons and groups more highly than others, and reward them accordingly.[37]

Carl Jung's discussion of the individuation process provides a more constructive interpretation of the centrality of values in the development of mature persons. Individuation for Jung is a "transcendent" experience in which the conflicting values between masculinity and femininity (animus/anima), shadow and light, ego and self, personal and collective, introversion and extraversion, thinking and feeling, intuiting and

85

sensing, and judging and perceiving are united in a creative synthesis characterized by synergy.[38] Synergy, as we have seen, can be understood in process theology as the optimal combination of intensity and harmony of experience, and hence as good rather than evil.

In fact, the self is the term that designates the quality of the outcome or accomplishments of the psyche as these pertain to and are assessed by the person and others. Another term for the self is "personhood."[39] These concepts refer to the organized and unique quality of the psyche or soul that emerge from the interactional processes of living. Terms such as self-hatred, self-acceptance, self-fulfillment, self-esteem, and self-aware-ness point to the capacity of the psyche to establish an internal relation to itself. They also indicate the qualitative or value dimensions of the psyche's relation to its own self.

Terms such as self-giving, self-centered, self-aggrandizing, and self-denigrating point to the quality of the interplay between the psyche's relationship to itself and its relationship to one or more of the environments to which it is related. Additional terms of evaluation are "true self" and "false self." The term "false self" designates that the psyche has substituted a partial or distorted synthesis of experience for more complete and congruent experiences. The term "true self" designates that the synthesis of experience is comprehensive and congruent with the energies, values, and creative potentials of the psyche. Bernard Loomer uses the concept of "size" as the most fitting evaluative concept indicating the self's optimal relationship to itself and its environment. In this view, size points to the most inclusive synthesis of contrasting experience. In Loomer's words:

> The largest size is exemplified in those relationships whose range exhibits the greatest compatible contrasts, contrasts which border on chaos. . . . The achievement of the apex of size involves sustaining a process of transforming incompatible contrasts or contradictions into compatible contrasts and of bearing those contrasts within the integrity of one's individuality.[40]

Persons seeking the ministry of care are often impaired in the structure of selfhood. There is too "little" self available to sustain contrasts and centeredness. Symptoms such as anxiety and depression indicate that the self is overwhelmed by dynamic processes from its multiple environments, and must develop its size or stature to synthesize these transactions more optimally.

2. *The self as creator of value.* Though human persons reflect and are created by the values of their context, they are also transformers of values and creators of contexts. Creating contexts means modifying the

stuctures, power arrangements, and transaction patterns according to options differing from those that are currently predominating. Because persons constitute entities and systems in their own right, they, like other entities and systems, have a degree of autonomy, self-transcendence, or freedom, even in oppressing and victimizing situations. There is always a relative degree of contextual creativity, based upon the bi-polar character of power, to influence the values by which the context operates, and to participate in the selection of those that will be determinative in the life of the body and soul. The creative freedom to choose values and actualize potentialities is a limited freedom, but it is a real one nonetheless. It constitutes the basis for change and transformation in persons and their worlds.

An examination of the relationship between conscious and unconscious processes provides a striking example of how reciprocal transactions within persons, and between persons and their worlds, contribute to the creative development and transformation of values. When material from the unconscious breaks through, it almost always shows new ways of configuring the self in its internal composition and external relationships. This material is often both frightening and compelling. It is frightening because it beckons one to recognize that major shifts of status and power are about to occur, or are in fact already occurring. These shifts are not usually revealed to be unambiguous gains, but as terrifying challenges that may result in the annihilation of the self and its world. Unconscious material is compelling because the new status of power and value it reflects offers a novel occasion for fulfilling the person's destiny and for constructing a world of greater quality. When integrated into consciousness and acted upon behaviorally, unconscious material offers extremely potent resources for creating new contexts, or for recreating the person's relationship to the original context.

Another example of the contextually creative dimension of the human being is the capacity to survive, recover from, and even transform destructive personal and social circumstances. The process of moving from victim, to survivor, to transformer of the experience of physical and sexual abuse, is an inspiring tribute to the human capacity for creatively overcoming and challenging experiences designed to destroy human dignity and bodily integrity. In addition, the body's capacity for healing provides an organic foundation for transcending illness and trauma. The capacity of the self to create new configurations of meaning from trauma and loss enables healing to include the possibility for a spiritual advance as well as bodily recovery.

Although every human being has the capacity for transforming their destructive experience according to alternate value orientations, there are some persons whose contributions in these areas are stellar. An examination of the lives and contributions of persons such as Madame Curie, Martin Luther King, Jr., and Mahatma Gandhi indicates the degree to which human individuals are able to transcend the dominant values, organizational structures, power arrangements, and transactional patterns and to offer creative and more humane alternatives in these areas. However, without the stimulation and support of countless others who were able, alongside these leaders, to conceive and use their power for creating new personal and social structures, their work would in all likelihood have been idiosyncratic and ineffectual.[41] Thus, like all elements in the psychosystemic universe, creativity and value involve deeply personal and individual, as well as relational and structural, realities acting in reciprocally constructive ways.

3. *God, power, and value.* Examining persons in the light of their relationship to contending values brings into focus the relationship of God to the human personality. It also enables us to propose an interpretation of spirituality that is grounded in the actual realities of personal and social experience. In the view I am developing, God is inherently related to the value, or quality, of what comes to be in every unit of experience, including personal human experience. God is always present, giving to each moment of experience the best possibility for its own becoming. This interaction between God, persons, and world is an interaction characterized by contending values, the outcome of which contributes to an increase of good or evil in the experience of God, persons, and the structures of the world. This activity of value receiving and value creating is essentially a spiritual reality, insofar as spirituality is interpreted as the struggle of God and human beings to contribute to good and to overcome evil in the concrete experiences of personal and social living. Religious concepts such as love, justice, stewardship, blessing, righteousness, sanctification, reconciliation, salvation, and redemption point to the positive outcomes of this spiritual struggle to increase harmony and intensity of experience. Concepts such as estrangement, sin, oppression, bondage, and death point to the negative spiritual consequences emerging when triviality and discord, or evil, come into being.

This spiritual struggle between good and evil is palpably real, and has genuine consequences for persons and for the world which we are bringing into being. Each of us alone, and the race collectively, is enhanced or diminished by the outcomes of this spiritual struggle. Indeed, the positive and negative outcomes of our contending with multiple value options provides the basic structure of our personalities and constitutes the direction of our destinies.

SUMMARY: THE PSYCHOSYSTEMIC INDIVIDUAL

The human psyche is an ongoing and developing process, which is characterized by activities and outcomes. There are several interrelated processes identifying the activities of the psyche. First, there is a *receiving* dimension to the psyche. The psyche is a receptor of multiple influences from its environment, as well as from its own energies. It is acted upon and it is shaped by these internal and external actions. Through touch, perception, sensation, imagination, cognition, and the like, the psyche is constituted by its activity and capacity as a receptor. Second, there is a *synthesizing* or organizing dimension to the psyche. The psyche plays a part in providing meaning to these internal and external influences upon it. With relative degrees of consciousness, the psyche struggles with which influences to retain and which to release. It contends with multiple influences, and with the self-creative task of arranging these influences into some coherent pattern.

Finally, there is a *creative and transformative* dimension to the psyche's interactions with its world. The psyche—and the self which emerges in response to these activities—is a creative transformer of influences, generating novel configurations of its own experience and participating in new patterns beyond its own being. All of these transactions are reciprocal: they require one another, and they feed back in ongoing ways upon one another. They take place simultaneously, and influence one another.

To be a person is to be a psychosystemic unity in the process of coming into fuller being and relationship. Personhood, in keeping with systemic thinking, is an *organized* unity, with differing levels of structural influence and accountability. By differential organization I mean the relative degree of power or influence each element and subsystem has in relation to one another in the receiving, synthesizing, and transforming processes of the human being. When it is recalled that power has the bi-polar quality of agency and receptivity, those elements with the greatest capacity for receptivity and agency will have the greatest influence in the system. In mature human beings, it is clear that the psyche has the greatest capacity for receiving influences from itself, the body, and the environment and for synthesizing and transforming these processes according to the agency of the emerging self. Though each structural element of the body and psyche has the capacity for a measure of receptivity and agency, none alone can incorporate and transform the breadth and depth of experience to the degree that is possible for the self.

Likewise, the conscious elements of the person must be seen, in the final analysis, to have greater differentiation than unconscious materials in the mature adult. Jung's notion of the individuated self is very much akin to my view.[42] The individuated self is the center of the psyche that finally incorporates, but relatively transcends, all of the other elements comprising the person. The individuated self refers to the conscious and transforming synthesis of influences from one's body, the personal and collective unconscious, and the historical experience uniquely personalized in an individual human being.

Though it is optimal for the self to be individuated differentially, this is a potential rather than an accomplishment in most cases. At certain points of life, for reasons of development or impairment—or some combination of the two—more limited dimensions of experience may be in ascendancy in any given individual or group of individuals. Infants are receptors more than agents, and the capacity for consciousness is severely restricted. Some persons remain forever cut off from the creativity of their unconscious, or from the riches of their world, thereby impoverishing the quality of the self that comes into being. Others are so overwhelmed by bodily illness or impairment, that their capacity to encounter the world is grossly limited. The self that results may lack certain necessary elements, and its contents are diminished as a consequence. However, as indicated earlier, the truest, richest form of selfhood is one whose boundaries are selectively fluid, rather than porous or closed, in relation to the conscious and unconscious elements of its own being, and to the world in which it lives and which it shapes. It is characterized by "size" rather than autonomous self-reliance, inasmuch as it perpetually incorporates greater combinations of experience and connectedness.

When understood in psychosystemic terms, the person is to be regarded as an emergent entity, resulting from the synthesis of value-laden and power-influenced experience. The person is a unity of body and soul and a developing creator and receiver of influence. Personhood is richest when it is characterized by a combination of depth and breadth of experience, and of greatest intensity and harmony with family, society, culture, and nature. God is integrally related to this process of developing a rich personhood. Spirituality is characterized as the value outcomes of the receiving, synthesizing, and transforming process of becoming a person in one's multiple environments. We turn now to a discussion of how, through an analysis of symptoms and a theory of change, we, as pastoral caretakers, might best influence the quality of being that might actually emerge in the lives of persons and in the life of the world.

CHAPTER 4

SYMPTOMS, CRISES, AND CHANGE: PSYCHOSYSTEMIC CARE AS STRATEGIC LOVE AND REDEMPTIVE JUSTICE

All sin is the result of a collaboration.
Stephen Crane[1]

*I know the one thing we did right
was the day we started to fight.*
"Eyes on the Prize"[2]

Persons seeking the ministry of care are driven or drawn by crises and symptoms in their lives. They seek change, whether in the form of more adequate resources to cope with an unchangeable situation, or to transform that situation. One of the more gratifying aspects of being in the ministry of care is providing effective assistance in resolving crises. A great sense of satisfaction is the result when persons are able to make genuine advances in their lives and to overcome or find transformative ways of living with their crises. Joy is felt when systems themselves change, offering relief and greater opportunity to their participants. These successes provide a basis for hope in the healing and redemptive processes of life. They give deeper meaning to the caretaker's affirmations about faith, and provide an experiential basis for the caretaker's belief in a liberating, active God.

THE MEANING OF SYMPTOMS

The ministry of care is the dimension of ministry that is predominantly symptom responsive. It responds to symptoms that actually exist, and organizes much of its educational efforts to prevent the emergence of symptomatic behavior. It is usually under the condition of symptomatic crisis that the ministry of care is sought or responded to at new levels of significance. Thus it is essential that the caretaker have a clear conceptual grasp of the meaning of symptoms and symptom formation. He or she

91

must also possess some technical skills for intervening strategically in order to assist in the prevention and resolution of symptomatic crises.

The general goal of ministry and of religious living is to increase the love of self, God, and neighbor, promote justice, and work for greater ecological harmony. When symptoms emerge, they are best understood broadly as crises in one or more of these arenas. They provide an opportunity to assess where love has become impaired or blocked, injustice stabilized, and the environment neglected or decimated. In psychosystemic terms, symptoms indicate disruptions in and between the elements of the interconnected world. They reflect a disruption of optimal organizational properties, unequal power arrangements, conflicting values, impaired transactions, and lack of creativity in the symptomatic context. While symptoms and crises are carried by individuals and felt keenly by them, they are not to be regarded only as the individual's problems. They emerge within and regulate the larger systemic elements and structures of the individual's world. Diagnostic awareness of the symptomatic interplay of the person-world relationship enables the pastoral caretaker to know how to influence the crisis toward a positive rather than negative resolution.

The word *symptom* is derived from the Greek term meaning, "to fall," and refers to a happening or attribute that stands beside or outside what is normally expected of persons in their social context. It primarily refers to the subjective evidence of disease or physical disturbance, though it can, by extension, refer to something that indicates the existence of something else. Thus, depression can be thought of as a symptom of rage, or grief a symptom or indicator of love and deep attachment.

Despite its usual association and dominant use in the context of medicine, the concept of symptom can be extended to the social, religious, and moral arenas of life. It is common to say that society is "sick" and sickness-producing, implying both a medical and moral evaluation. There are longstanding religious currents that regard symptoms as indicators of sin and moral failure, pointing to the need for personal and social change. Illness is a metaphor for sin and healing a metaphor for salvation in much contemporary religious writing.[3] Modern pastoral caretaking can lead to a spiritual advance for the persons directly affected by it. It is axiomatic in most contemporary psychotherapy, and the pastoral caretaking that builds itself upon such psychotherapy, that "things are not as they seem." Symptoms are forms of indirect communication that invite deeper analysis and response. Behind the symptoms stand causative and healing realities to which the symptoms point.

Symptoms constitute a crisis, and serve a dual function. On the one hand, they reveal a real or potential breakdown in the person-world matrix. On the other hand, they reveal the urgent need for a corrective response. As indicators of crisis, symptoms are "dangerous opportunities" for change and transformation. They are dangerous because they cannot be avoided and they may be responded to in such a way as to make matters worse than they currently are. They are an opportunity because something better may result. In a world characterized by novelty and risk, there are no guarantees of the outcome beyond the symptom. Symptoms require new responses, but they cannot determine those responses. They can only provide stimuli and opportunity for response. This response can take either the form of restoration of original harmony or transformation to a new state in which symptoms are no longer necessary, or problematic. If no response is made to the symptoms, the underlying crisis to which they point is likely to escalate into destructive proportions, leading to catastrophic outcomes.

Symptoms, then, are to be taken seriously, and regarded as crises that may result in advance or loss, in sickness or health, in salvation or damnation. We ignore them to our peril! Theologically, the importance of positively valuing the symptomatic first became clear to me in reflecting upon the "little apocalypse" in Matthew 24–25. At the Last Judgment, Jesus is separating the sheep and the goats according to the way persons responded to the most acutely symptomatic persons on earth (those with handicapping conditions, the ill, the imprisoned, the demonic). Jesus said that he was "hidden" in these people—they were symptomatic of his presence—and their treatment of these least and lost reflected their treatment of him.

This passage metaphorically links the destiny of each of us to one another—and especially to our response to the most symptomatic among us—and provides the systemic foundations for the Christian's relationship to God in Jesus Christ. The God Christians worship can be found in the symptoms of the wounded. God and our salvation are made present through those crushed or marginalized by the systems constituting our world. For pastoral caretaking to be Christian, it must involve a strategic response to both the acute and chronic symptomatic crises confronting us in these realities.

There is a discernible process of symptom formation and resolution. The psychosystemic matrix is characterized by a variety of tensions, including those between homeostasis and change. While there is relative durability throughout the system, there is also internal and external pressures for novelty and change. The psychosystemic matrix is inherently unstable, though relatively predictable. Thus there are always general background stressors that function as precursors to crisis and symptom formation. These have to do with the interplay of values, power, transactional messages, and creative options in relation to the existing structure.

The first phase of actual symptom formation is the *onset phase*. This may be gradual or sudden. A dissonance emerges. The dissonance may be between family members, between individuals and the workplace, or it may emerge as individual discomfort with things as they are. Anxiety, depression, acting out, and underfunctioning in one's environment are some common expressions of psychosystemic dissonance at the individual level. Marital affairs, chronic underemployment, anomie, and civil disobedience are some random examples of psychosystemic dissonance in the larger milieu. More particular patterns of dissonance will be developed later.

At the onset phase of symptom formation, dissonance is often experienced as unpleasant, intrusive, and perplexing. Anxiety and pain attend its presence. It is sometimes initially denied or avoided. When faced, dissonance is often removed by simple changes of attitudes and behaviors, or by straightforward communication. Simple change of location, such as moving to a new community or finding a new place of employment, reestablishes the former security. When these attempts to avoid or resolve the dissonance at the onset phase fail, symptom formation escalates.

The second phase of symptom formation is the *escalation phase*. During this phase the symptom becomes more painful and forms the central gestalt in the system. The system organizes itself to accommodate the symptom. That is, the system becomes stabilized around the centrality of the escalating dissonance. Thus, when an adolescent in a family becomes troubled, the symptom stabilizes the family in avoiding possible conflicts between the parents, or the family in the larger system, and mobilizes resources to attempt to help the teenager. Thus the family's organizational pattern may for several months, or even years, be focused upon managing a troubled member.

The escalation phase may be characterized by acute and/or chronic dimensions. Acute escalation is relatively temporary and responds to interventions to reestablish the former order or to move to a new level. Chronic dissonance means there is neither a resolution nor a return to a former state of being. The symptoms become the organizing center for the family and remain stabilized at a high level of crisis. There are families and individuals who have multiple crises, characterized by chaotic functioning, because symptoms have remained escalated without resolution. In more extreme cases this can lead to death or severe forms of emotional and physical injury in the context of family. In the larger social system, unemployment, war, or civil disturbance are examples of chronically escalated symptoms, with little sign of resolution in the near term. As we shall see, it is during the escalation phase that persons often seek pastoral assistance and are most likely to move to some type of resolution.

The third phase of symptom formation is the *resolution phase.* Resolution means that the symptoms have led the system in part or in whole to modify its organizational structure, power arrangements, value patterns, and transactional arrangements in some creative way. Resolution may be better for all concerned. It may also mean diminishment or overall loss for the system. The resolution phase emerges as a result of some combination of strategic influence and focused openness in the system. Resolution may come about as a result of new information, new exiting or entering persons or organizations, and changed patterns of response by the players in the system. Because systems and subsystems are dynamically construed, the exact form of any resolution cannot be predetermined or technically manipulated. But the caretaker can take confidence from the reality that systems move toward new forms of being, and that it is possible to anticipate at least partially positive resolutions, even when loss is apparent.

Resolution may take the form of restoration of original function, as when a plant decides not to close and lay off workers in the community. It also may consist of an extinction of the dissonant behaviors without either a restoration of formal functioning or development of dramatically new functioning. For example, an acting out adolescent child may begin to act responsibly and autonomously, without being dependent as earlier, or requiring dramatic new family changes such as launching the child from the home. Finally, resolution may take the form of transformation within the system, which means that dramatically new patterns of relatedness, values, and structural organization may emerge. Examples of transformation in the system are seen in the recent news when the former Soviet Union withdrew from its empire, freeing many of its allies to seek their own national interests. Another example of transformation is when persons who have undergone a major life crisis, such as illness or an identity and relational crisis, develop values and orientations to life that are more fulfilling and expressive of their social consciences. Many second career persons in seminaries, who are preparing to use their talents in the service of others, represent a manner in which earlier symptomatic crises may be resolved in a transformative manner.

Symptomatic crises are frightening and unpredictable. They create intrapsychic and interpersonal disorder. They threaten the larger social network, and sometimes tax its resources and challenge its organizing principles. They operate at many levels, usually ravaging much of the established order in the escalation and stabilization phase. Even recovery from crisis in the resolution phase requires much rebuilding and is often characterized by grief and chaos. When crises persist without adequate resolution, they contribute to evil in the world, especially when evil is characterized as some combination of triviality and disharmony. When optimally resolved, however, they may contribute to beauty, which is an increase in the intensity and harmony of living and patterns of relatedness. Thus, crises may in fact lead to a greater capacity to love self, God, and neighbor, to promote justice, and to increase the capacity for ecological partnership in the universe. They may also eventuate in the opposite, as every minister and caretaker knows.

GOD, SYMPTOMS, AND CHANGE

Crises and the suffering they reflect indicate a need for change in the existing order, including the transactions and values undergirding that order. Pressure for change is built into the nature of reality. Symptomatic behavior gives structure and focus to these pressures, and contributes much to bringing about change. The direction of the change may be in the interests of greater or lesser value.

The ministry of care is a particular context in which the suffering connected with symptomatic crises may be contained, their causes and meanings explored, and new patterns of relatedness fashioned. The ministry of care seeks to promote change. In general terms, change is understood as an effective increase of love, justice, and ecological partnership throughout the psychosystemic matrix. More particularly, the ministry of care seeks to promote a creative modification of the power arrangements in the existing structure of things. It attempts to reorder the values that are contributing to symptomatic behaviors. It identifies and modifies transactional patterns that eventuate in limiting or destructive outcomes. Thus, for the pastoral caretaker, symptomatic crises are an invitation to be a participant in changing the fundamental fabric of personal and social reality, and to reconstruct the environment.

The reality of symptoms and the suffering they occasion, raise acute questions, conceptually and existentially, about who is responsible. Are sufferings and symptomatic crises to be accounted for by individual failings? Or are they to be ascribed to an impersonal, systemically oriented world that grinds on inexorably indifferent to the virtues and vices of individuals and their subgroups? Or, does God somehow directly cause events to happen that must be dealt with at a personal, historical, and natural level? Responsibility implies agency. In questions of agency lie questions of values, power, and creative transformation of meanings and structures. Transactions between individuals, God, and the world become acutely focused in such instances. Questions about who is to be regarded as morally accountable for symptomatic crises and their resolutions are often at the heart of the ministry of care, and must be responded to both conceptually and pastorally.

In the context of tragic loss and suffering, the relation of God to human welfare becomes most acutely salient. Persons commonly ask questions such as: "Why did God bring this about in my life?" "What is God's purpose in this?" "What did I do wrong to deserve this punishment from God?" In some cases, persons are angry when they ask these questions, leading to a repudiation of any belief in a benevolent and providential God. Others feel overburdened with guilt and remorse, and seek forgiveness and new life. Some are confirmed in their belief that God has no positive relationship to their suffering and crises. Still others find comfort and a deepened relationship to God through their tragedies.

From a psychosystems perspective, it is to be expected that there would be a multiplicity of responses to such events, since the world itself is multiply complex. Accordingly, a psychosystems view affirms that there is no single causation for symptoms. Since the world is multiply conjoined by multiply contending values, structures, and power arrangements, to ascribe causation to any single agent is highly problematic. In psychosystemic theory, there are multiple agencies. God is one agency among many, though God is the agency with the greatest degree of agential and receptive power. The vast array of agents and receptors that make up the world contend with one another, thereby accounting for the possibility of symptomatic behavior. Thus, even when the responsibility for disorder and sufferings appears to be located in one person, or one sector of the psychosystemic matrix, that person or sector is operating out of a history of multiple influences, and with certain tacit support from the larger environment. Accordingly, even so great an agent of evil as Adolf Hitler is widely regarded to have been a victim of certain forms of abuse and racism as a child, and he was supported by a nation whose injuries were enormous for several generations before the onset of his leadership. This means that larger cultural, religious, and economic realities, as embodied in the consciousness, social institutions, and behavioral patterns of millions of persons over hundreds of years, must also share the culpability.

God is an agent and receptor, and as such has power to be influenced by and to influence every element of the psychosystemic matrix. But God does not have power to coerce and control, since all other entities have power as well. God can influence and stimulate, but there must be a focused openness to God's power for God's aims to be realized in concrete terms. God's agency is never toward evil, but always toward higher value. I have characterized this value as an increase of love of self, God, and neighbor, the capacity to promote justice, and the ability to build partnerships with the natural order. God is a reservoir and pioneer of value. Because God is one agent among many, God cannot prevent tensions and conflicts from emerging that sometimes lead to suffering and evil. Such outcomes are always against God's intentions. Yet, even in the presence of these losses and disorders, God continues to be present to influence new and vital possibilities for something redemptively novel to emerge and to shape the future.

Since there are multiple causations of symptoms, change requires multiple responses. There is no predetermined formula that can apply to every situation, since every situation is relatively novel. God's way with the world is to envisage all possibilities for the world's becoming, and to strategically select the *most* appropriate possibility or set of possibilities for each unique situation. While God's love is pervasive and all-embracing, it is also focused and particularized. It is strategic love, inasmuch as it selects from a multiplicity of options the most promising opportunity for each given particular situation. In this respect, strategic love is realistic, moving incrementally from things as they are to new patterns. God's strategic love is not passively accepting, nor does it assume that change comes only from the situation itself. Rather, it actively apprehends the situation as it is, while energetically influencing novel configurations. Strategic love therefore has a causative dimension, and works to change things while at the same time accepting persons unconditionally. God's strategic engagement with reality is witnessed to in the doctrines of continuing creation, incarnation, and resurrection. Events such as the Exodus from Egypt and healings in the Gospel accounts underscore the strategic particularity of God's love, which undergirds and empowers change throughout the psychosystemic matrix. The "little apocalypse" referred to above indicates that God's love is strategically focused upon the "least and the lost" in this world; to respond to God's love is to generate strategic love to these unloved and victimized persons.

One of the contemporary convictions in much feminist and liberation theology is the need for strategic love to be linked to redemptive justice. Love affirms, embraces, unites, and heals. It also eventuates in justice, which liberates from captivity and oppression. Love pushes for an embodied justice, which changes the conditions of social living. It seeks to lift out, or redeem, those who are caught in systems of domination and subordination by changing the value orientations and power arrangements that exploit them. This includes changing the external structures that oppress, as well as changing oppressed persons' internalized relationship to their oppression. Redemptive justice identifies and requires accountability for injustice, and leads to more mutually harmonious patterns of relatedness. Strategic love and redemptive justice assume and eventuate in partnerships between persons, culture, and the world that enhance the fecundity of each and minimizes exploitation and toxicity.

To promote optimal change, the caretaker must look for the causation of symptomatic crises in the interplay of forces operating in the psychosystemic matrix. Symptoms will not be fully understood if they are sought only within individual persons or entities. Rather, symptoms are to be understood in terms of how they reflect unjust power arrangements in and between entities, and how they reveal lovelessness and environmental rapaciousness operating at multiple levels throughout the system. Further, the pastoral caretaker must become an ally with the God who apprehends symptomatic situations and provides occasion for novel, more optimal configurations. Just as God strategically seeks to increase the welfare of those caught in symptomatic crises, so also the caretaker seeks to embody a strategic love that might provide acceptance and transformation. Just as God's redemptive justice seeks to liberate persons from patterns of domination and subordination, and to create harmonious relationships between human beings and nature, so also the pastoral caretaker promotes such outcomes. The ministry of care therefore is understood to participate in and to reflect God's strategic response to crises. Since it is grounded in the loving activity of God, the ministry of care is also ordered by strategic love, redemptive justice, and efforts on behalf of ecological partnership. The goals of care are also reflected in the means of care.

THE GOALS OF CHANGE

To respond to symptoms, the pastoral caretaker must have some way of understanding and assessing what is wrong. There must also be some explicitly normative ideas about what constitutes desirable patterns of living. What does love, justice, and ecological partnership look like in concrete operational terms? How is lovelessness, injustice, and ecological destructiveness manifested in the daily crises and experiences of living? This section will try to provide an overview of diagnostic criteria by which symptoms may be interpreted. It will also profile the positive outcomes of effective care undertaken from a psychosystems perspective. Each of these goals will be discussed in subsequent chapters. They are placed here so that the reader may gain an overview. They are outlined in the Appendix.

The first goal is to move from contextual impairment to contextual integrity. Contextual impairment means that there is a fracture in one or more of the structures comprising the psychosystemic matrix. Overwhelming anxiety on the part of an individual, for example, indicates impairment in the structure of the personality, and has consequences for the integrity of the family, and so on. An identified patient in a family system indicates impairment in the family structure, especially when parents are conflicted about the nature of the values organizing the family, and specifically concerning how to respond to the symptomatic individual.

There are three particular expressions of contextual impairment. First, contextual impairment is expressed in ruptured boundaries, which may take the form of too much openness on the one hand or too much rigidity and impermeability on the other. Second, impairment is expressed in disordered accountabilities. Focused accountabilities maintain order and regulate exchanges of energy and indicate the degree to which a system is adaptable. These become disordered when they are absent, unclear and hidden, unaccountable, unresponsive, or irreplaceable. Finally, contextual impairment is indicated by a runaway system. A runaway indicates that the mechanisms maintaining a system are no longer operative. The system is out of control and in danger of destroying itself or incapable of protecting itself. Contextual impairment most clearly reflects injustice in a system, but also results from and leads to lovelessness and ecological disharmony.

Contextual integrity means that the structures comprising the system are intact and endure in a manner that protects the system from internal and external threat. This means that internal and external boundaries are clear and flexible without too much openness or too much rigidity. It also means that accountabilities within the system are clear and not unfocused or disordered. In addition, it means that the transactional processes within the system, and between the system and other entities, are predictable and ordered, rather than out of control in a threatening and chaotic manner.

The second goal is to move from power imbalances to synergistic power arrangements. Power is symptomatic and evil when it is victimizing, chaotic, unaccountable, intractable, exclusive, and inaccessible. When crises occur, there is always an imbalance of power needing attention and correction. It is particularly dangerous when it leads to victimization, chaos, and permanent unjust and oppressive situations. Many single mothers find that they have little access to economic and legal power. They become a permanent underclass, subject to the power of mostly male lawmakers whose policies make their success as mothers extremely difficult. At the same time, male fathers of children are not held accountable for their power to beget, contributing to extreme imbalances in child rearing and family responsibility.

In place of unjust and unloving imbalances such as these, there needs to be synergistic power arrangements. Synergistic power arrangements are characterized by the mutuality of give-and-take and of reciprocal, life-enhancing influence. These are most clearly expressed when the power arrangements are cooperative, accountable, and modifiable. A synergistic power arrangement is further characterized by sharing and accessibility. Thus, in terms of child rearing, more synergistic power arrangements will pertain when men and women have shared power to make laws about their common life, and to share more equal and mutual responsibility for the consequences of their emotional and sexual liaisons.

A third goal is to move from destructive value conflicts to synchronized value orientations. Though it is normal in a psychosystemic matrix for values to contend as a part of the natural order of things, it also follows that values will often be in discordant conflict. When such conflicts become too discordant, the system goes into crisis and requires change or stabilization.

There are three sub-patterns of destructive value conflicts. The first involves lovelessness and enmity toward self, neighbor, and God. Such lovelessness is reflected in a fracturing of the values necessary for the promotion of individual and social welfare. Lovelessness and enmity toward oneself is reflected in estrangement from important elements of one's own being, or deprecation of one's personal value and creative power. Lovelessness toward one's neighbor is reflected generally in indifference, rejection, denigration, and the like. Lovelessness toward God is reflected in indifference, idolatry, and despair regarding God's benevolent action. The second form of destructive value orientations is injustice, which is expressed in the domination of persons or groups, abuse, and marginalization. Pastoral caretaking seeks to influence liberation from domination, to replace marginalization with participation, and to rework abusive relationships into nurturing relationships. The third form of destructive value orientations is ecological exploitation. This is expressed in a chronic humanocentrism, which understands the natural order purely as a resource for human welfare. It is reflected in policies of economic determinism and materialism, which overplay the importance of control and manipulation of the natural order for narrow ends. And it shows itself in the acquisitiveness and greed that contribute both to natural disaster and to unjust distribution of resources. To transform these symptoms into more positive values, humanocentrism needs to be replaced by ecocentrism and mutuality with the natural order. Economic determinism must give way to economic planning. Acquisitiveness and greed must be changed to relinquishment and sharing. Pastoral caretaking may be able to assist with these macrosystemic value disorders by looking, at the microsystemic level, at how personal anxieties about survival and finitude intersect with life-style and larger economic and nationalistic values.[4]

Psychosystemic care promotes synchronized value orientations, recognizing that there will always be relative degrees of contention. Too much unity leads to trivia or boredom. Too little unity leads to chaos and disintegration. The pastoral goals of increasing love, justice, and ecological partnership reflect the concern for a positive interplay of different values. In particular terms, this means that different world views and their moral orientation within a given system and between systems come to enhance the welfare of each entity within the system and the system as a whole, rather than to tear apart and disintegrate persons and their worlds. When values harmonize, relatively speaking, an active and vital wholeness is achieved, as well as movement toward expanding inclusiveness and novel opportunities throughout the psychosystemic matrix. In terms of our earlier discussion, this is reflected in an increase in "size."[5] It is also characterized by an increase in beauty, or a more optimal intensity and harmony of experience. It is opposed to evil, which is expressed in triviality and discord.

The fourth goal is to move from vitiated creativity to vital creativity. Every system is characterized by contextual creativity, or the capacity for novelty and creative advance. This dimension of the system connects present structures to new possibilities. A symptomatic crisis occurs when no creative options are apparent, or where there is no power to carry out the options before the individual or larger entity. There are three particularly common symptoms of vitiated creativity emerging in the ministry of care: discounted creativity, paralyzed creativity, and underground creativity. For example, women and other oppressed classes of people in our culture have had their creativity negated; certain roles have been consistently denied them, and certain aspirations discounted, leading to their subsequent paralysis or subjugation. Depression and anxiety in women is often accounted for by these dynamics, and not necessarily by intrapsychic factors such as immaturity, defiance of their biological destinies, envy, and the like.[6]

An entity or system characterized by vital creativity means that the impulses and forces for novel change are not discounted, but affirmed. Indeed, they are effectively appropriated as tangibly palpable realities. They make things different. In vital systems, creativity is relatively apparent and protected rather than underground, denigrated, or marginalized. Its discoveries lead to new value arrangements, new organizational structures, and to a reworking of power dynamics within the system. It opens communication, resulting in surprise and novel opportunities. It also occasions loss and dislocation, and the need to integrate diminishment as well as gain.

Finally, psychosystemic care seeks to move from transactional impasses to transactional effectiveness. To exist is to transact, or to relate, reciprocally with one's world and with one's own being. The quality of being within an entity and between systems is reflected in the quality of the transactions.

Much symptomatic behavior occurs when transactions become stuck, or unable to meet the challenges faced by persons in context. Transactional impasses exist when systems are impervious to change, or creativity. Transactional impasses are most clearly seen in three symptoms: frozen roles, tangled messages, and disparate rules. Frozen roles exist when people and groups become rigidly bound. Tangled messages are most commonly indicated by lack of clarity, distortion, and indirect communication. Double-binding, blaming, deceiving, and discounting are the more virulent and most serious forms. Disparate rules reflect which conflicts about mores will govern the system, how power shall be arranged, and which, or whose, values will predominate. For example, couples and families often reach an impasse over who will make decisions and whose wishes will be followed because they cannot harmoniously blend their aspirations.

Transactional effectiveness means that the reciprocal transactions that formally characterize any entity or system are stimulating and affirming. It means that they are open to modification, correction, and multiple levels of meaning. Transactional effectiveness means that there is flexibility within roles, that messages are clear, and that the rules by which the system operates are fair and affirming. It also means that the exchanges of power, values, creativity, and information between levels of the system are positive rather than negative. That is to say, if a psychosystemic matrix is to be characterized by justice, it will not have influences at one level in the system discount and undermine those at another. Thus one would not expect the person to be a responsible agent in one system and an automaton at another level in the system. Double standards would also be inappropriate in a positively functioning system.

Though the goals of pastoral caretaking may be stated in linear, sequential, and quantitative terms, it is important to underscore the principles of organicity and simultaneity outlined in chapter 1. The principle of organicity recognizes that all elements of a system interconnect, and must be examined as a whole. This means, for example, that the impairments in a given structured context reflect particular patterns of contending values, power dynamics, and the like. Or, looking at the quality of the creativity and transactional exchanges in a particular context, also requires examining the power and value issues in that context, and between that context and its larger world. The principle of simultaneity reminds us that change in one area will have consequences for change in all the other areas. While these elements may be discussed singularly and linearly—and responded to in planned sequential fashion—to provide psychosystemic caretaking one must learn to think systemically and to plan interventions according to their strategic impact on the whole system.

STRATEGIES OF CHANGE

Change is based primarily upon the concepts of creativity and bi-polar power in psychosystemic theory. The possibility of change is built into the nature of reality, and is assisted by God's ongoing stimulation of new possibilities. Change is most optimal when it results in the increase of organizational integrity, transactional effectiveness, synchronized values, synergistic power arrangements, and vital creativity. Fuller descriptions of the means by which change might be influenced in each of these particular areas will be developed in subsequent chapters. For now, it is important to have a general overview of the process of change, and the general strategies for implementing it.

When rooted in the ministry of care, change results from two interacting conditions. First, there must be strategic influence in the symptomatic crisis. Second, there must be a focused responsiveness to the strategic influences employed by the caretaker or the caretaking system such as the congregation, hospital, counseling center, or social service agency. Strategic influence, grounded in the reality of God's strategic love discussed above, seeks to move from symptomatic crisis to more optimal functioning. Without influence, little change takes place. The world, including the world of symptoms, is interactive, conflicted, power-infused. Without countervailing and stimulating influences, change is not possible. Thus, the pastoral caretaker and the caretaking community must claim their own values, authority, history, and social situation as a basis for their strategic response to persons and systems in crisis. Some of the more common strategic influences utilized in caretaking are accepting, interpreting, restructuring, coaching, advocating, and consciousness-raising.

Focused responsiveness is the second condition necessary for change. Strategic influence must be matched by a focused response. Strategic activity can influence such a focused response, but it cannot control it. Every entity determines what it will respond to, so coerciveness and manipulation have little positive effectiveness. Focused responsiveness is expressed in altered consciousness and behaviors. Altered consciousness and behaviors reflect and lead to modified power and value arrangements and to an increase in creativity and transactional exchanges both within persons and in the psychosystemic matrix. When focused responsiveness leads to a more optimal level of functioning, there is often an attendant sense of joy, blessing, and liberation.

Psychosystemic change, more precisely defined, is the process by which God's strategic love and redemptive justice are embodied in the pastoral caretaker's role and activities. Pastoral caretaking comprises the efforts of the caretaking agent(s) strategically to influence the renewal, development, or transformation of the behavioral consciousness of persons and their contexts. It seeks to influence a focused responsiveness by which symptomatic crises are transformed into greater occasions for love, justice, and ecological harmony. Such change reflects and necessitates particular modifications of the pertinent systemic social structures, power arrangements, value commitments, and creative options related to the pastoral situation.

There are several practical strategies for engendering the focused responsiveness necessary for change. These are tied to some roughly predictable processes or stages in the caretaking relationship. More specific and detailed examples will be provided in the second half of the book.

For change to occur, the caretaker must first effectively join the symptomatic situation and develop a working alliance with the parties. The principle of organicity is particularly helpful to understand this point, inasmuch as it underscores how the pastoral care agent must become an organic part of the situation or there is little basis for significant exchange of influences. Joining is accomplished by the strategies of empathic mutuality, by which is communicated that the caretaker is available and connected meaningfully to the situation. Empathic mutuality is communicated by unconditional positive regard toward the persons in the situation, and by self-disclosure on the part of the caretaker. It is enhanced by active listening, and by communicating that the caretaker has enough strength to challenge as well as to affirm each person and each element in the situation as a whole.

It is critical for joining to occur in relation to the situation as well as to each individual. This involves a rather early redefinition or reevaluation of the symptomatic crisis in psychosystemic terms. For example, a family dealing with a suicidal child may be asked about how they handle anger or despair as a whole, and how this confirms or challenges what they think their religious faith teaches them. Or, a verbally abusive husband who parades his wife's shortcomings may be asked what would happen if the power arrangements in the marriage changed so that the wife stood up to him as an equal partner. Such early maneuvers begin to break up the power dynamics and value orientations reflecting an impaired context. They reframe the symptomatic crises in systemic rather than individualistic terms. They lay the groundwork for new transactional patterns, and for a creative restructuring of the symptomatic behaviors. By means of such initial joining interventions the groundwork is laid for more specific goal-setting at a later point in the helping process.

Second, for change to occur, there must be a means of illuminating awareness and changing behaviors. Individuals, couples, families, and groups become symptomatic when they are not able to mobilize energies to live out their conscious values and aspirations. Their interpretations and level of awareness of what is happening and what needs to happen are in conflict, or for some other reason not sufficient to account for what is going on. Their behavioral attempts to change things are futile, and even destructive on occasions. This frequently results in a crisis of meaning. Hence, there is need of strategic influence to help them change their interpretations and behaviors related to their situation. In the concrete process of helping, this requires that persons and groups expand their awareness of their situation, and energize effective response to it. This sometimes necessitates that they become aware of and accept responsibility for their collusive participation in destructive patterns, and that they rebuild their world views.

Specific strategies for enhancing and expanding behavioral consciousness are numerous. Journal keeping, dream-work, body-work, guided imagery, visualization, and exploration of one's narrative history and significant memories are essential devices for expanding phenomenological awareness of individual dynamics. Some of these methods also apply for assessing the life of larger groups, such as families, and congregations.

Expanding consciousness also involves facilitating insight into the meaning and function of the materials that have come to light as phenomenological awareness has been expanded. For example, helping persons identify how their concept and image of God has functioned to limit (or enhance) their outlook and actions, provides the foundation for helping them rework their consciousness of God in a manner more congruent with their situation. Or, assisting families to identify transgenerational alliances and roles enables them to understand why certain patterns of difficulties persist over time. Once identified, it is possible to consider ways to change them, or to neutralize their negative consequences by incorporating more effective countervailing interpretations and behaviors.

Consciousness and behavioral options are also expanded by conscientization. This is a specialized concept deriving from feminist and liberation theology, and refers to interpreting how one's difficulties derive from one's social location in an unjust social order. In the context of the ministry of care, this includes teaching about oppression and its consequences, gaining clarity about the real differences between victims and perpetrators, and heightening awareness about the process of moving from victim, to survivor, to transformer of one's subordinated position.

All three of these modes of expansion of consciousness may be enhanced by and eventuate in energized action in relation to one's situation. I have found that change may occur in consciousness by means of behavioral change (people who learn to act effectively may also by this action come to feel effective), and that changes in consciousness may lead to a change in behavior (people who recognize that their failure pattern stabilizes their parents' dead marriage may choose to begin to garner successes while finding more positive ways to support their parents). Liberation thinkers emphasize that conscientization involves an interactive process between awareness and consciousness about the social realities contributing to one's distress and the strategic individual and collective behaviors or actions that need to be mobilized to change these circumstances.

The principle of conscientization leads quickly to the principle of advocacy. The advocacy role of the pastoral caretaker strategically enables the careseekers to become advocates in their own contexts. Advocacy has two dimensions. First, advocacy involves the strategic effort to enable persons to hear their own voices and to perceive the dimensions of injustice contributing to their situation. Second, it involves the strategic attempt to struggle with the prevailing social situation for the purpose of making it more just. Thus, many victims of childhood abuse are encouraged as part of their healing and transformation to confront the larger social and cultural forces which perpetrate violence against women and children.

Third, for change to occur, there must be strategies for restructuring the larger system itself. Certainly heightening awareness and advocating more strategic behavioral change have consequences for whether and how a system may or may not change. But there are additional strategies, which have a greater chance of modifying impaired or entrenched structures. These include establishing viable accountabilities, promoting viable roles, and establishing viable rules.

To establish viable accountabilities, by which the system is enabled to rework its power arrangements and to make its communication processes more open, it is necessary to differentiate and detriangulate individuals and subgroups in the system. When, for example, the parents triangulate a child into their marital system as a symptomatic person to detour their conflicts, they also undermine their power as individuals and further negate their accountability as parents. They also undermine the integrity of the child, diminishing the child's opportunities to engage in responsibilities and activities appropriate to his or her status as a child. Pastoral caretaking must therefore reorganize the family structure by detriangulating the child from the parental system, differentiating the marital dyad from the parental dyad. Each individual parent needs help to engage the other from a position of strength rather than to continue a futile power struggle.

Coalition building, or restructuring subsystem alliances, and developing the capacity for oppositional protest are two other strategies to promote viable accountabilities by which a system might change. At the personal level, it is sometimes powerful to build a coalition between the self and neglected parts of the unconscious to overcome symptomatic crises and to change persons' relation to themselves and to their world. At the family level, it is often fruitful to build alliances between adult siblings in caring for elderly parents, rather than to overburden one or two of the children with this responsibility.

Coalitions can be mobilized for protest and opposition, as when family members join together to confront the problematic behavior of one of its members. At the social and cultural level, the black freedom movement made significant advances by building internal coalitions and by incorporating outside groups into their strategy of public protest of unjust patterns. If the one thing the black freedom movement did right was to start to fight, as the documentary "Eyes on the Prize" makes poignantly clear, the second thing it did right was to decide not to fight *alone.*

Systems may be restructured by promoting viable roles. To be viable, roles must be accessible and flexible. Persons or groups of persons who are locked into certain roles reveal an impaired or underfunctioning system. Creativity is low, and usually the power arrangements are intractable. Thus, if persons are only in oppositional and never in generative roles, the system underfunctions or malfunctions. When only women rear children and only men make money and control the lawmaking process, the roles in a system are not viable. When persons of one racial or ethnic group constitute a disproportionately high percentage of persons in prison and poverty, the roles in the system are not viable. Psychosystemic pastoral caretaking seeks to change roles by extinguishing negative roles such as scapegoat and identified patient, and by providing occasion for sharing equitably and flexibly in the many necessary positive roles necessary to the well-being of persons and their larger worlds. When a number of blacks, and later middle-class whites, said, "Hell no, we won't go" to Vietnam in the 1960s and early 1970s, serious questions were raised about the nature of our social order and the values by which it would organize itself. Some important structural changes were made possible, at least on a temporary basis, as a result of this protest concerning the roles of black and white young men in our society.

Finally, systems may be restructured by establishing viable rules. Rules are the mores and processes that become established to maintain order and regulate power and transactions in the system. They constitute the operative values that govern and maintain the psychosystemic structure. When symptomatic crises emerge, there is usually a conflict in the rule-making processes, and a need for more viable arrangements. There are at least two levels of conflict over rules. The first is conflict over what the rules will be. The second is conflict over who will make the rules.[7] Systems can come into great tension when there is conflict and confusion about the rules and who makes them. When the rules subordinate one set of realities to another, rather than blend entities harmoniously, great difficulty can ensue. Thus the pastoral caretaker must assist the system to identify its operative rules and to negotiate more effective rules. This means that the pastoral caretaker helps people move from coercion to cooperation and from avoidance to constructive engagement in establishing the vision and purposes by which the system shall be organized, and for setting the goals necessary for accomplishing its purposes. The pastoral caretaker helps the system find viable rules for handling its conflicts in a creative rather than a destructive manner, and for sharing the responsibilities, opportunities, and rewards of the system in a loving, just, and ecologically responsible manner.

Fourth, for change to occur, there must be strategies for relinquishing and terminating the caretaking relationship. When crises have been resolved, or when it becomes clear that they cannot be resolved through continuing the caretaking relationship, a process of terminating the working alliance is necessary. The idea of termination relates to an ending of a working agreement. It includes review of the work accomplished, and a sharing of appreciation of the relationship established. It provides an occasion to deal with unfinished business and any residue of negative feelings that may remain. Termination allows other issues to emerge, and an occasion for recontracting or referral. Sometimes the need to terminate the helping relationship uncovers deeper unresolved terminations and new levels of fear of change in the system. These dynamics need to be acknowledged and explored.

The pastoral caretaker must relinquish his or her position in the caretaking subsystem of the individual and of the family's life, and renegotiate the larger basis for engagement. There may in fact turn out to be little or no basis for engagement beyond the caretaking role. On the other hand, there often will be numerous occasions to participate together in the larger work of the congregation and in the public arena of religious faith. Some brief informal liturgy of blessing and handing over may assist this transition, while affirming and celebrating the meaning and accomplishments of the pastoral caretaking relationship that is ending.

Joining, illuminating, restructuring, and relinquishing are various strategic means by which the principle of adventure becomes a reality in pastoral caretaking. The principle of adventure affirms that through the caretaking process, novel and unpredictable configurations of experience come into being, to the potential enrichment of all. The principle of adventure is rooted in the concept of God as one who seeks a new thing of beauty to emerge from present circumstances. This principle underscores that while all those in the caretaking subsystem are important players, there are creative realities beyond any one's control. God is a player too. During the relinquishment phase in particular, the novelty of what has come about is most clear. Relinquishment involves recognizing that while the outcome was influenced by our efforts, no one alone controlled or manipulated it. To relinquish means to recognize that what has come into being will have a life of its own beyond our control. When symptomatic crises have been resolved in transformative ways, there is a great sense of wonder and joy. When not, there is often a sense of sadness and dread. All of these must be relinquished to God, and taken into account for the next moment of care that presents itself.

SUMMARY: THE MEANING OF CHANGE

In a psychosystemic view, change is not simple, automatic, or predictable. It is rooted in the nature of God, who desires and seeks to promote a new thing of beauty, characterized by an increase of love, justice, and ecological partnership. Since the psychosystemic matrix is simultaneously stable and unstable, both the basis for change (and resistance to it) are built into the nature of reality, including the reality of God. For change to occur, there needs to be a stimulus upon the system as a whole, or from pressures between subsystems. When these pressures mount and create dissonance, symptomatic crises result, which threaten the stability of the system and require a response. The response that occurs will contribute to change, particularly if the response is received by the symptomatic parties in the system.

For change to occur, therefore, there must be dissonance, in the form of symptomatic crises, followed by a strategic influence that engages the symptomatic situation. If the strategic influence is effective, it will stimulate a focused responsiveness from the symptomatic parties. The specific nature of the focused response will shape the precise nature of the change. Since the receiving agent of the strategic influence also shapes what is received, change will not be a simple replication of the original stimulus. Rather, it will be a novel appropriation, and will in itself create a novel influence on what follows from it.

There are several operational goals of change, and numerous interlocking strategies to realize these goals. These goals and strategies reflect the principles of organicity and simultaneity, inasmuch as they recognize that everything is connected—including the pastoral care-taker—and that change in one area coincidentally leads to change in another, at least in part. The goals and strategies reflect the principles of conscientization and advocacy inasmuch as they require an illuminating interpretation of the total situation in which the symptoms function, and push for public efforts to bring about new structural models of organizing the institutions of our world. These goals and strategies reflect the principle of novelty inasmuch as they promote the possibility of surprising change, which increases the values of love of self, God, and neighbor, and promotes a just social order and a more livable world.

PART II
PASTORAL ANALYSIS AND RESPONSE

OPENING EARS TO HEAR: RESOLVING TRANSACTIONAL IMPASSES THROUGH THE MINISTRY OF CARE

Ships are only hulls, high walls are nothing,
When no life moves in the empty passageways.
Sophocles, *Oedipus Rex*[1]

TOWARD TRANSACTIONAL EFFECTIVENESS

Symptomatic crises are centered in transactional impasses of one kind or another. Blocked or impaired transactions render persons and systems less effective in maintaining themselves, and close them to possibilities for change. A central goal of the ministry of care is to promote transactional effectiveness instead of transactional impasses. Concretely, the ministry of care seeks to replace frozen roles with flexible roles. It promotes energizing messages in place of tangled messages. It helps negotiate congruent rules instead of disparate rules.[2]

The importance and power of transaction became clear to me in a class I once taught with James Lynch, a medical psychologist from Johns Hopkins University. We taught a class on "Healing and Theology," at the institution where I teach. The purpose of the class was to demonstrate the interplay between physiological, emotional, and environmental factors. Lynch had done considerable research on the psychological consequences of loneliness, the effect of pet care on depression and sociality among the criminally insane, and the relationship of interpersonal processes on blood pressure.[3] He was to show the effect on bodily processes of interpersonal transactions. My role in the course was to interpret this dynamic interplay in the light of process theology and pastoral care. There were about thirty-five persons in the class, which consisted of one cardiologist, several psychologists, a number of therapists and parish ministers, and a variety of lay persons who work in the church. The class met five days a week for about four hours each day. The format consisted of lecture, discussion, and role play.

Lynch brought a blood pressure machine that was hooked to a computer and monitor. On several occasions, he hooked persons to the blood pressure machine while he interviewed them or while the class went about its work. If the screen was turned on, the class could see what was happening to the person's heart rate and blood pressure during the interaction. It was predicted that certain kinds of interactions would raise stress, as registered by an increase in heart rate and blood pressure. On several occasions it was demonstrated that blood pressure and heart rate rose alarmingly, depending on the exchanges of information that occurred.

In one particular case, a woman in her sixties volunteered to be interviewed. She was a widow of a very renowned minister in her community. She began to tell her story in a very quiet, calm manner. She said that she was very happy to be a minister's wife, though sometimes she thought she was not able to develop some of her own interests and talents because of expectations others had of her. She realized that she spent long hours alone at home and had primary responsibility for the care of their several children. All of their children were grown adults and were doing well in their professional and family lives. She was grateful for that. She thought it was a privilege to be a minister's wife and to serve the church. She talked about some of her avocations throughout her married life, and now through her semi-retirement years. She particularly talked of her love of the arts and of her leadership and growing contributions as a composer. She said that her arthritis made it difficult for her to do as much composing as she would like, and occasionally she was in so much pain that she despaired. But she knew that her faith and courage were strong and that she would continue to endure her pain for the sake of the joys of her work. She then went on to tell of a recurring dream. In her dream, she saw herself sitting in the front of a church. As she sat, all of the parishioners from all of her former churches passed in front of her. Each person smiled at her, and reached over and took a piece of her and walked on by. When she was diminished to nearly nothing, her children came before her in the same way. Each took a piece. Finally, her husband came and stood before her. He took the last piece of her body.

As she recounted her dream, it was clear to all in the class that her blood pressure and heart rate were rising astronomically. Lynch seemed calm as he continued to interview her. She showed no external signs of distress, discomfort, or pain. She was calm and matter-of-fact, almost as though she were conversing quietly over tea with close friends. As Lynch intervened, neither her blood pressure nor her heart rate diminished. In fact, they continued to escalate, and there seemed to be no way to stop this transactional pattern. The room seemed calm during the interview; however, in debriefing afterwards people said they were in fact quite alarmed.

As the blood pressure and heart rate continued to climb, however, a black minister interrupted the process. He said something like this: "Mrs. Jackson, I understand from what you are saying that you love music and have been a composer. I, too, am a musician and have been a performer. I love music and I can tell from what you're saying that you also love it. I would appreciate knowing more from you about how you came to love music and what it does for your life."

She smiled, took a deep breath, and began talking about the songs that she had composed and her feelings about them. She talked about them as an expression of her love for God and the world. She shared how gratified she was that people performed them and that they brought joy to other persons' lives. For several minutes she continued in this vein.

As she continued talking about her love for music, interacting with this compassionate and interested minister, her blood pressure and heart rate decreased in dramatic fashion. It returned near the baseline level of her typical functioning, which, incidentally, was higher than normal. The participants in the room breathed a collective sigh of relief and began to feel less anxious. Finally, Mrs. Jackson finished the interview process and returned to her seat that she had occupied during the class. We finished out the class session, though I dare say that few of us remember very much what happened after the interview.

As we later debriefed the session, Lynch said that this pattern was quite typical. He described how blood pressure and heart rate would rise dramatically for persons with whom he worked as they discussed painful parts of their past, especially when they seemed calm in the telling. The cardiologist in the room told us that he was extremely worried about what he was seeing, because the blood pressure level was "at emergency room proportions." He said that the likelihood of her having a stroke or heart attack was very high, and that he was deeply concerned about what was happening. The members of the class were appreciative of the black minister's sensitivity and his willingness to enter the process to shift the dynamics so that Mrs. Jackson became less physiologically and psychologically distressed. Mrs. Jackson did not come back to class the next day, saying that she had taken to her bed after the session and slept all afternoon and all night. She was too exhausted the next day to attend class. When she did return, she expressed deep appreciation to the class for listening to her and allowing her to share very painful material. She also expressed particular appreciation to the black minister who had let her talk about what she loved and to feel accepted and valued for this side of her personality.

This vignette is not strictly from the context of the ministry of care, in which one person who is experiencing crisis formally seeks help from another. However, it amply illustrates that the need for care and the possibility for the onset of symptoms is pervasive in a psychosystemic environment. Mrs. Jackson carried in her memory, anchored in her bodily processes of heart rate and blood pressure, a history of transactional impasses that have diminished her life. In the context of recounting these in an environment of apparent acceptance, learning, and collaboration, she was, without being aware of it, driven to a situation in which a tragic crisis might have eventuated. Inadvertently, the class exercise had replicated the very position in which she spent much of her life, freezing her in the role in which something was taken from her rather than developing a flexibility of roles in which mutual give-and-take was the norm.

On the other hand, one of the members of the group recognized the imbalance in the transactions and connected with her in such a way that messages were exchanged about what she loved and valued. He was able to join her at a deeper level than merely the symptomatic. He also found a way to reciprocally join, through his own participation in similar interests, her love for music, and to reduce her stress by reconnecting her with her positive attributes. The feedback of this transaction upon her bodily processes was dramatic. Rather than taking her power away, it energized it. Rather than further threatening to impair the structure and viability of her personality and bodily life, it contributed to relief and, perhaps, restoration. Instead of perpetuating the values in which she was sacrificing her personhood through her love, it provided a form of mutuality in which something was received as well as given. In this respect, she was no longer a victim of the injustice of others who used her for their own growth. She experienced a measure of liberation, participation, and nurture in this loving connection with the black minister. Finally, it demonstrated that care does not always come from where one would expect within the system. The leaders and the class as a whole were helpless to provide positive care. We were somewhat paralyzed by the dynamics that were taking place, though they were engineered by us for what we thought would promote the greater good. In this respect it is always essential that the caretaker examine the structure of relationships, and their consequences, that emerge from the quality of transactions that are employed or neglected.

SUPPORTIVE CARE OF THE DYING

Frequently the ministry of care is asked to respond to persons and families facing dying and death. It is in this context that transactional impasses are often paramount. Long-standing frozen roles sometimes persist. However, the reality of dying and death provides the occasion to develop more flexible roles and to sort out tangled messages and to resolve conflicting rules and values. Sometimes, however, these transactional impasses are unresponsive to attempts to promote transactional effectiveness.

An example of the virulent, or evil, effect of long-standing transactional impasses presented itself in a recent verbatim. A student chaplain in a local hospice described her interview with a mother of a twenty-five-year-old man dying of AIDS. The nursing staff asked the chaplain to talk with the man's mother. She had expressed pain because her son did not want to see her but had invited another older woman to his room to be with him in his last days. The mother had traveled from another state to be with her son. The parents were divorced and nothing was said about the father. The chaplain was called to help the mother deal with her ambivalence about leaving the next day for home. The chaplain was not able to work with the son, or with the mother and son together, since the son had left word in the chaplain's office that the chaplain should not visit him under any conditions. Clearly there were transactional impasses between the chaplain and the son, and between the mother and the son. There was also a transactional impasse between the nursing staff and the mother. The chaplain was asked to resolve the impasse by ministering to the mother.

S-1: Hi, my name is Susan and I'm with the pastoral services here at the hospice. Ellen told me that you might need someone to talk to.

C-1: Oh yes. It's that lady. She's lying across his bed now, so I can't talk to D.

S-2: That lady?

C-2: You know, the one D gave power of attorney to, the home nurse.

S-3: Tell me more about her. It seems you're really upset.

C-3: Well she's completely taken over D. She's here all the time, and D seems really to like B a lot. She really helps him and I'm glad he has someone since I can't be here with him. I have to go home tomorrow.

S-4: I'm sorry. I'm not really understanding why you're upset. On the one hand I hear your concern that B is taking D's time away from you and on the other hand, it sounds like you're relieved she's here.

C-4: Well, I guess I'm glad D has someone here since I can't be. I don't know if I should go home tomorrow or if I should stay until he dies.

S-5: Are you feeling like you would be abandoning him if you go home tomorrow?

C-5:   (starts to cry, cigarette case and lighter are in constant motion)

S-6:   Do you wish to smoke? I really wouldn't mind going with you to the smoking area. We can talk about D there.

C-6:   Oh yes. I'm sorry. I've been smoking a lot these last few days, but it calms me.
(We walk down the short hall to a smoking lounge. She lights her cigarette and inhales deeply.)

C-7:   I always tried to be a good mother, but I failed him. His father and I were divorced when he was six, but I always tried to give him things boys need. I bought us each a set of boxing gloves and would box with him all the time in the living room, trying to teach him self-defense, thing[s] like that. He never played with dolls or things like that, but he became so unhappy about boxing, I had to stop it. I made sure he was in Boy Scouts but he didn't take to that, either. I remember when he was about ten, I had an intuition something was wrong with him. He was so quiet and wanted to be alone a lot.

S-7:   Did you ever talk to him or anyone else about your feelings?

C-8:   No. But I remember reading about how boys turn out to be homosexual when they have absent fathers and domineering mothers. I really tried not to be domineering though. I had to spank him once in a while when he got out of hand, but don't all mothers have to do that?

S-8:   Yes, they do, of course. It seems to me that you're blaming yourself for D's being gay.

C-9:   (Starts to cry.) I always tried to be a good mother. I don't know what I did wrong.

S-9:   Have you ever talked to D about your feelings?

C-10:   Yes, but he just tells me I'm silly. He doesn't want to hurt my feelings.

S-10:   So, you think you've caused D to be gay, by something you did as a parent?

C-11:   Yes. (crying)

S-11:   Do you know that most authorities in the field of psychology would not agree with you?

(Here follows a review of homosexuality as an alternative life-style. What caused her to choose her heterosexuality? Does she think she can be counseled into loving women? And, what makes her think her son can change then? As we talk, she becomes more relaxed, leans forward, talks with more animation. There are longer periods of eye contact, less fidgeting with her cigarettes and lighter. Conversation goes on in this vein for approximately one-half hour.)

S-12:   It feels to me that if you go home tomorrow that would be one more example of your "poor parenting" (finger quotes). You've been awfully hard on yourself about this, haven't you?

C-12:   Well, I didn't know. I never talked about it before. I guess I felt like I'd be letting him down if I go.

S-13:   And it's really hard to know whether to go or to stay. Know that we'll take good care of him if you're not here. He'll not be in any pain and we'll help him die. You do what you have to do, but recognize that this is not an issue of your being a good parent—your staying or not. My view is that you tried very hard to be a good parent. I can't see one thing you did to cause D to be gay. Take care of all your unfinished business before you go, then decide with him what to do. Be open and honest, as much as you can.

(Here follows a discussion of what might constitute unfinished business. I make a final suggestion to her to try to contact a counselor in California to talk some more about her guilt and grieving issues. D passed away in the early morning hours, four days later. D's mother was not at her son's bedside when he died.)

This poignant verbatim illustrates both the difficulty and importance of the pastoral caretaker's role in establishing reciprocal transactions where impasses have come into being. The chaplain was helpful in opening communication at some deeper level regarding the messages the mother was giving to herself about her son's homosexuality. At the intrapsychic level, the chaplain helped the mother at least begin to consider that the messages she was giving herself about her son's homosexuality might be incorrect. This strategic intervention, which included giving other messages and communicating different values, helped promote a measure of focused responsiveness on the part of the mother regarding her valuation of her son's homosexuality. However, the long-standing roles between mother and son, and the apparently absent father, were not amenable to change in the present circumstance. Thus, while the mother's intrapsychic attitudes toward homosexuality may have been modified to some extent, there is no evidence that this was translatable into the interpersonal relationship with her son. Here is an example of how the ignorance and negativity toward homosexuality within the larger heterosexist culture, as internalized in this mother, functioned to freeze the roles and keep a destructive distance between them.

A second issue that emerges is whether the mother should return home or stay with her son. It appears that the mother prefers to leave, but feels guilty about it. It also looks like the son is making it difficult for him and his mother to reconcile and say goodbye at this critical time. The distance that has emerged between them over life is maintained reciprocally by mother and son, partially through the triangulation of a third person into the maternal role with the son.

The chaplain's interventions at S-12 begin to help the mother focus on leaving for her home state. The chaplain is not as helpful here, tending to give advice and support before exploring what it would mean for the mother to leave or to stay. The transactional exchanges here tend to be from a one-up position on the part of the chaplain, rather than mutual exploration of what might be appropriate for the mother. Specifically, the chaplain could have helped the mother better explore what unfinished business she had with her son, and how it might be introduced effectively in her relationship with her son. The chaplain could have become a coach by advocating for more open communication at this time and empowering the mother to take an effective step in changing the transactional impasses that have remained. The chaplain encourages the mother to do something like this, without knuckling down and actually assisting her to do it. In this respect the chaplain missed an opportunity to help empower the mother and son to connect at a deeper level interpersonally, and to disengage and relinquish their relationship in a more holistic fashion.

It is also striking that while her son's dying is the reason the mother has traveled from another state, issues of death are not addressed. The major issues attended to in this pastoral exchange are the mother's attitude toward her son's homosexuality and the distance between them that had developed over time. There is no explicit reference to the mother's feelings about her son's dying and to what she needs to communicate to her son. At a time when the very fabric of the structure of their relationship is under the hand of death, no explicit communication is taking place about the impact and meaning of this. The love and affection that the mother and son may have once had for each other seem to be lost in anger, estrangement, and misunderstanding.

There is no opportunity to say "good-bye" or "thank you" for the impact of each other's life on the other. Nor is there much creativity between the mother and son during this critical period in their lives. The power imbalances that have existed throughout their relationship seem to dominate. It is unclear why the chaplain in this instance stayed focused upon the issues of homosexuality and estrangement without taking pastoral initiative to strategically focus upon the transactional impasses pertaining to death and dying, grief and loss. In supervision, questions such as these would be important. Unfortunately, in these circumstances, it was too late for a supervisory process to occur and to possibly influence the subsequent outcome of the interaction.

A contrasting example of effective transactions during the crisis of death and dying is recounted by Chaplain Stuart Plummer.[4] Plummer argues that Christian faith in its most positive sense helps persons face the reality of death by approaching it with "courage, dignity, and hope." Persons who face death in such a manner have effective communication and transactional processes with the persons around them and with their own internal life. Plummer recalls meeting a twenty-two-year-old man dying of leukemia. He recounts the family's reflection in the period of his dying and death:

Mrs. L: It was the most memorable experience of our lives. We didn't want to lose him, but to share it, to talk about things that were really important to us, made it easier for us *and* Dick.

Chaplain: Things such as?

Mrs. L: All sorts of things. We reminisced about experiences we had shared, as well as ones we had hoped to do together but never did. Some were funny while others were sad, but they were all important because—I guess because they had been ours to share.

Chaplain: It meant very much to you, didn't it?

Mrs. L: Oh, so much. You see, we knew and Dick did too; so there were no barriers left between us. Sure, there were things we regretted, things we would have done differently. But that was no longer important. We just wanted to be together for as long as possible. Near the end we kissed each other and cried. Dick, even though very weak, told us again that he loved us and not to worry, that he'd be all right. And then in a few moments he closed his eyes—and was gone.

Chaplain: You have much to be grateful for, even in the midst of your loss.

Mrs. L: That's true. We're just thankful to have known him, and have had him as long as we did.

In this brief vignette, it becomes clear that the chaplain enabled greater transactional effectiveness during this crisis in the life of the young man and his family. Rather than being frozen in roles and cut off from each other, this was an occasion for people to share more deeply. Mrs. L regarded the transactional processes as leading to ". . . the most memorable experience of our lives." They were able to talk about the things that were most important to them, including their disappointments at what they would not be able to share in the future. They were open to sharing their histories, feelings, hopes, and losses. As Mrs. L says, ". . . there were no barriers left between us." This is an example in which the structure of their family life was strengthened and advanced through the transactional messages that were allowed to take place. They were able to relinquish each other. Though there was deep sadness, there was also a sense of harmony and synchronicity rather than tearing and estrangement. Clearly this is an example in which an increase of love took place between family members. There was a creative resolution to the impairment in the structure brought about by the premature death of the son. This family, in contrast to Mrs. C above, can relinquish its son with gratitude and joy. And while grief is certainly a part of their ongoing heritage, the grief is not underground, hidden, or paralyzed by unresolved power and value issues. Rather, it is suffused with joy and memory, as well as sadness at missing someone who was dearly loved.

TRANSACTIONS WITH A CHAUVINIST

Gender, age, and role are virulent contextual factors that influence whether transactions are effective or not. A striking example of just how tangled messages can become when these factors are at work occurred in a verbatim presented by a first-year, lesbian, M.Div. student. Sherry is about twenty-five years old. She worked in a field education setting in a local hospital. In this setting she reported that she was more comfortable visiting women, but forced herself to make a visit to at least one male patient each time she was on duty. On this particular occasion she chose to visit a man whom the nurse said was lonely. Sherry said, "I was a bit nervous upon entering the room, as always, and hoping that in spite of my issues with men, I would be available to him, as well as a comforting presence." Already her internal transactions are struggling to move from frozen roles in relation to men to more flexible capacities for relating. She is struggling not to avoid her conflict with men, but to affirm the conflict and to move beyond it.

Sherry said that when she greeted Bill, he was sitting upright on his bed looking out the window. She described him as "a grizzled-looking man with two tatoos on both arms, and a leathery face. His eyes were red and his hands shaking, giving him the appearance of someone in for detox." She went on to say that he was a seventy-five- to eighty-year-old man who was in the hospital with "lung problems." She said, "He smiled and seemed glad to have me there, which made me feel a bit more at ease." The interview proceeded as follows:

C1: Hi! I'm Sherry. I'm with the chaplain's office. I came by to see how you're doing this afternoon.

P1: Oh! Sit down right over there. Just throw that stuff on the floor and sit. Good to see you. Pretty young thing like you. You're a minister? (He is noticeably looking at my breasts.)

C2: Well, yes. I'm studying to be one. (I take his hand) Your name is . . .?

P2: Bill.

C3: How do you feel this afternoon, Bill?

P3: Oh, not too good. My lungs hurt. I've got lung problems. So I'm just sitting here wasting the time away . . . all cooped up looking out the window.

C4: It must be hard to have to stay in bed all day. What do you wish you could be doing?

P4: Oh yeah (nodding). Well, I used to be outside all the time. I used to ride broncs on the rodeo circuit. I'd ride anything that moved. (He looks me in the eyes.) I still like to ride anything that moves, especially pretty young things like yourself. (He laughs.)

C5: (I laugh nervously, thinking I must have misunderstood him.) Well, do you have any idea when you'll get to go home?

P5: Tomorrow afternoon.

C6: How do you feel about that?

P6: Oh okay. It'll be lonely though. There's no one there to visit me. I'm just a lonely old man.

C7: Hmm . . . How does that feel?

P7: Well, I can't get out and do half of what I used to do. I just sit around brooding. Look at me. Do I look like I could do much? Ha! It's just my wife and me, and she still works a lot. She's not home that much, so I'm alone most of the time. I would really like to get to know you, though. Are you married? (Most of this time he is looking at my chest, avoiding eye contact.)

C8: Nope, I'm not. (Pause) But let's talk about you. I'd like to hear more about how you're feeling. Are you saying you wish your wife was around more?

P8: Ha ha ha. Oh, no . . . well, I really wish I had someone to visit me. Do you think you could? I could really use some company, and I would really like to get to know you. You sure smell good. Mmmm. I would like to get closer to that.

C9: Why do you think you want to get to know me?

P9: Well, I'm just a lonely old man and I could do with some pretty company. Why can't you come? I'll pay you fifty dollars. Wouldn't you like to earn fifty dollars?

C10:   Oh, I don't think so. (nervous laughter)

P10:   Well why not? I could sure use a minister with the way my life is going.

C11:   How would a minister be of help?

P11:   Oh, you know. Someone to make me feel better. Life isn't what it used to be. I know you could make me feel better. I can tell that right now. (He is staring in my eyes with a smirk.) Can't you see how badly I'm feeling?

C12:   Yes, I think I do. It sounds like it's something other than a minister that you want though, and I don't think that I can really make you feel any better, though I wish I could.

P12:   What? (laughter) You're just nervous. You really make me feel better by being here. No one ever comes by like this. God bless you for being so sweet, honey. Why don't you come visit me? Let me give you my address and phone. Can I have yours?

C13:   Ah . . . Bill, I'd really like to listen to you and help, but . . . ah . . . I just don't know if that will work out.

P13:   Here's my address and phone. (I go ahead and write them down as he dictates.) Why don't you hold my hand? An old man like me doesn't get much touch.

C14:   (I take his hand and sit for a moment.) Well, I think I'll let you rest now. (I rise still holding his hand.) I need to go.

P14:   Why? I don't want to rest. I think you know what I want to do with you! Ha ha ha. Why don't you say a little prayer for me? I could sure use some comfort.

C15:   Okay. (I put my hand over both of ours and say a little "Help Bill get well prayer," after which I let go of his hand but he won't let go of mine.) You take care, Bill.

P15:   Oh don't leave, honey. (He looks desperate with tears in his eyes and his hands clenching both of mine.)

C16:   Okay, but tell me what you want, Bill.

P16:   I just want some love. Is that so bad? Look at me. Don't I look like I could use some? You've really cheered me up. Why leave now? I could make you feel good too. (At this point he shoves his hand all the way up the sleeve of my dress and rubs my upper arm.)

C17:   (I grab it and yank it out as hard as I can and give his hand one last squeeze and then jerk my hands away.) I need to go, Bill. Take care. Bye. (I march out of the room and begin to cry as I walk down the hall.)

P17:   Honey! Honey!

In her conclusion, Sherry observes that the transactions here were multileveled. She says, "I don't know what to take at face value, and what to doubt. For example, does the fact he wants me to pray for him convey a belief in God and a longing for God's comfort and healing? Or does he simply want to hold my hand? I honestly do not know. Maybe both are true." As she reflects further on her own performance, she says:

> I don't know why I reacted so strongly to this encounter. I hate to admit that I left crying. I'm not really sure of the reasons behind that sudden emotion except that I felt powerless and run over and disgusted that he stuck his hand into my dress. I am angry at myself, that my own issues got in the way of effective ministry, and that some deep down childhood view of what it means to be a minister, or Christian, allows me to play the victim. I was careful not to misunderstand or "reject" him, and in doing so denied my own power and feelings. Yuck. I am angry at sexism—that I am a young, female chaplain to people who don't respect me as a woman, who most often look at me as their daughter, and who think they can grab my hands and not let go. . . .
>
> Oh, this is difficult . . . I really did feel his loneliness and isolation, and in this hospital setting I see my ministry as one of being a comforting, loving presence, and of creating a space where people can express their feelings and doubts. With this in mind, I was hesitant to sound harsh, or to focus the conversation on his behavior rather than on his feelings, which I wanted to encourage him to explore. So, ironically, it was my hesitancy to confront that actually allowed little ministry to take place.

She concludes:

> From this experience I have learned . . . that to subvert my own power and self in hopes of not offending a man, or seeming harsh, only perpetuates the unequal power relationships between males and females. I realize that I need to work hard to define my own boundaries and respect them as much as I do others', or I will be a burned out, used, and bitter person someday.
> . . . I have to work very hard at seeing men as unique, separate human beings with whom I share a common humanity instead of lumping them all together under the title of "Jerks like Bill." Of course I know all men are not like Bill, but it takes work to continue to live openly, trustingly, and uncynically.

This rather candid and engaging episode in ministry highlights how sexism and heterosexism are structured into our psyches, our behaviors, and the total fabric of our lives. It shows how the attempt to have a human-to-human, pastorally centered encounter is rendered extremely difficult by these larger systemic realities. Bill had a difficult time unfreezing his expectations to allow Sherry to be a chaplain to him. He continued to see her as a sex object, and a source of gratification to him apart from her role definition and personal integrity. She became confused about the role of the chaplain and how that related to her own personal authenticity as a lesbian woman worthy of respect in her own right. Pseudo-Christian notions of love and acceptance became the vehicle by which these deeper cultural issues concerning sexuality overtly emerged.

The rules of the game in this situation were clearly oppositional. Fundamental values and moral orientations were in acute conflict. Bill's sexism and sexual harassment of Sherry reinforced Sherry's oppression as a lesbian and as a woman. It was not possible for them to negotiate mutual rules for their interaction and for Bill to find an occasion to deal with his relationship to God and the totality of his life in a more substantial fashion. Sherry was particularly ensnared in Bill's tangled messages, double entendres, and ambivalence about what he wanted from her. She faced an unarticulated double bind, which contributed to her paralysis. Bill's double-binding message was: "If you love me the way I need to be loved, you will let me control you sexually and not persist in trying to be a minister to me. However, if you refuse to let me have my way with you sexually because you are a minister, you will not really be loving me."

These tangled, double-binding messages contributed to rendering Sherry relatively powerless in this situation. She did make valiant attempts to give "I" messages and to maintain her integrity as a person and as a minister. But as she pointed out, she was too overwhelmed to break through Bill's stereotyping.

TRANSFORMING THE GENERATIONS

Some time ago, I worked with a very complicated, transgenerational family system that was in deep crisis because of transactional impasses persisting over at least three generations. The frozen roles, tangled messages, and disparate rules that led to chronic symptomatic crises needed strategic intervention and fundamental restructuring for healing to occur. Through therapy and ongoing support from a local minister, this family was able to move from transactional impasses to transactional effectiveness. A detailed discussion of this pastoral therapy allows specific techniques for changing transactional processes to come into focus.

Sharon sought pastoral counseling because she was very depressed. In her early thirties, she had just had an abortion because her live-in lover refused to marry her and raise the child together. He wanted her to have the child so that he could have the experience of being a father, but would make no commitments to the child or to the relationship. She felt guilty for betraying him and for betraying the Roman Catholic faith that she held. She was not aware of the anger that she held for Dick. Her internal transactions and her transactions with him consisted mostly of her sense of shame and failure at having an abortion and for being unable to convince him to marry her. Since she was already divorced and the mother of two boys, ages ten and seven, fathered by her former husband, she particularly felt like she was an unworthy person religiously speaking. The messages that she was giving to herself were: "I am a bad person. Dick does not love me enough to marry me, and though I tried to keep Jack in our marriage, I have not been able to save him from his alcoholism and his inability to hold a job and be with a family." She felt frozen in the role of scapegoat. She was the target of the anger of her in-laws, lover, and former husband because in their minds she was selfish and not adequate to meet their expectations. As hard as she might try, she was unable to satisfy them. She also felt diminished in her own eyes because her boys were having school-related trouble. The oldest boy was diagnosed as schizophrenic and was continually fighting with other kids in his class. Her youngest boy was diagnosed as school-phobic. He was passive and withdrawn most of the time.

Sharon's life was complicated in other arenas. She was the manager of a busy legal office and was required to handle the professional affairs of many persons. In addition, those with whom she worked and those working for her confided in her about many of their personal and family situations. She was continually on the phone trying to help other people manage their lives, even while she tended to her own life and the troubled lives of her sons. Her ex-husband was a continual worry besides. He was in and out of jail and lived the life of a homeless alcoholic. He would frequently turn up in a disheveled state, needing money for one thing or another, wanting to see his sons. She would usually give him some money, allow him to see the sons, and then shove him off. At times he would kidnap the boys and take them to a friend or relative's house, forcing her to take time off work to track them down.

Moreover, her mother and sister made great demands upon her. Her sister was involved in a conflicted relationship with an older man, and her mother was in an after-care facility from being released from the state mental institution. She had spent twelve years in the institution, diagnosed as schizophrenic. She went into the institution when Sharon was five, because Sharon's father had shot himself to death and the mother could no longer cope. Sharon and her sister were raised by nuns in an orphanage. Sharon's mother was released from the hospital when Sharon married her husband, Jack. She did not live with Sharon, but called upon Sharon for much support and help.

The therapy began to help Sharon look at the messages she was giving to herself about herself and to the transactional patterns throughout her interlocking areas of living. She began to realize that she was angry at Dick for wanting her to have a child while not being willing to commit to her in marriage. Further, she was angry that he went home every weekend to be with his widowed mother in another state and insisted that she not date anyone while he was gone. He was about fifteen years older than she. He said that as long as his mother was alive, he could not see his way clear to marry her. She realized that she was in an untenable situation in which the rules were imposed rather than negotiated, and that they did not lead to a mutual sharing of responsibilities and losses. She began to think that this was unjust and began to touch her anger about it. Dick was invited to counseling to help them clarify their relationship. He came reluctantly and was not willing to make any changes. He was a physician, and she found out that he was dating and having sexual relationships with one of his patients. In the light of this information and his unwillingness to make any changes in relation to her, she ended the relationship. He was much aggrieved that she ended the relationship. She felt a mixture of relief and guilt.

The next phase of the therapy process was to restructure the transactions between Sharon and her ex-husband. She stopped letting herself be scapegoated by him and triangulated into a relationship between him, the courts, and her sons. She found a better way to protect her sons from being kidnapped by their father, while at the same time giving them supervised access to him. This relieved the anxiety of the oldest boy, who verbalized that he could not function well in school because he was continually worried that his father would not be permitted to see him, or that his father would die on the street. His behavior problems diminished greatly over time, as his relationship with his father became less triangulated with his relationship to his mother. Sharon stopped giving Jack money and asked him not to come to the house unannounced in the future. She quietly and patiently encouraged him to reconnect with his own parents when he needed help. She also set limits on the continued expectations of people in her office to meet their needs. She encouraged her sister to get counseling for her relational problems. Sharon also drew upon an older male friend for support and advice during this period, and felt less guilt about doing so. Instead of feeling responsible for her mother in all cases, she also began to ask her mother for advice and support, including some help with watching her sons. She was surprised that her mother was able to act effectively upon these requests. This made their relationship more mutual than impositional.

Sharon began dating. She went out with several men without becoming over-involved with any one. After a time, she began to be interested in a man her age who was a successful FBI agent. He had never married. He had positive relationships with his family of origin. He enjoyed Sharon and treated her with respect. He was a nominal member of the Presbyterian Church and found his faith helpful to him. He showed an interest in her boys and befriended them. He took them camping, hiking, and encouraged them in the interests that they had in Boy Scouts, athletics, music, and school. After about a year, Sharon and Harold decided that they wanted to marry. Harold helped Sharon keep boundaries between them and Jack, while also supporting Jack's relationship to his sons in a supervised environment.

Sharon became quite anxious and depressed when she realized that she loved Harold and wanted to marry him. This brought her in touch with the loss of her father and unresolved grief about it, as well as the need to confront her relationship to the Roman Catholic Church. As long as she had not remarried her divorce did not affect her relationship to the church. She had confessed her abortion and felt a measure of forgiveness. Still, she was not a communing member of the church and had increasingly grown distant from it. In the psychotherapeutic process, she reworked her covert transactions with her dead father and the impact of his suicide upon her attitudes towards herself, her choice of men, and her overall life-style. She was able to let go of the impasses connected with her unresolved grief and to find new energy for living her life in the present. After much difficulty, she decided to leave the Roman Catholic Church and to join the Presbyterian Church. She and Harold began to connect with a parish and a minister, and received pre-marital guidance and consultation. They were married in the church and maintained an active relationship with it.

Though I lived in a separate city from Sharon and Harold for several years, I annually received Christmas news from them. Jack continued his basic pattern of being homeless. He did occasionally contact his boys. Sharon and Harold prospered in their careers and became more active in the church. Each of the boys became symptom-free and was quite successful in school, Boy Scouts, sports, and their social lives. They had an active relationship to the youth group in their church and, the last I heard, were preparing for college.

The symptomatic crisis that began with Sharon's depression, when analyzed, revealed transactions that occurred over the generations and persisted throughout them. The chronic depression and underfunctioning in the family, which was connected with the father's suicide, continued with a hidden virulence into Sharon's and her sister's life, as well as into Sharon's children's lives. Sharon was frozen into a role of feeling underpowered and unworthy, while over-responsible and unsuccessful. She colluded with these frozen roles that kept her at an impasse. She was unable to be more flexible, interdependent, and differentiated in relationship to herself and those around her. The message given to Sharon was: "Even though you are inadequate, you are responsible for taking care of us at your own expense." She avoided conflict by taking all of these responsibilities upon herself, rather than setting limits and asking for something back.

She also was crowded into a frozen transactional pattern in which it was assumed that she had enough power to benefit others, while having none for her own benefit. The reverse side of this coin is that other persons did not have power for their own welfare, but were dependent upon her for it. These messages were untrue. They were restructured so that mutuality and reciprocity of power came more into the foreground. The rules, which were largely covert, became more overt. As Sharon gained power, and the rules became more overt, the patterns of relatedness could be negotiated to a greater extent, and were not as dominantly imposed on Sharon.

There were many strategic influences within therapy, as well as from life in its larger sense, that helped this family disentangle itself from the multi-leveled impasses that had persisted over the generations. Learning to give "I" messages rather than accepting the projections of others was important. Teaching persons to negotiate rules and to set limits on undesirable behaviors was involved. It was necessary to build more optimal generational coalitions while dissolving other unhelpful coalitions. Persons needed to be taught how to confront conflict from a position of strength rather than avoiding or detouring it. Through these interactions, assisted by the local minister, school counselors and psychologists, other family members, and life itself, changes were made over a two- to three-year period of time, which led to a transformation of this family and each individual's life. There was focused openness to the strategic interventions, though that openness sometimes eventuated in disconnecting relationships and creating restructured patterns, such as in the case of Jack and Dick.

In my judgment, this pastoral psychotherapy eventuated in change of behavior and of self-understanding or consciousness. The structure of the family's life and its relationship to the larger social order were simultaneously changed. Rather than continuing as a dysfunctional family that called on multiple community resources merely to sustain it, this family became characterized by contextual integrity instead of contextual impairment. And while, like all families, it still needed larger social support, it was able to be a contributor to the health of the larger social order by having worked its way to more just and loving patterns of relatedness.

PASTORAL STRATEGIES

The process of diagnosing and fashioning strategic interventions begins immediately when persons seek the ministry of care. Indeed, one of the reasons people seek the ministry of care is because they are at a transactional impasse, feeling stuck in their attempts to solve their crises. Seeking pastoral assistance is in itself a behavioral step, indicating that there is at least a general openness to redefine and modify their situation. When the pastoral caretaker accepts the role as helper, there is an immediate diagnostic intervention, which indicates that the pastoral caretaker also expects help to take place. Diagnosis and intervention coincide, however momentarily, in such instances.

I have found several procedures helpful in assessing and intervening. These procedures underlie all human communication and may be strategically employed in general living, as well as in a more particular responsibility of the caretaking ministry, whether in short-term or long-term situations. Though I will list these strategic interventions in a certain order, it should be obvious to the reader that they interrelate and may be employed in whatever fashion seems timely.

First, it is helpful to explore why the particular transactional impasses persist when other individuals, families, and groups do not have them. This communicates that the impasses are particular to this situation and might in fact be otherwise. Such awareness enables the participants to recognize their own behavior and explore creative ways to modify it. At this juncture it is also helpful to explore steps that have been taken which have not worked, so that the caretaker and careseekers do not persist in futile directions.

It is extremely useful to explore which patterns from the past are being preserved in the present situation, including the benefits and costs involved in maintaining or changing the patterns. A specific question to ask to highlight all of these concerns is: "Who, besides yourself, are you protecting from pain by keeping this pattern going? That is, who benefits and who loses in this arrangement?"

In the case of Sherry and Bill, above, it seems clear that she was struggling to integrate her lesbian and feminist understandings of love and gender justice with her little-girl notions of Christian ministers as "nice." Her agenda clashed with Bill's struggle to balance his needs for companionship with his needs for sexual conquest and masculine domination. To change this pattern would be costly for both. Neither was able to negotiate it under the circumstances. I recall another example—a counselee who was frozen in her job and unable to resolve ambivalence about her economic goals. To resolve this impasse this meant deciding whether to identify with her mother's side of the family and

133

become wealthy, or to maintain continuity with her father's side and live in relative poverty and underachievement. This conflict was a transgenerational conflict, which meant that change would shake the family structure throughout. She particularly realized that acting on behalf of her aspirations would further pain her father and alienate her from him. Once she saw this, she was able to maintain a relationship with her father while she pursued economic goals that were appropriate for her.

A second strategic influence is to reinterpret, or reframe, the diagnosis of the impasse held by those in it. Relabeling, or reframing, assists people to mobilize positive energy to deal with their circumstances. In the case of Mrs. Jackson, the black minister reframed the class situation by having the woman discuss what she loved rather than persist in the expectation that she explore painful areas. This restructured the situation from making Mrs. Jackson an object for the class's gratification and requiring us to see her as a valued individual whose achievements were taken seriously in their own right. By redefining her as a positive, healthy human being, the minister restructured the transactions so that they might be more enlivening for all.

Another example of relabeling is the common practice in family therapy of reframing moralistic interpretations into medical or developmental terms and of reframing medical diagnosis into interpersonal terms. Thus, it is not uncommon for a juvenile delinquent to be labeled as immature rather than criminal, while a depressed or anxious person is labeled as selfish or adaptive, rather than sick. I remember a videotape of Salvador Minuchin making a breakthrough with a family when he rediagnosed an acting-out young adult as selfish rather than sick. Such relabeling gave the family some power to deal with him from a position of strength, rather than feeling victimized by his problematic behaviors— which were otherwise presumed beyond control because he was ill.

A third strategy for changing transactional patterns is to escalate the transaction pattern and thus destabilize or unbalance the system, stimulating it to new patterns. As a youngster, I remember that the father of a friend of mine caught him smoking. He at least temporarily cured my friend's desire to smoke by buying a carton of cigarettes and forcing him to smoke one after another until he became so sick that he was adversive to smoking.

Similarly, a few years ago, an M.Div. student was in a conflict with his supervising minister. He felt that the supervising minister did not allow the student to demonstrate his competence. The student believed that the minister was threatened by the student's greater competence and undermined it as often as possible. The student and I explored ways in which the student could become more incompetent than he already was feeling. After some hesitation, and with not a little anxiety and suspicion, the student began to act as incompetently as he felt in the congregation. The minister then began to explore ways in which the student could become more competent and successful! As the student and minister explored this, new patterns were found and the supervisory relationship took on more significant meaning. The student did begin to feel valued for his competence by the supervisor and the congregation, and he was accordingly able to act competently. Such paradoxical interventions need to be structured with care, but they can sometimes lead to transactional breakthroughs, especially when there is a great deal of covert resistance to change.[5]

A fourth mode of intervention to help move from transactional impasses to transactional effectiveness is to increase the "I" messages given and received. Impasses occur when people give "you" messages, directing energy away from them and to the other. This invariably puts others in a defensive, resistive, and reactive position. When persons give messages such as "I feel," "I think," "I want," "I won't," it helps clear the system and resolve impasses, though it often escalates affect and conflict.

Helping persons give "I" messages is particularly important when they are caught in double binds. A double bind means that they have to respond to two opposite commands and cannot avoid responding. At the same time, there is a negative consequence for whichever response they make. Thus, rather than accrue such a painful response, no decision is made. But this is also punished! Often there is a prohibition about describing the double bind or having it openly acknowledged since that puts those sending the messages into accountability, which would rather be avoided. I have already indicated how double-binding occurred in the woman who was caught between her mother's family's expectations about wealth and her father's about poverty, or Sherry's bind between being a minister or a sexual object to Bill. In the case of Mrs. Jackson above, it might be possible for her to resolve her double bind by finding ways to see that acting on what she loved is also a way of service, while providing people what they want is not necessarily serving them.

A fifth strategy for resolving transactional impasses is to assist persons to change their role position in the situation, while still maintaining contact with the players. Kantor and Lehr identify four "player parts" or roles, organizing family life.[6] These are: mover, follower, opposer, and bystander. In healthy families these roles are flexible and interchangeable. When there are transactional impasses, these roles become frozen. Helping persons move from opposer to joiner can help change a family transactional pattern in a very short time. To move from mover to observer or bystander will accomplish the same.

I remember a situation in which two sisters were allied against their older brother about allocating their father's estate. The three were at an impasse. The family therapist suggested that one of the sisters join rather than oppose the brother, especially on matters that she could genuinely affirm him about, without relinquishing her position concerning the allocation of the inheritance. She began to compliment him on his many accomplishments and fine qualities. In their discussions she agreed with him wherever possible and even disagreed with her sister on points that she genuinely held in difference. It did not take long for the brother to begin to moderate his position about allocating the inheritance. While tensions continued to persist because of the strong alliance held by the sisters, there was clear resolution and increased appreciation and cooperation.

In a similar way, I find it helpful to instruct students and others who are returning for home visits on school breaks to strategically change their role position in relation to one or both parents. For example, I ask them to change the pattern of opposing their father and joining their mother by observing mother and joining father. I have yet to find students and counselees say that this was not a positive experience in their relationships to their families.

Finally, it is important to look for resources from active imagination and dream-life when persons are in transactional impasses. Sometimes the unconscious process generates the crisis and provides guidance for how it ought to be resolved. Exploring inner work is crucial during these times. Mrs. Jackson's dream gave a clear indication that she was in deep pain and needed to be moved to a situation of mutual partnership and fulfillment. The situation of self-giving abuse in the context of ministry and marriage needed to be modified if she were to flourish. For instance, I recall the client who had a dream that her older sister might engulf her at the next home visit and family reunion. She woke up from the dream terrified and immediately knew that she needed to find ways to protect herself while at home. She decided to protect herself by staying closely allied with her husband while visiting her family, and not being alone with her sister or mother for extended periods of time.

I remember at one transitional point in my life I knew that I had to leave the denomination that reared me. I was stuck, knowing I had to go on the one hand, and terrified to leave on the other. In the midst of this impasse, I dreamed that I was scaling a building alone. On this building was the symbol of my denomination, to which I was holding. Suddenly the symbol came off the roof and I began to fall. I realized that the symbol was being held up by balloons and I was caught between flying away or crashing to the ground. I began falling toward the ground, holding on in terror. I realized I was coming down on a paved driveway which had a grass lane in the middle between tire paths. I fell onto the grass, thinking I would be killed. When I surveyed the damage, however, I saw that I only had grass stains on my pants, and that I was uninjured. Upon waking from the dream, I realized that I could leave my denomination and survive. And, while it actually took me years to reestablish a viable relationship to another Christian denomination, I knew that this dream represented the resolution of my painful impasse on this matter.

CONCLUSION

To move from transactional impasses to transactional effectiveness, a variety of strategic influences are necessary. Since healing and aliveness come from appropriate transactional connectedness rather than isolation on the one hand or codependent enmeshment on the other, the quality of our transactions is crucial. Transactions create and reflect accountabilities, distribute power, and enhance the quality of love, justice, and partnership with the larger environment. In the following chapter, we will explore the relationship of transactions to power, examining particularly the relationship of transactional impasses to power imbalances, while exploring strategies to enhance effective transactions in the interest of synergistic power arrangements.

CHAPTER 6

DETHRONING THE DEMONIC: REARRANGING POWER THROUGH THE MINISTRY OF CARE

[Women] can use their abilities to support each other, even as they develop more effective and appropriate ways of dealing with power—sorting out its appropriate use and reacting to its inappropriate use in themselves and others.

Jean Baker Miller[1]

POWER IMBALANCES AS DEMONIC HEGEMONY

Power imbalances partially account for the symptoms arising in personal and environmental crises. Every entity, system, subsystem, and macrosystem must have power to exist, adapt, and change. Power is the bi-polar ability to influence and be influenced. It is the capacity to exercise agency or influence in relation to others and to be a receptor of the agency or influence of others. When crises occur, there is always an imbalance of power needing attention and correction. Imbalanced power is dangerous and destructive when the imbalance leads to victimization, chaos, and permanent unjust situations. Under such conditions, a demonic hegemony of power arrangements has come into being. Unless such a hegemony is challenged and modified by more positive configurations, great evil can occur.

To say that power is demonic is not to say that there are actual personal beings such as "demons" that inhabit individuals and social groups. Rather, the concept refers to destructive personal and structural forces transcending individual will and consciousness, yet affecting personal and social behavior. The concept of the demonic, as I am using it, refers to the "principalities and powers," or to the pervasive social and cultural conventions that distort our lives by elevating some partial good or truth into a dominant position from which all other good or truth is evaluated. Hence, Dana Wilbanks, a Christian ethicist, contends that the overreliance upon militarism to preserve liberty in the United States has become demonic and functions in idolatrous fashion.[2] Archie Smith, a black liberation ethicist and pastoral counselor, argues that the social conventions we hold about autonomous selfhood and individual

138

responsibility obscure the destructive social consequences of our pastoral care and counseling.[3] Rollo May, a humanistic psychologist, argues that the demonic refers both to the positive powers of the human personality, and accounts for the distortions of positive human qualities into something destructive and evil.[4] Demonic hegemony occurs when social convention and personal need elevate certain persons, qualities of being, or dimensions of experience over others with little or no provision for a corrective countervailing influence. Power is imbalanced; one element is locked into an ascending agency, the other into a descending receptivity. The symptoms generated by such a situation can be extremely acute, as we shall discover.

DIAGNOSING POWER IMBALANCES

There are predictable patterns of imbalanced and destructive power underlying crises. I will map some of these and relate them to the case of Joan and Mike, as well as to other examples.[5] Joan and Mike are a married couple in their early forties. They have a five-year-old son, Mikey. Joan is a successful corporate office manager; Mike is semi-employed as an entrepreneur and property manager. He is a Vietnam veteran and an intermittent member of Gambler's Anonymous. They sought personal help because Joan feels overwhelmed with all of the financial and emotional responsibility for Mikey and depressed about Mike's financial drain on her. She is also afraid that Mike will injure Mikey in one of his rages; he apparently has already shaken Mikey violently on several occasions. She has reported this to Social Services and Mike has been encouraged to get professional help for himself. Mikey is now living with Joan's parents. Joan has become suicidal on occasions and is in the care of a pastoral counselor and psychiatrist. Mike refuses to get professional help and tells the minister that everything is Joan's fault: "She should be a more dutiful wife, more submissive and patient like the Bible says. If she solves her problems, we won't have any problems. She doesn't trust me, which undermines my confidence and keeps me from being more successful." The pastor visited with Joan's parents and learned that they agreed with Mike, and that their relationship paralleled Joan and Mike's. The father is a retired military officer who is highly critical of his wife, Joan's mother. Joan's mother struggles to keep peace in the family and is angry at Joan for trying to set limits on Mike. She too feels that Joan should be more patient and accepting. Joan's parents are happy to have Mikey with them, and believe that their life is much calmer and more purposeful with him there. Mikey appears to be tolerating these stresses, but on occasion has blacked out and is scheduled for tests to see if he has epilepsy or some other brain disorder.

Victimizing and chaotic power exists when either one person or group is coerced into becoming the receptor of the influence of others quite apart from their own desires, needs, and aspirations. It also exists when there is such a power vacuum that legitimate desires, needs, and aspirations of individuals or groups of individuals have no viable means of validation or fulfillment. Such conditions result in the lack of genuine agential power on the part of those victimized, or those living in a chaotic situation. The opposite is cooperative or shared power, which is expressed in reciprocal agency and receptivity in a respectful covenantal framework.

When power becomes victimizing, a person or a group is unwillingly oppressed, abused, or exploited by another. Rape, battering, incest, racism, colonialism, sexism, and ageism are blatant examples, but there are numerous other expressions of such coercive, victimizing power. Being ignored, discounted, marginalized, and frozen in unsuitable roles are also expressions of victimizing power.

In the case cited above, Joan struggles not to be victimized by the overwhelming power of her husband, Mike. She is too much a receptor; he, too much an agent. There is an unbalanced exchange of power and influence for mutually chosen aims around mutually congruent values. Mike's power is reinforced by Joan's parents and the larger society, making it extremely difficult for Joan to discover her own power to choose and bring about her own desires. Achieving power to refuse the expectations of others is in itself a major task for her. Little Mikey is in a vulnerable position. He has the protection of his mother and grandparents, on the one hand, but the price he pays is separation from his father and mother, on the other. Such a situation may make him feel powerless in relation to his parents, while he finds some basis for influencing the world he is creating with his grandparents.

Chaotic arrangements of power exist when there is little or no viable means of validating or fulfilling the needs, aspirations, and desires of certain persons or groups in the social system. In the case of Joan, Mike, and little Mikey, little Mikey exists in a chaotic situation. His parents are struggling with victimizing power in relation to their families of origin, their marriage, and the social and cultural milieu in which they live. The net effect creates a largely chaotic situation for little Mikey. The extent to which his legitimate personal needs, desires, and aspirations can be validated and fulfilled in this context largely remains questionable.

The most pernicious dimension of victimizing and chaotic power arrangements is their imperviousness to change. Countervailing elements are denigrated, suppressed, or ignored. People seeking to remain in a dominant power position usually interpret the symptomatic behavior of others to their own advantage. Thus, symptoms such as illness, rebelliousness, depression, suicide, and violence are not interpreted by those on top to mean that something is wrong with the power arrangements and organizational structures in the social system. They are interpreted to mean that something is wrong with the symptomatic person. The person is then "treated" ro make his or her behavior and attitude more compatible with the expectations of those in power. These attitudes and behaviors will not be seen as indicators of a need for more cooperative and shared power distributions between the symptomatic and the nonsymptomatic.

Unaccountable and intractable power arrangements exist when a person or group disowns responsibility as either an agent or receptor of power, while simultaneously refusing to relinquish their current power position. In such cases, power usually operates covertly rather than openly, and is not subject to modification through reciprocal exchange of influence. In the more extreme examples of these situations, one person or group always is, or believes it should be, in power over another, while the other thinks it has no right to power aside from what is delegated by the dominant party. The patterns are set, and often are sanctioned by those in the more dominant position by an appeal to "the natural order," "God's will," "national security," or the like. Those with lesser status maintain their position by some combination of fatalism and protest, however active or passive. Military dictatorships and tyrannies are the most extreme examples, but passive-aggressive persons in smaller social systems are also notorious for their effectiveness in wielding power over others in an unaccountable and intractable manner!

There are four types of unaccountable and intractable power arrangements commonly emerging in pastoral caretaking. These cluster around projective bonding, triangling, internalizing blame, and discounting oneself and others. It is not possible to provide a full discussion of these topics, but it is important to analyze their relationship to imbalanced power and their potential contribution to an evil, demonic hegemony.

Projective bonding, more commonly known as projective identification, refers to the largely unconscious identification with a power center outside oneself. This identification has an ongoing, usually hidden, influence upon one's attitudes, belief systems, feelings, and behaviors. A common expression of this is in unresolved grief reactions to the death of an important attachment figure, such as a parent or close friend. Hidden attachments may function to inspire sustained efforts in the interest of important values, or they may function to keep persons from discovering their own values and working to fulfill their aspirations.

One's "invisible loyalties" to others in the family system and to heroes and ideologies in the wider milieu in which one lives may also constitute projective bonding. The common factor underlying projective bonding is that one's own agency is often diminished, and the ongoing agency of others is dominant in the personal lives of those so attached. Often persons become symptomatic when these attachments conflict with other loyalties and desires. It then becomes important to rework these attachments so that they are accountable and modifiable, rather than unaccountable and intractable. Much pastoral counseling and psychotherapy consists of this very activity. It may be that Joan is unable to become more powerful in relation to Mikey and Mike because she is projectively bonded to her own mother's role as the longsuffering, powerless one in relation to her own husband and children.

A second expression of unaccountable and intractable power is found in the phenomenon of triangling. A triangle in systems terms is, according to Murray Bowen and others, a stabilizing arrangement that reduces tension and moderates the exchange of power and values between two persons, or two subsystems, by involving a third person or subsystem.[6] A triangle is a normal phenomenon, and every system consists of multiple interlocking triangles. The more differentiated and complex the system, the more complex and multivalent the triangles. In times of stress, however, the triangle can function to avoid conflict, and, paradoxically, to increase it. Thus, a child may deflect parental conflict by becoming symptomatic and force the parents to cooperate around his or her care. Or one parent may make a hidden alliance with the child's symptoms as a means of winning the battle with the other parent. In such a situation, the child has now enormous, though hidden, power to influence the relationship of his or her parents. In severely conflicted families these triangles take on a life of their own, becoming intractable and unaccountable. We see this happening in Mikey's case, inasmuch as he seems to be the key element linking the parents and the two families, as well as a major source of conflict between them.

Virulent triangling is a common phenomenon and impossible to avoid in both large and small social systems. It is a form of structural or organizational impairment that operates through power imbalances. Parentifying children, engaging in incestual relationships, and conducting sexual affairs between bosses and employees, and between professionals and their clients are examples of triangling in which people with unequal power are brought into usually hidden and often intractable power alliances.

On a larger scale, it is not difficult to see how the superpowers triangulate smaller developing nations into their conflicts—and how some smaller nations allow themselves into this role—as a means of moderating or diffusing the intensity of conflict with one's enemy while providing one's supporters evidence that progress is being made in advancing one's cause. The important point to note in all of these examples is that triangling functions to detour a usually much more threatening conflict hidden somewhere else in the system, while creating a serious, but apparently less dangerous, conflict at some more manageable point. By failing to resolve the apparent conflict, while simultaneously avoiding the generative conflict, such power arrangements remain intractable and unaccountable.

Internalizing blame is a third form of unaccountable and intractable power. Closely related to projective bonding, internalizing blame refers to an ongoing sense of failed responsibility for one's own welfare and for the systems in which one resides. However, the internalized sense of failure is not based upon any real failure, at least with respect to what one is blamed for. A "false consciousness" occurs in which the oppressed wrongly believe that they deserve their situation, or victims wrongly believe that they had the power to prevent their abuse. The main psychological components are shame, guilt, low self-esteem, and depression. The main social dynamics are expressed in scapegoating, deviance, marginalization, or overcompliance. In terms of power imbalances, those who internalize blame are usually too much the receptor of the expectations of others, without the agential power necessary to either fulfill appropriately held internalized expectations, or to reject inappropriate expectations. Hence, they feel that they have failed themselves and those who count on them the most. Power becomes unaccountable through misplaced or unbalanced accountability, and intractable through denial of what is taking place.

Joan is the one in her family system who has internalized the blame projected upon her by other family members. She is struggling to find the power to moderate this self-blame and to work for more shared and reciprocal responsibility. Another place where we can see clearly the effects of internalized blame is in the case of victims of sexual or physical abuse and victims of oppression, as well as in the theories about these realities. Victims of abuse and oppression often internalize their victimization and become intractably locked into the existing power arrangements. Some family therapists and many persons of good will and "common sense" have argued that this makes the victim equally responsible for what the perpetrator of abuse does. Drawing upon the concepts such as collusion, masochism, laziness, hysteria, attention-seeking, sense of entitlement, and so on, the victim is blamed for being a victim. There is the sense that he or she—or the group as a whole—deserved what they got, or at least could have prevented its reoccurrence, if not its onset.

To be sure, some victims internalize their victim status and contribute to its perpetuation. Or, as Jean Baker Miller points out, they avoid their own power and the responsibility to act on behalf of their welfare by being locked into blaming others.[7] But it must be remembered that a victim status is initially a reactive status to the abuse of power by someone else. Someone else—often a prior victim—perpetuates an act of victimization and must finally become accountable for that act, no matter how otherwise provoked, deprived, or discounted. It is a further abuse of power to blame the victim or someone else in the system for not preventing it, rather than to hold the perpetrator accountable.

In cases of father-daughter incest, for example, both the daughters and mother have been held responsible along with—or even instead of—the father who perpetrated the act. The mother is blamed for not being sexually or emotionally available to the father, and the daughter for being sexually precocious, seductive, or, in the very least, unwilling to protest or disclose the activity. Such an approach fails to recognize proper accountability. Minor children do not have the capacity for informed consent, even when they and others think so. Mothers who actually participate in the abusive behaviors are accountable in a different manner than those who did not know about it, or who knew about it but were too paralyzed to try to stop it. Thus, simply because mothers and daughters may play some role in an abusive situation, it does not follow that they are accountable in the same way as the adult who actually perpetrates the offense. Indeed, one of the most dire consequences of abuse and oppression is the extent to which it diminishes self-confidence and the capacity to believe that one is worthwhile and can act on behalf of one's own welfare. The inability to prevent ongoing victimization—or to mobilize external help—is, indeed, one of the ongoing consequences of victimization in the first place.

Discounting is the fourth common expression of unaccountable and intractable power. Discounting refers to attitudes, messages, and behaviors that keep the needs, aspirations, and perspectives of one person or group in a disadvantaged relation to some other individual or group. Their aspirations to be an agent are frustrated by someone with greater power; or, someone with less power uses their passivity or helplessness to hold back someone dependent upon them. In pastoral care, it is not uncommon to see persons who have come to believe that they do not deserve to stand up for themselves, or who discount their aspirations for fear of being injured by the retaliation of others close to them.

In marriage and family work, it is not uncommon to observe the ingeniously multiple ways that couples and family members discount themselves and one another. Failure to listen, inability to understand, changing the subject, minimizing the thoughts and feelings of others, telling others what they think or feel, leaving the scene, intellectualizing, emotionalizing, scapegoating, and triangling are all forms of behavior involving discounting. On a larger scale, racism, colonialism, and various forms of oppression are extreme forms of discounting: those in the disadvantaged position are commonly blamed for their condition, while those in power are excused and justified.[8]

When the discounters and discounted begin to find a basis of power parity from which to treat each other openly and with mutual respect, taking one another seriously as both agents and receptors of influence, they will have learned to make their power arrangements responsible and flexible rather than unaccountable and intractable. Such changes must begin with the discounted protesting their status, and the discounters ceasing to discount other people. The process of change finally results in an organizational structure that arranges power so that none are intractably disadvantaged and all are held accountable.

Exclusive and inaccessible power means there is too little sharing of power or influence. There is not adequate diversity and inclusivity in the power arrangements, leaving some marginalized and disadvantaged, and others with excessive influence. The net effect of this arrangement is evil, inasmuch as there is either too much discord on the one hand, or too much triviality on the other. Persons and their world are diminished rather than enhanced. Injustice is the result.

In the realm of bodily life, AIDS is an example of the exclusive and inaccessible elements of existing power arrangements. The AIDS virus comes into virtually exclusive dominance in the life of the person and, to date, has proven to be ultimately inaccessible to moderating influence. The result is intense discord and ultimately premature death, or evil in the form of triviality. Because persons and their worlds are less than they otherwise would be, AIDS must be understood, theologically and morally, as an example of demonic hegemony or genuine evil. Persons with AIDS, along with their loved ones, truly are victims of the demonic hegemony of the AIDS virus, which overwhelms the immune system of the carrier as well as the medical and social resources of the human community.

In the psychological, social, and cultural arenas, when any element wields its power—as either receptor or agent, or both—in an exclusive and inaccessible manner, great dangers lurk. When thought processes exclusively dominate and are impervious to influence from the emotions, schizoid existence—or worse—results. When the family dominates the individual, enmeshment, isolation, and/or fragmented selfhood results, as in the case of Joan, Mike, and Mikey. When social forces ignore the necessary conditions for optimal personal and family life, fractured families emerge, engendering enormous social consequences in loss of production, cost of health care and rehabilitative services, legal and judicial fees, and so forth.[9] When only one type of person—or certain groups of people—are allowed access to the responsibilities and benefits of their worlds, power is arranged exclusively and inaccessibly. Family oligarchies, "the old boy network," sexism, racism, ageism, and nationalism are examples in which power is ordered exclusively on the basis of certain group characteristics, and is not accessible on an equal or merit basis.

In conclusion, it should be noted that power imbalances overlap. The characteristics of one type of imbalance assume and promote the characteristics of others. For example, to maintain a situation in which power is held exclusively and inaccessibly, power must also become coercive, unaccountable, and intractable. The covenantal framework is torn as a result and power takes the form of a demonic hegemony.

Before proceeding, it is necessary to clarify a central issue related to power and care. One might ask whether power can be mutual, just, and accountable when it is arranged hierarchically. A corollary of this question is whether power should be structured hierarchically in the helping relationship, or whether the careseeker and the caretaker should be regarded as having mutuality with respect to all elements of the caretaking encounter. My position is that hierarchical organizations of power are usually damaging, especially when they are unaccountable, intractable, and exclusive. But when they are temporary, mutually chosen, accountable, and flexible, they may serve important tasks. Such temporary hierarchies may function positively to protect children from being parentified or adultified by recognizing that there are in fact real power differentials between parents and children.

Likewise, recognizing situational power differentials between careseekers and caretakers is essential to maintain boundaries necessary to prevent abuse of the careseeker by the caretaker. Thus, while a philosophy of mutuality and justice makes hierarchical distributions of power highly suspect, it does not rule against the recognition of necessary and inevitable power differentials and clear boundaries. These differentials are not in themselves unjust, and in fact may be necessary for "otherness" and justice to exist in the first place. The main issue is whether hierarchies and power differentials are accountable, flexible, temporary, and accessible. It is their quality rather than their existence that needs to be assessed for an accurate moral appraisal to be made about them.[10]

It is also important to underscore that we are discussing systemic power, not the power of individual persons alone. Systemic power transcends the will, values, behaviors, and personal relationships of individuals within the system, though it accounts for and is influenced by these as well. Thus, it takes only a few individuals in strategic positions to act powerfully as agents of the intact social system—even when they disagree with many of the elements comprising their social system.

STRATEGIES FOR CHANGING POWER DYNAMICS

There are several interrelated strategic influences that might be brought to bear on symptomatic power arrangements. In order to promote effective change these strategic influences must result in focused openness on the part of individuals and the system as a whole. Power is necessary for life and must be arranged optimally for life to continue and expand. In psychosystemic thinking, power is not a negative term. It only becomes a problem when it is arranged in such a manner that symptomatic behaviors occur. Indeed, for any change to occur, there must be an effective expression of power. Power is a positive reality when it is joined with values, structures, creativity, and transactions in such a manner as to increase love, justice, and ecological partnership. It is when power works against these positive values that it is regarded as problematic.

Before describing specific strategic influences by which power might be changed, it is important to review the goals of psychosystemic care in respect to power. In chapter 4, the goals were summarized as moving from power imbalance to synergistic power arrangements.[11] Synergistic power arrangements are characterized by the mutuality of give-and-take and of reciprocal, life-enhancing influencing. These are most clearly expressed when the power arrangements are cooperative, accountable, and modifiable. A synergistic power arrangement is further character-ized by sharing and accessibility.

At the present time, most people seeking the ministry of care are those who are in the victimized, or powerless, role. Hence, the burden of this chapter will be upon empowering the powerless. Less attention will be paid to neutralizing the powerful.

The two interlocking strategies, generally conceived, for empowering the powerless and restructuring power arrangements in the system, consist of *individuation* and *participation*.[12] Individuation, refers to the greater awareness and ownership of what is actually happening in the consciousness and behaviors of the individuals in the situation. It particularly focuses upon the stories, feelings, perceptions, and inten-tionalities of those who are locked into the receptive mode. Thus, it tends to focus upon those who are more symptomatic and in greater distress. Participation, addresses the embeddedness of the symptoms and the power dynamics in the larger system. It involves conscientization as well as a variety of activities such as boundary setting, alliance building, and rule changing. In the pages that follow I will illustrate the ways particular strategic interventions increase the capacity of persons and systems more effectively to individuate and to participate. Thus, what follows is an attempt to show some sequential interventions that might enable the ministry of care to facilitate moving from victimizing and chaotic power to cooperative power, from unaccountable and intractable power to accountable and flexible power, and from exclusive and inaccessible power to shared and accessible power arrangements.

Persons who seek the ministry of care are suffering from a sense of too little, or inadequate power, to address their situation from a position of strength. It is important to help them interpret their situations in power terms. To do so will create a capacity to join them empathically, and to help them to understand what is happening in psychosystemic terms.

First, the caretaking process begins with listening to the story of the symptomatic person or persons. Listening to these stories provides a basis for empathic connection and for beginning assessment and intervention. More important, in cases where individuals are made powerless by their symptoms, the very active telling of one's story and having it listened to with respect and appreciation in itself begins to empower. Having center stage with an appreciative audience in the form of the caretaker is a powerful experience that begins to correct for the consequences of being discounted by primary others in one's world. Listening to the stories of those who are wounded and underpowered is a way of "hearing into speech" experiences that are too painful to verbalize. In cases where there is extreme physical and sexual abuse, it may take months or even years for people to recall, let alone share, their stories.

In listening to the stories of the powerless, it is essential that these stories be believed. Respect for the teller, and for the difficulty of telling, must be communicated verbally and nonverbally. Interpretations should be at a minimum. They should be self-affirming rather than denigrating. The caretaker should be sensitive to discover the emotional meaning of the stories to the teller, rather than impose his or her own framework upon them, no matter how supportively intended. One of my counselees told me, for example, how offended she was at her minister. After telling her minister how relieved she was that her abusing father was dead, the minister replied, "You know you are probably a stronger person because you've had to overcome an abusing father." The individual felt betrayed and deeply misunderstood by her minister. She was unable to confront the minister. She withdrew from him, effectively ending a very important relationship. Whether it will be repaired remains to be seen.

In addition to listening to the stories with belief and respect for the teller, it is essential, secondly, to uncover whatever hidden agency that remains underneath the abusive reality. Usually this comes in the form of a creative vitality that has not been lost in the core self. This vitality is often disclosed in some unrecognized talent, or in an unrecognized intentionality to make a certain contribution to the world. Because the victim is so wounded, and so reactive to the agential power of others, this creative agency is hidden or unrecognized. Discovering it through dream-work, guided imagery, visualization and the like, helps to regain the agential power that was shattered or driven underground through abuse or other overpowering social circumstances.

I remember how striking this truth became in my work with Karen.[13] Karen was referred for pastoral psychotherapy by another client because she was very depressed. It was difficult for Karen to describe very much about herself, including her symptoms. She was extremely frozen, underpowered, and withdrawn. I found it difficult to stay in the room with her, but sensed it was important to keep trying. I asked her about her college major, and she informed me that she had majored in art, with a focus on sculpture. I asked her who her favorite sculptor was. She replied, "Rodin." She began to become more animated as she described what an excellent sculptor he was, in her opinion. I asked her, "On a scale of one to ten, how good a sculptor are you compared to Rodin?" She did not hesitate and said, "Seven."

This interchange initiated a turning point in our relationship. It was the basis for a long-standing therapeutic relationship. She began to communicate her inner state by artistic drawings. Later she represented it through sculpture. This not only enabled me to understand the fragmented nature of her life, but it also enabled her to tell her story of multiple sexual abuse more fully and directly. Moreover, her therapeutic drawings and sculpting became the basis of a substantial career as an artist. By uncovering this hidden talent and intentionality, it is clear that Karen has found new power to become increasingly whole and integrated as a person. Through her art she has become able to make an increasingly powerful statement about the nature and consequences of abuse, and to protest against it.

Many examples could be given of the empowering impact of discovering the hidden agency and intentionality in the talents of symptomatic persons. In every case, this discovery has been startling. It did not emerge from simple application of logic and technique to the careseeker. It rather came as a surprise to all, with a sense of awe. There is always enormous anxiety connected with naming this power. There is fear of punishment or further injury. It is no simple task. Yet it is an essential task in helping people move from being the victimized recipient of the agential power of others, to a position in which the individual is able to claim his or her own power.

A third strategy for empowering the underpowered is to uncover the primal wounded child who was and remains injured by the circumstances perpetuating the symptoms. Until the wounded child emerges, it is often unlikely that further empowering can take place. Karen has worked for several years to try to directly recount the multiple wounding she has had. Unfortunately, this is still rather dissociated, though it has emerged symbolically through a variety of personas appearing in her psyche. One of these personas is a bereaved child who grieves the loss of her little sister. Many of Karen's artistic drawings show the injury to this dead child, and testify to Karen's woundedness as the consequence. These symbolic images are not yet attached to specific memories of injury, which need to emerge for fuller recovery to occur. Nonetheless, even symbolic awareness of an apprehension of the wounded child has increased her capacity to function as a vital agent. Karen is now more able to protect herself in her world, and to accomplish goals related to her talent as an artist.

When the wounded child appears, there is a sense of horror and sorrow. It is the feeling one would have watching a baby crawl across a major highway at rush hour. The sense of helplessness, horror, and injustice of what is happening is paralyzing. While in touch with these memories and symbolic meanings, persons literally cannot breathe. The wounding is so primal that it interrupts life at the point where it occurs. There is often an attendant sense of shame, guilt, and failure for neither being able to prevent it nor to heal from it. It is as though life, love, and hope are forever arrested in time and space. When this moment of horrifying wounding is recognized and shared with another, the healing process is allowed to emerge more directly. It cannot be rushed, manipulated, or managed. It presents itself as a sacred moment in its own unfolding. It is at this point that the psyche's capacity to creatively rework its own experience becomes assisted through the relationship with the caretaker. The caretaker provides a protective place, a sacred space, where further injury will not occur as this material is examined and experienced. Thus, for the healing agency of persons to work there must be receptive power on the part of the caretaker that does not overpower the emerging agential healing power of the careseeker.

The fourth strategy for helping persons experience their agential power is to recognize and mobilize the attending rage. Usually when persons uncover their intentionality, and recognize the depth of the wounding that has kept them from realizing their agential power, a deep sense of rage emerges. When owned and integrated, rather than acted out or disowned, the rage can mobilize deeper analysis and strategic action in the larger world. When joined with the person's previously unrecognized vitality, the rage can be used to help the individuating person participate more optimally in the larger arenas of his or her life. It can mobilize the energy to overcome obstacles, to prevent further abuse, and to hold offenders accountable for their acts.

I know of two brothers who sought psychotherapy because their business was not going well. In the course of psychotherapy it turned out that as young boys they were both severely abused by their father. The abuse was both physical and psychological. The father communicated to them that they would be failures unless they did things his way. He expected them to choose the same education and career paths that he chose, and to assume his pattern of life. Anything that they produced was never good enough. They felt deeply ashamed and enraged at his humiliating impositions. They found some comfort from their mother, but the psychological drama was mostly between them and their father.

As they worked in therapy to understand how they had internalized this set of expectations, even as they fought against them, they recognized how enraged they were at the deep wounding that their father had perpetrated upon them. One of them said, "For forty years I have been robbed of my life." Ron went on to say, "Someone has to pay for this. I have been paying too long." Deep pain and considerable rage attended this awareness. The son recognized that he had been living a script that both reacted against, and led to a fulfillment of, his father's expectations. He realized that he had not been able to ascertain his own talents and intentionalities.

As he began to be in touch with his rage and his pain, he also began to realize that there were a number of recreational interests that had long been denied as he pursued the fulfillment of his father's expectations of failure in business. From this, he was able to decide in his own terms how successful he wanted to be. He was also able to balance his life better between his own newly-recognized desires about his relationship to his spouse and to his avocational interests. He found that he was able to use his rage to energize his goals, as well as to set limits on those who imposed their values on him in his workplace.

A fifth strategy of increasing power on the part of the underpowered is to interpret the systemic realities contributing to the sense of powerlessness. In the case of Ron mentioned above, it was helpful for him to recognize his father's status as an immigrant who had lost his father at an early age and subsequently felt a need to be hypervigilant and overachieving in order to survive. Ron began to recognize that his sense of failure was exacerbated by having internalized the dominant culture's values that males must be overachievers and invulnerable to be regarded as successful.

Further, Ron was married to a highly achieving lawyer, who on the one hand understood his struggles, but on the other was increasingly tired of being isolated and financially responsible for both of them. He also recognized that he was caught up in his brother's struggles to individuate from his family. He was doing too much of his brother's emotional work, and taking on too many of his brother's responsibilities in the business.

He began to be clearer about the structure of domination/subordination in which he had been reared, and in which he was living out his life. He came to interpret his wife's messages as attempts to restructure their relationship on a more mutual, egalitarian basis than as attempts to dominate him. He recognized how his own voluntary commitments falsely came to be experienced by him as impositional expectations of others. He recognized how much his brother was dominating him and how much he and his brother were entrenched in a power struggle of domination/subordination. He recognized a fundamental double bind on achievement: if he fulfilled his father's expectations of failure by failing, he could only be diminished in his own and others' eyes; if he defied his father's expectations by succeeding, he would be unable to have his father's badly needed approval, and would feel guilty for besting his father.

Recognizing these larger patterns helped him to make choices about how he wanted to live, and to do so more congruently. As he gained more understanding of his father, he was able to forgive him rather than to retaliate against or dominate him. He began to find that mutuality with his wife was fulfilling and nurturing rather than an admission of weakness or failure. He found that he could be a brother to his brother, rather than trying to be a father, son, or boss.

A sixth strategy for increasing power is to mobilize the capacity for boundary setting. To set boundaries requires and promotes greater differentiation, as well as more loving and just relatedness. A boundary may protect from further abuse, as well as let in nurturing elements, depending on where the boundary is set and with whom it is set. Victims are unable to set and maintain boundaries. Moving from victimization to survivorhood involves a capacity to set boundaries. Setting boundaries also involves holding persons accountable for their abuse and neutralizing their capacity to continue abusing self and others.

I have found a great deal of assistance in thinking about this dimension of empowerment by reflecting on *The Autobiography of Malcolm X*.[14] Malcolm recounted the many wounds that he had early in life, connected with his father's death for racial reasons and the impossibility of fulfilling his own vocational dreams for the same reasons. He recounted a life of drifting into crime and self-indulgence. Finally he was arrested, and imprisoned for burglary. While in prison he had a transformation. Through the faithfulness of his brother, who had become a Black Muslim, Malcolm was converted.

With the onset of his conversion came the onset of new boundaries. He held himself apart from the prison population. He ate only a certain diet, which further maintained boundaries between him and the prison environment as well as separating him from Christianity. As he read voraciously, informing his keen intelligence about the nature of the power realities of the racist world in which he has been reared, he gained new insight into his own experience. He further recognized that these situations would not change without strategic action on the part of those victimized by the white power structure. Through joining the Black Muslims, and throughout the odyssey of his life, he pushed for clearer boundaries between those who are oppressed and those who oppress. Through advocating self-help and self-protection, he attempted to mobilize the black community to protect itself from further injury by the white man's system. He attempted to neutralize those abusing power in relation to blacks and to increase the power of self-determination on the part of blacks. Further, he held the white man accountable for his abuse. He did not allow the black man to blame himself for what has happened to him.

All of these are powerful and instructive examples of the importance of boundary setting in the process of moving from a powerless to a powerful position in the larger social matrix. We also see the connection between Malcolm X's differentiation as a powerful black male and the differentiation and empowerment of the black community. It is exactly this parallel process that needs to occur for all individuals, subsystems, and oppressed groups if the world is going to be characterized by more loving and just relatedness. It is unfortunate that too many persons responding to Malcolm X saw only the rage and the separatism, without seeing the context and larger meaning of these. In psychosystemic terms, the rage and separatism were necessary forms of agential power in a system that kept blacks in an exclusively receptive mode. This separatism and self-defensive posture was denigrated by the white power system. A transactional double standard was in place. Blacks were regarded as culpable for using their power for equality and self-defense, while whites overlooked their own culpability for using their power for the ongoing violent subordination of blacks. This is a common power tactic. Jean

Baker Miller observed that "dominant groups tend to characterize even subordinates' initial small resistance to dominant control as demands for an excessive amount of power!"[15]

The seventh strategy for changing power imbalances is to build workable alliances. Because power is systemically interactive, individuals alone have little chance of changing the power arrangements. New alliances need to be fashioned in order to neutralize the dominant arrangements. Building an alliance with a pastoral counselor is one such experience, though not finally adequate. In this respect, I differ with those who think that seeking individual care is in itself an accommodation to the individualism of our day. It would depend on the focus and scope of such care whether the alliance between the careseeker and caretaker perpetuates a truncated individualism. By contrast, that alliance may be the very beginning of a pattern of opposition to the dominant power structure. In some ways we already know that it is, particularly when the pastoral care office allows persons to experience feelings and thoughts, and to try out behaviors that are denigrated or prohibited in the larger culture. For example, it is commonly held that we live in a death-denying culture. The pastoral caretaker's office is one place where persons are encouraged to deal with their thoughts and feelings about death and dying, grief and loss. We also know that this larger culture uses sex and sexuality in abusive and denigrating manners. The psychotherapeutic enterprise has been one setting in which sexuality could be explored and understood more fully and channeled more constructively.

However, alliances broader than the individual-caretaker relationship are essential if the psychosystemic vision of care is to be fulfilled. We have seen how Malcolm X drew upon the broader religious context for his own self-understanding and to implement his vision of changed power arrangements between the races and religions in North America. Karen has been seeking a broader network of support, using the artistic community as a medium to express her protest against abuse and to further her vision for healing and justice.

One common place in pastoral care where power alliances need to be modified is in triangulation between children and parents. It is not unusual for one parent to be allied with the child against another parent. Or, for the parents to be divided in their sense of what is appropriate for a child and to fight about behavioral rules and the consequences for breaking them. Such misalliances of power are extremely troublesome and need to be changed outright for effective transactions and positive outcomes to occur in these situations. The parents need to find ways to become more unified as parents in relation to their children, allowing their differences to be a source of creative opportunity rather than negating the power of the players in the scene.

One of the unfortunate consequences of misalliances is that the child gets a degree of power in relation to the parents that is destructive for the parents as well as for the child. Such power imbalances need to be addressed and modified or severely negative consequences will inevitably emerge.

Another place where strong alliances need to be forged is between siblings in relation to the care of elderly parents. In North American society it is not uncommon for the responsibility for elderly and needy parents to fall to one of their children. The other children tend to be unavailable, unwilling, or unable to provide this care. The consequences of such arrangements are usually negative for all. The under-involved children often feel guilty while others miss an opportunity to have important experiences with their parents. The sibling subsystem becomes divided by guilt and resentment. It becomes further disengaged. The parents do not get the balance of care that they need. The primary caretaker in the family becomes overburdened, often causing personal distress to them and negative consequences for their own families. They may also be less effective in their larger social involvements. In such cases it is important for the pastoral caretaker to help build stronger alliances within the sibling subsystem so that it might better share the task of caring for elderly parents.

It is increasingly clear that if pastoral caretakers are to be helpful to careseekers who have been physically battered, raped, or sexually abused by a family member, they will need to build strong networks of care and advocacy. The increase of such cases and the greater awareness that we have of how to respond to them is forcing the minister to move from an insular position to being a member of a comprehensive community of care. Such cases inevitably will involve alliances with legal resources and law enforcement agencies. It will involve building strong relationships with the shelter community. It will require a reassessment of our diagnostic categories and therapeutic strategies. It will force a revisiting of the laws by which we hold persons accountable and the philosophy by which we incarcerate or rehabilitate offenders. The religious community will increasingly be required to take leadership in this area, since so much abuse of power in this area lies in the abuse of notions of love, self-sacrifice, sexuality, forgiveness, and reconciliation. We are increasingly being asked to rethink all of these concepts so that they do not serve to keep one group in a dominant position relative to another group. Our understandings of forgiveness and reconciliation cannot work to keep victims at greater risk, while failing to hold accountable and insist upon meaningful rehabilitation of the perpetrator.[16]

The final strategy for changing power dynamics involves changing the rules and the roles by which persons live. As I indicated in a previous chapter, one of the core power issues involves the rules persons will live by and, more important, who will determine these rules. Anne Wilson Schaef argues that one of the major characteristics of the dominant white male system is that it makes all the rules and says that anyone who has a different vision of reality is simply wrong.[17] The empowerment strategy of Malcolm X was to change the rules by which the black community related to Christianity and to the white power structure. Martin Luther King, Jr. also wanted to change the rules by which the people of the United States would live their lives. On the one hand, he wanted to move from a domination/subordination model to a model of shared humanity. On the other hand, he wanted to move from a violent to a nonviolent mode of relatedness. He saw this transformed vision grounded in the rules that were generated by Christianity, as well as grounded in the self-understanding of the American people as reflected in the Constitution. By confronting the rules by which we live, and by advocating a new set of rules that were more congruent with who we profess to be, Martin Luther King, Jr. illustrated a powerful form of moving from power that is unaccountable, intractable, and coercive, to power that is accountable and flexible.

One of the common rules regulating the interchanges of people seeking help is to regard whoever is most symptomatic as the real problem. This rule operates as a power dynamic to keep all members of the situation from being accountable for their interactions and for implementing change. Usually, the identified patient colludes with this rule by being enough of a real problem to enable the system to avoid larger systemic dynamics. After a time, however, it becomes clearer that this rule, and the power relations that it disguises, is inadequate. This becomes especially clear when the identified patient begins to act normally, and nothing changes in the larger family, except, perhaps, that someone else becomes the identified patient. Usually such dynamics hide the deeper pain and the symptomatic power relationships, which in themselves need to be changed.

In their book, *The Family Crucible,* Augustus Napier and Carl Whitaker demonstrate how a family moves from one identified patient to another, until they begin to see larger family issues.[18] First one, then another, of the adolescent children of the family are focused upon as the problem. However, it soon becomes quite evident that the daughter's acting out is fueled by her mother's power struggles with her own mother. It also becomes clear that there are power struggles in the marriage that also affect the children. Finally, it is revealed that the father's unresolved dependence upon his own father, including the power dynamics between them, has been affecting the whole system in a hidden way. While these are not all resolved in the course of the book, it becomes apparent that to treat individual symptoms requires that each member of the family, and the family as a whole, look at the power dynamics between the generations over time. Rules then need to be modified about how all persons will live in relation to each other rather than just about how the family would accommodate the symptomatic individual.

Karen, the abused sculptor, changed the rules of secrecy and accommodation by which she lived by symbolically addressing abuse and recovery from abuse in her sculpture. She still has some way to go to change the rules in relation to her actual abusers, but she has begun the process. Uncovering secrets and challenging those who use power to the disadvantage of others are ways in which rules are being changed in relation to power. By hearing and believing these stories, and by supporting those who are telling them, the pastoral caretaker is also playing a part in changing the rules of silence. By assisting victims to recover and to confront their abusers and the abusive culture in which we live, the pastoral caretaker is taking an advocacy position, however indirectly, on behalf of redemptive justice.

I have illustrated eight strategies of intervention primarily in terms of individual functioning. It needs to be underscored that these also apply to groups and subgroups of persons. For example, I recall being a consultant to an organization in which the committee in charge of personnel decisions was given a great deal of responsibility, but was increasingly frustrated because it was not able to discharge its duties effectively. There were serious morale problems throughout the organization because the personnel committee continually failed to discharge its responsibilities in a suitable manner. As I explored the situation with the organization, it became evident that there were several powerful individuals, as well as other committees, who undermined the personnel committee's ability to function. The personnel committee also was not comfortable with conflict among its own members or between itself and the larger system. Indeed, there was a larger ethos in the system requiring that conflict be avoided and agreement maximized. Finally, the exact mandate of the personnel committee was unclear, and it was not evident who would implement any strong action it recommended.

Once trust was established, members of the personnel committee told many stories of frustration. They recognized the wounding that occurred to them as a part of this committee and how angry they were about it. They began to identify the multiple sources of this wounding, and to be more specific about their anger. They began to set boundaries between them and the rest of the organization, including those they were responsible to evaluate. They began to hold others accountable for their behaviors. They became clearer about their own mandate, and they did not let people talk them out of it. They built alliances and procedures with other structures in the organization without handing over their responsibilities and power. Finally, they changed the procedural rules by writing out protocols and insisting they be implemented in timely fashion.

As the personnel committee took more power, but functioned cooperatively and accountably with that power, the morale in the system improved. The personnel committee found ways to neutralize the discounting, intractable, and unaccountable power elsewhere in the system, and to make things more open, flexible, and accountable. Such processes are also useful with families, or with subsystems within families, that are wounded and bifurcated. They also extend to larger systems such as congregations and classes of people organized by gender, sexual orientation, and/or race and ethnicity.

CONCLUSION

The ministry of care is ultimately grounded in the power of God. God's power receives lovingly whatever is presented to it. God's power also takes strategic action to enhance the agency of the world, and of each entity within it. When responded to with focused openness, God's loving power transforms unjust patterns of living. It modifies the dominant power configurations underlying symptomatic crises. It makes unaccountable power accountable to love, justice, and ecological harmony. It makes intractable power flexible and creatively responsive to the situation. It modifies discounting and chaotic transactions throughout the system. Its goal is to bring about an increase of value throughout the universe. It is to the relationship of power transactions and the increase of value throughout the psychosystemic matrix that we now turn.

CHAPTER 7

LURING TO SHALOM: HARMONIZING CONTENTION THROUGH THE MINISTRY OF CARE

The Bible never treats justice as a lesser order than that required by love, but as the objectification of the spirit of love in human and divine relationships.

Daniel Day Williams[1]

With shalom as its motivating vision, justice finds its finest expression in the realization of community in which human diversity in all its forms is affirmed and celebrated instead of being seen as lines of division that could become the basis for discrimination and oppression.

D. Preman Niles[2]

Persons seeking the ministry of care do so because they are often conflicted over values. A couple may seek pastoral assistance to help them become unstuck from an impasse about whether to have an abortion or not. One party may believe abortion is evil and argue for bringing the fetus to term. The other may believe that abortion is a morally acceptable procedure and try to convince the other party to seek one. The impasse and power struggles over these conflicting values may threaten the very life of their relationship. Or, it may lead to a creative advance in their relationship and to new arrangements of power. It may also eventuate in a heightened moral orientation on the part of one or both parties.

A psychosystemic interpretation of reality is realistic about the presence of serious conflict because it recognizes that the elements comprising the world are neither benign nor neutral. They are value-laden. Because values are linked to power, structures, and creative possibilities, there is an obstructive contentiousness built into the nature of reality. Obstructiveness is not in itself bad. The outcome with respect to beauty or evil determines whether conflict is regarded positively or negatively. When obstructiveness leads to disharmony or triviality, it is valued as evil.

One of the principal forms of obstructiveness in our current world is the organization of much of our personal and social life in terms of domination and subordination. This form of social living means that conflict over values is simply given. Contention about who is to remain dominant and who is to remain subordinate, along with the rules by which such an order is to be maintained, is built into our lives. As I have indicated earlier, such arrangements severely curtail possibilities for loving partnership and for just relatedness. Intractable arrangements of domination and subordination represent unjust structures of related- ness. When these emerge in the psyches and interpersonal relationships of those seeking the ministry of care, it is incumbent upon the caretaker to try to change the value system into more just and loving terms. The linking of redemptive justice and strategic love form a unity in such an approach to the ministry of care.

Shalom is the religious reality from the biblical and theological heritage that joins love and justice for the sake of greater community and harmony. According to a penetrating study by Perry B. Yoder, shalom is a "powerful symbol of God's purpose and will for our world."[3] There are three interlocking dimensions to shalom. First, shalom is expressed in prosperity and material well-being. Second, shalom is an active "working for just and health-giving relationships between people and nations."[4] Third, it has the moral dimension of "working to remove deceit and hypocrisy and to promote honesty, integrity, and straightforwardness."[5] Thus, to be an active participant in making shalom is to "act from love through justice to liberate those in bondage since only through liberation can shalom be experi- enced."[6] Shalom links concepts of love, justice, and deliverance from bondage to an increase in health for individuals, families, and nations. Shalom is the activity of a divine-human partnership by which the whole of creation is brought to greater well-being and prosperity characterized by loving, just, and liberated relationships.

Most writers on the relation of love to justice, drawing upon the Judaic and Christian heritages, emphasize that God's love and justice speak to concrete human need, rather than deriving from abstract principles applied to situations. For example, Daniel Day Williams writes that "the biblical writers on the whole do not interpret justice in the form of general principles, but as a universal personal concern for every man [sic], for the strangers and alien as well as the elect people."[7] D. Preman Niles says that "biblically speaking, justice is not a general or abstract concept about the rightness of things. Rather, it has to be grasped and practiced in concrete situations where justice is denied—the economic exploitation of people, sexism, racism, casteism, landlessness, torture, etc."[8]

Further, God's justice and love are related to shalom inasmuch as both seek to meet the real needs of persons, whether expressed in particular acts of mercy and kindness to wounded individuals, or in efforts to change larger structures of society and organizations. There is no ultimate conflict between the personal and the public when love and justice are united in shalom. God's justice, which is expressed in shalom, is moved by love "since the standard for shalom justice is not whether people deserve it but whether they need it."[9] Shalom justice is based not upon merit or proportionality, but upon the divine activity that responds to persons on the basis of what they need. Persons need shalom, or the quality of well-being in which they can prosper, find fulfilled integrity, and live in a transformed egalitarian relationship with the natural order. In Daniel Day Williams' terms, "the Bible never treats justice as a lesser order than that required by love, but as the objectification of the spirit of love in human and divine relationships."[10]

If symptomatic crises largely emerge from a variety of forms of lovelessness, injustice, and ecological disarray, God's shalom is the response by which there is a unified emergence of love, justice, and a new ecological partnership. This psychosystemic affirmation is supported by a statement of indigenous peoples formulated at the Granvollen meeting on the Integrity of Creation sponsored by the World Council of Churches:

> We must now clearly understand that justice is the maintenance of the wholeness of creation. Justice involves the righting of relationships not only between human beings, but between human beings and the earth and the things of the earth. Our concept of justice must shift away from being that which protects possessions toward that which provides healing of relationships between human beings, between cultures, and between human beings and all of creation. The indigenous concept of justice is such a process of healing. If we begin with the perception of ourselves as a part of the wholeness of creation, and if we understand justice as a practice of human beings in maintaining the inter-relatedness of all creation, then peace will flow naturally.[11]

The ministry of care, when informed by such prophetic and ecumenical perspectives, understands that justice making is a work of love that transforms social relationships and extends to the natural order. The result is shalom. Pastoral caretaking arises when mutual obstructiveness leads to symptomatic crises in the context of personal, interpersonal, and family life. Pastoral caretaking also indirectly seeks to harmonize contentions in the larger social, cultural, and natural environment.

In the sections that follow we will examine some ways by which love, justice, and ecological partnership might be increased. Though these will be examined separately, it is important to recognize that they comprise a unit and are interconnected. Shalom is the religious power that informs this unity, as well as reflects its accomplishments. The task of the ministry of care, therefore, is to move from destructive value conflicts to increased harmony and intensity of experience characterized by love, justice, and ecological partnership. When this is approximated, there is a greater degree of shalom and the salvation that it signifies.

DIAGNOSING LOVELESSNESS IN THE MINISTRY OF CARE

What, more precisely, is the character of the love that the ministry of care seeks to promote? It is more than affection and more than "proper action," though it may include both of these. Love is an ethical, psychological, and relational category. Love is "the will to communion" with oneself and others, and to committed action on behalf of the welfare of the loved one. It is also the recipient of the committed action of the other on behalf of one's own welfare. As lover, I am giver as well as receiver; love creates a covenant of committed giving and receiving on behalf of the welfare of the lovers. Love creates a community of lovers and builds bridges across communities. Many things are exchanged between loving partners: material goods, ideas, values, relationships, goals, and achievements. The most important exchange, however, is the exchange of selfhood; love is above all the communion of inner being to inner being in a covenant of faithfulness. Love actively seeks, affirms, cherishes, and accepts one's own inner being, as well as the inner being of God and neighbor.

Love harmonizes discordant values; it allows differences to exist as sources of creative good rather than destructive negation. Love recognizes and promotes uniqueness and individuality; love is freely given and received in a commitment to an unknown future; love suffers on behalf of the other and receives the suffering of others on one's own behalf; love challenges the destructiveness and lovelessness of the other and seeks to establish conditions where lovelessness is opposed and loving enhanced; it is impartial in its judgment and sets priorities for overcoming obstacles to its increase.[12] Love is based in the nature of reality, embodied in individual persons, and extended through human institutions and culture. Love is the drive to overcome estrangement.[13] Love opposes discord and triviality of experience. It expresses the most desirable synthesis of harmony and intensity of experience.

Lovelessness and enmity toward one's own self is reflected in estrangement from important elements of one's own being, denigration of one's personal value and creative power, and domination by some aspect of one's personality or some element within one's social system. It is the refusal or inability to affirm, cherish, and employ the fullest array of possibilities within one's own being. It is the inability to use one's power creatively in the interest of one's own welfare. One is afraid of claiming one's fullest array of resources to engage one's world. Persons so oriented become unduly reactive to others and violate their own integrity. In the worst cases, persons give up on themselves entirely, and take their lives by suicide or live an otherwise destructive life-style. More commonly, persons live a mixture of love and hate toward themselves: partially affirming their personhood while simultaneously neglecting and denigrating it. Symptoms such as depression, guilt, shame, and low self-esteem reflect lovelessness or enmity toward one's self.

In the case of Joan, Mike, and Little Mikey, Joan's symptoms of anxiety and depression reflect her inability to love herself. She is afraid of her power to set limits and of her desire to look after her body. She does not believe that she is valuable. She is dominated by the internalized belief instilled by her family and culture that she is flawed and immature. Consequently, she is estranged from other elements of her being. She is not able to be as strong as she needs to be nor to find nourishing outlets for her legitimate dependency needs. Her counselor has helped her connect with some of her deeper resources and has challenged her low self-esteem by treating her as a person of value and worth. Where there is lovelessness toward the self he is helping her sow the seeds of love.

Lovelessness and enmity toward one's neighbor is reflected in a variety of ways. The most common are indifference, rejection, hate, violence, and greed. Lovelessness toward one's neighbor is largely an outgrowth of lovelessness toward one's self, and reflects lack of proper neighbor-love from parents and other significant persons at certain formative stages in one's own development. Loving environments contribute to the conditions in which love of self and neighbor may grow; unloving and unjust environments create the conditions for lovelessness and enmity toward self and neighbor. The interplay between the quality of neighbor-love and love of self is most clearly evident in pastoral caretaking involving issues of family enmeshment and isolation, double standards, and vocational malaise.

Lovelessness toward neighbor is seen in families that are either enmeshed or disengaged. An enmeshed family is one that does not let its members differentiate socially or psychologically. Rather than growing up and emotionally separating in order to establish their own lives, they become and remain part of the "undifferentiated family ego mass."[14] They denigrate the individuality and particularity so cherished and promoted by love. Disengaged families do not provide enough structure of belonging for its members. There is often little sustained intimacy and interaction. Persons "do their own thing" as best they can. There is little loving commitment, freedom, and positive influence upon members of the family. If enmeshed families set too many limits, disengaged families set virtually none. In Joan and Mike's family, there is both enmeshment and disengagement resulting in a virulent emotional culture. Joan's attempts to differentiate as a self were thwarted in her family of origin and continue to be thwarted in her present circumstances. The value by which she is supposed to live trivializes her potential as a person; her revolt against those values have put her in discord with her spouse and parents. Mike refuses to be engaged with her on a viable and consistent basis. The net effect is that the struggle among contending values with respect to personhood and family have contributed to a dangerously neglectful and occasionally abusive environment for Mikey, the five-year-old son. He is alternately disengaged from his parents and enmeshed with his grandparents. The extent to which he will subsequently be able to develop his individuality is in considerable jeopardy as long as the family system remains so dominated by the lovelessness of enmeshment and isolation.

In the larger social arena as well as in small groups, including families, another expression of lovelessness toward one's neighbor is the so-called "double standard." The double standard holds one person or group accountable for values from which another is exempted. James Nelson argues persuasively that the double standard is opposed to an ethic of love, since it impedes mutual communion and perpetuates other forms of exploitation and oppression resulting from imbalanced power arrangements.[15] Double standards operate when marriage is given a higher status than singleness, heterosexual experience is valued over homosexual or bisexual experience, and bearing children is regarded as morally superior to remaining childless. Further, a double standard is at work when men and women are not paid equally for their work, when housework and child-rearing are disproportionately the responsibility of the female— even when she is employed outside the home—and when sexual fidelity is required of women but not also of men. As any alert person can determine, the existing culture is based upon a plethora of double standards, which function to normalize unequal power arrangements and keep one group in a vulnerable, and often symptomatic, condition. Phyllis Chesler's *Women and Madness*[16] and Frantz Fanon's *The Wretched of the Earth*[17] are extremely incisive accounts of how double standards lead persons to become emotionally ill and relationally dysfunctional. Those in the more vulnerable positions either must remain disadvantaged and symptomatic by fulfilling their culturally expected role, or labeled as ill when they rebel against it.[18]

When persons are in crisis, one must ask if their symptoms reflect the consequences of complying with double standards, or their struggle to overcome double standards. In the case of Joan and Mike, we see how she is expected to take responsibility for the home, birth control, and child-rearing—while making a living and supporting his adventuresome risks. He is allowed irresponsibility. It is apparently acceptable for Mike to underfunction and to not be held accountable for his domestic violence, addictive behavior, financial neglect, and parental abuse. She is in a great deal of personal conflict and the marriage is in crisis as she attempts to develop an internalized single standard that holds both of them accountable for their household, birth control, child-rearing, finances, careers, and relationships to their families of origin.

A third form or expression of lovelessness toward neighbor is vocational malaise. Vocation, in Protestant circles, refers to the call to love one's neighbor as oneself as an expression of one's faith in God. Vocation encompasses every personal and social dimension of one's life. Vocation includes how one relates to nature, government, business, education, and the social order. In the Protestant vision of human love and service we are to be responsible for the welfare of others, and responsive to their concern for our welfare. When egocentric values and inadequate visions of reciprocal care dominate attitudes and behaviors, vocational malaise has come into being. Under these conditions, the person and the group or groups to which one belongs become "curved in upon themselves," and sources of evil rather than beauty in the world. The horizon of one's vocational vision becomes too closed and limited; one's own welfare or the welfare of one's group becomes the exclusive parameter of one's concern. Rather than appreciatively grasping and seeking to positively influence the broadest possible interrelationships in one's psychosystemic world, some smaller part is exclusively chosen to the diminishment of the whole. Anxious self-preoccupation and exploitive greed take the place of sustained participation in the search for terms by which the self might be in "communion with every other life."[19]

Mike's vocational malaise is expressed in his desire to control Joan and Mikey, and to organize both his and their resources solely for his own benefit. He is unable to define their value in terms other than their value to him. He can neither see them as persons in their own right nor extend himself very far in the direction of their welfare. Joan has a broader vision, but it is still limited to the horizon of her own family. She cannot yet see that to take Mike seriously as a person she must also learn to say no to him. She cannot affirm her value as an office manager. There is little energy available for service to the larger world. A vocational malaise has grasped them. It both expresses their limited capacity for neighbor love and keeps them from developing a greater capacity.

Lovelessness toward self and neighbor are closely related to lovelessness toward God. In Christianity, God is viewed as unreservedly gracious and benevolent. God takes strategically loving action for the sake of increasing intensity and harmony of experience, or beauty, at every level of the universe. Lovelessness toward God means that through indifference, idolatry, and despair God's loving action and the ends that it seeks are refused, neglected, or opposed.

In idolatry God is made into something God is not—God's purposes are distorted and employed toward ends which are opposed to God's nature and hopes. By intention, ignorance, or shortsightedness, some lesser or partial good is set in place of God's nature and will, replacing God as the center of faith and loyalty. One's nation, family, personal fulfillment, or social group becomes the object of devotion. One's view of God is ordered by these loyalties, rather than these loyalties being transformed by the will of God. The result is evil, in the form of discord and triviality. Sources of potential blessing have become contentious. Persons settle for less than is possible for them. Rather than communion and loving partnership with God, there is exploitation and indifference. God becomes an extension of one's own egocentricity and politicized affiliations rather than the loving partner who lures all dimensions of relationship into reciprocal sharing and collaboration.

Indifference toward God's reality and purposes is another form of lovelessness toward God. An attitude of indifference discounts God's generosity and creativity. It posits a self-reliant orientation to life and cuts persons off from the deepest source of their being. Persons may believe that God is irrelevant or powerless. They may simply be uninterested in discovering how God might be a factor in their experience. Like so many in our secular and materialistic culture, Joan and Mike do not seem to hold a concept of God that is relevant to their situation. Indeed, they seem indifferent and unresponsive to exploring this dimension of their lives.[20]

Despair is another form of lovelessness toward God. As the opposite of idolatry and indifference, despair assumes that God is my enemy rather than a benevolent center of my existence. A sincere desire for loving communion with God may stand behind despair; more often despair results when one is no longer able to maintain an idolatrous or indifferent relationship with God. It is therefore made up of disillusionment and meaninglessness. If despair continues it may eventuate in hostility toward or rejection of God. It also may be resolved through a fresh and transformed discovery of God in personal experience. In pastoral work I have spent hours with persons experiencing acute despair because God did not seem to be able to protect them from unjust suffering and to provide resources for helping them through it. For some, this despair led to a deep inner sense of impoverishment and estranged them from the capacity to find a meaningful experience of God as one "who is a very present help in time of need." Other sufferers found a great deal of comfort from God's presence in their suffering. Their despair became an occasion for an even greater apprehension and deeper understanding of God.

Lovelessness toward God refuses to let God be God, and to let God be a loving and effective influence in one's life. Through idolatry, it makes God into something God is not; through indifference it discounts God's creative freedom and agential power to be a source of value in one's experience; through despair it makes God into an enemy.

Lovelessness toward self, neighbor, and God are interrelated. Ana Maria Rizutto has written in her insightful book, *The Birth of the Living God: A Psychoanalytic Study*,[21] about how one's view and emotional experience of God is a transmutation, psychologically speaking, of one's early object relationships. Thus, one's experience of God reflects the positive, negative, and ambivalent relationships through which one's psychological development has been fashioned. God may therefore be a reflection of an abandoning or abusive father, or a nurturing and sustaining parental unit. Correctives and elaborations of these early experiences are provided by the culture in which one lives. One's subsequent experiences in the family, school, church, synagogue or mosque, work, and life-experience modify or confirm one's early belief system. Indeed, an examination of pastoral caretaking with persons reveals how the pastoral relationship itself effects change in the experience and view of God in both the caregiver and care receiver. Don Browning in his *Atonement and Psychotherapy* describes how the experience of nonjudgmental acceptance by the caretaker enables the careseeker to experience God as forgiving and gracious rather than as rejecting and punishing.[22] In this instance, love toward God is increased by the love offered by and received from neighbor.

In turn, when one has a positive experience of God's love and neighbor love there is an increased capacity for love of self. Many persons have testified how their "hearts are strangely warmed" by a sense of God's loving, accepting presence. We have discussed at length how positive feelings toward oneself result from the loving concern of significant others. Thus, to increase love in any dimension of experience is to potentially increase love in all dimensions of experience. A psychosystemic view of experience affirms that if one area of experience is affected by an increase in value, all areas potentially benefit. In training for pastoral care and counseling, this dynamic interplay is called "parallel process." Parallel process is the term used to describe the phenomenon which occurs when either symptomatic or beneficial patterns in one subsystem appear in another subsystem to which one is emotionally connected. The concept of parallel process is important both for understanding the meaning of symptoms and for understanding and promoting change. Paradoxically, symptoms of lovelessness provide the basis for understanding how love might best be increased in the world.

DIAGNOSING INJUSTICE

Injustice is a form of lovelessness toward neighbor that denigrates shalom by harming others through domination, marginalization, and abuse. By contrast, shalom justice seeks fairness and positive access to both the benefits and responsibilities to be found in the personal, familial, social, cultural, and ecological arenas of life. Justice is based upon a positive understanding of human welfare and of human nature; it is a concept that regulates social intercourse so that concrete needs are met in the most beneficial way. Lack of justice fractures relationships at all levels of the psychosystemic social order. Justice, along with love, is a value that determines how power relationships, transactional patterns, creativity, and other values will be organized and structured in relation to one another. Justice is relevant to a theory of pastoral caretaking by offering in the context of pastoral caretaking a way forward from oppression, abuse, and burdensome transgenerational indebtedness.

The concept of justice has not been utilized in relation to pastoral caretaking, at least until rather recently. Nagy's concepts of family loyalty and the family ledger infer that justice as an integral part of transgenerational family dynamics has only been recently appropriated in pastoral care and counseling.[23] Marie Fortune and others working with victims of domestic violence have come to see that justice needs to occur for family healing to begin.[24] She has rightly criticized the pastoral caretaking movement for moving too quickly to acceptance and reconciliation, without moving through accountability and restitution.[25] She and others are recognizing the need to link justice and peacemaking in the macrosystem with the need for justice and peaceful ways of living in microstructures such as families and congregational communities. The reader is also reminded that the previous discussion of Chodorow provides a social-psychological analysis of what might be regarded as the developmental structure of injustice.[26]

In pastoral care the dynamics of oppression are pervasive and inescapable. The white, middle-class, male dominance of ministry and pastoral caretaking reflects the sexist, patriarchal structure of the North American church. The structure and philosophy of caregiving is often oppressive, since it operates on a largely elitist professional model and requires high fees for service. In spite of the attempt of pastoral caretakers to liberate persons from bondage, and to make the structures of the family more just and democratic, the social and cultural standpoint of pastoral caretaking is pervasively sexist and racist with respect to our own population. It is largely colonialist, sexist, and racist with respect to the Third World. Paradoxically, by helping our "clients" become more autonomous and less conflicted in their personal and family lives, we may be helping them to more fully participate in larger economic and cultural structures that perpetuate racist and sexist realities in our own nation, operate unjustly with respect to the Third World, and function militaristically with respect to everyone else.

While it is relatively easy to demonstrate the oppressive structure of pastoral caretaking, it is more difficult to draw direct lines between specific symptoms and oppression. Since the whole context of sickness and healing occurs in an oppressive situation, it follows that every symptom and its resolution in some way derives from and relates back to the oppressive social matrix in which our lives are lived and our care offered. But more particularly, despair and depression in women, gays, and persons of color can be demonstrably linked to the dynamics of their social location in an oppressive situation. Their familial structures, developmental patterns, and social opportunities are highly stressed by the unequal power arrangements and creative options of an oppressive society.[27] This means that members of an oppressed class as a group have ongoing health, emotional, social, and economic problems on a far larger scale than the oppressor class. The many psychological and social problems experienced by these persons differ in kind, if not degree, from the oppressor class inasmuch as they are generated and maintained by the social location of the oppressed in an oppressive society. As Edward Wimberly sagely points out in *Pastoral Care in the Black Church,* there can be no complete personal healing in an oppressive racist society until the racist roots of the wounding are removed.[28]

The oppressed are more likely than the oppressor to be symptomatic and seek the ministry of care. They are usually the victims of some situational or chronic injustice who need help with their pain. Joan sought help because the oppressive white male system kept her in a state of insecurity with a lower paying job than those available to males. It enabled her husband to be cavalier with her money and body and permitted the males in her family to separate her from her child through threats of violence and attacks upon her own self-esteem and confidence. The white male therapist and pastoral counselor took a supportive and advocacy role on her behalf. They did not see her as inferior, sick, or immature, but symptomatic of an unjust system that took away her creative power, the fruit of her labors, and her own perceptions of reality. By defining her symptoms as a function of an unjust social order, she was helped to mobilize her own power around more loving and just values, and to struggle to free herself and her family from the oppressive structure that held them all.

To be sure, the oppressor suffers and knows pain. But the nature of the pain differs and is not of the same social or moral status. The pain of the oppressed is largely the pain of the victim and exploited; the pain of the oppressor is that of the perpetrator and exploiter. The one lives by despair and shame; the other by violence, pride, and anxiety. The oppressor uses agential power to unbalance organizational structures and control the interchanges within them. Particularly, the oppressor wants control over the definition of reality, of good and evil, of appropriate and inappropriate roles, of labor and production (including childbearing and the values by which children are reared), political and informational processes, economic and social benefits, and even the definition and punishment of crimes. The oppressed are the receptors of these values, and protest them at core levels of their being.

Oppressors in pastoral care situations are not always aware that they are oppressors, and in fact sometimes are symptomatic and the identified patient. For example, a father and husband may show signs of acute emotional stress because he is unable to control his family adequately or because he is being held accountable by law for abusive overcontrol. He comes to the pastoral caretaker to gain help in controlling his family, much like in the case of Mike and Joan. The pastoral caretaker must be careful not to be inducted into an oppressive collusion, but struggle to find a working alliance with the oppressor in order that his or her symptoms might lead them to a more equitable and fulfilling partnership.

INCREASING LOVE AND JUSTICE
THROUGH THE MINISTRY OF CARE

We have been following the case of Karen, a woman who was multiply molested as a child, and sexually assaulted as an adolescent. Her depression and isolation led her to pastoral psychotherapy, at the onset of which she was extremely alienated from herself and from others. She had little ability to remember or to describe these assaultive events in her life. Early in the therapy she became aware that she was probably gay. Her fantasy life included a desire to be connected intimately with other women; while she did not have any behavioral intimacy with women, she had a high degree of fantasies and desires about being with women. This realization further estranged her from herself, leading her to feel that she was unworthy and dirty. The estrangement that she experienced in relation to herself took many forms. Her thinking and feeling were incongruent. She was unable to identify her core talents and to act on them meaningfully in the world. She felt she deserved a better life on the one hand and punishment for her unworthiness on the other. At times she became self-punitive and, on frequent occasions throughout the course of the therapy, she thought seriously of taking her life. This extreme lovelessness towards herself, as introjected from her experience with others and perpetuated by her own self-organizing capacities as an individual, was extremely debilitating to her. She was virtually unable to act on behalf of her own welfare, even as she began to discern what would bring her pleasure.

The basic pastoral strategies to counter this self-loathing and lovelessness took several forms. First, there was the unconditional positive regard and empathic connection learned in basic clinical pastoral training. Active listing skills were indispensable for communicating a deep acceptance of her in spite of her estrangement and brokenness. I did not put a demand upon her to be more whole as a condition for sustaining our relationship. A second strategy was to challenge the enmity she held for herself and to raise her consciousness about its source. Thus, while recognizing and accepting her estranged selfhood, I did not define this as the norm. I pointed to a deeper selfhood that survived the abuses and in fact challenged them through her desire to live, seek therapy, and later to act more consistently in relation to her own interests. A third way of affirming her was to explore and become acquainted with the many dimensions of her personhood, even as these were disengaged from each other and disenfranchised by other elements within her personality.

As time went on, Karen began to recount through left-hand writing, guided imagery, and dream-work, stories from her past as told by dissociated selves within her personality. Over the years, several dissociated personalities have emerged. These represent various components of her total selfhood. These selves are contenders for dominance among the other personalities and the conflict between them at times has been excruciating. One figure is extremely hostile toward her and believes that she has betrayed her core identity by sharing with me secrets about her life. Other selves counter this hostile person within her and push her to be more creative in her healing process and in her relation to the larger world.

The depth of her estrangement from an integrated center reveals the depth of the injustice perpetrated on her. One of her artistic productions particularly reveals the source and consequences of this injustice. Karen painted a picture of a beautiful woman tied to a large post shaped like a penis. She is chained to this structure in a posture of physical agony, her body bent back from the waist in obvious discomfort. Her face is blank, with several masks descending in a large arc from her face to the ground. She is situated in a moonlit desolate landscape. Above some rocks a short distance away is the face of a woman watching her agony. The woman is impassive and seems both unwilling and unable to help. Karen interpreted this painting as a metaphor for her situation. She realized that through the social institutions of patriarchy, and her own specific abuse at the hands of two rapists, an uncle, a religious cult, and, quite possibly, her own father, she was subordinated by the domination of others. The observing woman represented for her other women who were helpless to intervene or to prevent such injury. They too were the wounded and the underpowered.

The acceptance and affirmation that she received in the pastoral psychotherapy enabled her to tell these stories, to have them heard and believed, and to explore the depth of her estrangement and enmity in relation to her own being. This process also helped her uncover healing resources within her in the form of a persona she called "Christopher."

Christopher truly was for her a "Christ bearer" inasmuch as he praised her for surviving the multiple abuses. He convinced her that God was on her side to further heal and transform her experience into service for others. Christopher was able to blend the contending voices and persons within her personality so that a greater working harmony emerged.

This striking figure not only helped her coalesce and mobilize her powers as an individual, he also helped her explore more symbolic material. The most noteworthy contribution that Christopher brought, however, was a viable and powerful belief in a transforming God. When Karen began pastoral psychotherapy, she professed no belief in God nor any meaningful experience with God. With the emergence of Christopher she began to experience that she was not alone and that her life was rooted in a divine agency that was powerful, sustaining, and transforming. This was a discovery for her rather than an accommodation of anything explicitly interpreted to her in the pastoral psychotherapy. In fact, her conceptualization and experience of God differ considerably from mine. Nonetheless, I received her experience appreciatively and explored its meaning to her with genuine respect. She has continued to find in Christopher a powerful divine image characterized by healing love. Christopher has mediated a cosmology by which she understands her experience in a larger framework. He has also mobilized her to seek ways to thematize her experience in her art and to be more confident in putting her art into the larger culture as an expression of her loving advocacy for victims of abuse.

Karen is still estranged in many respects from her fellow-humans as a result of the abuse. Despite her attempts to address the larger public arena through her art, she is still rather isolated socially. It is difficult for her to reach out for larger support and social stimulation. Her recovery process has been slow and difficult. And while she is gaining a measure of liberation from the patriarchal system that enchains and abuses her, her capacity to participate in and to receive nurture from the larger world is quite limited. My pastoral psychotherapeutic work has tried to connect her with shelter groups, women's support and therapy groups, and other larger networks by which her artistic work might be conveyed to the public. So far she has not been able to take advantage of many of these suggestions. She has, however, encouraged me to use her story and our work together as a way of communicating her protest against injustice and her hope for a more loving world.

It is clear to me that to increase love toward self, God, and neighbor and to promote justice in the larger world are not easy tasks. Insofar as my work with Karen is transferable to others, I have found that it is essential to be faithful to the processes and timing of the other, rather than to induct them into one's own ideology and agenda. Further, it is extremely important that one learn to confront and handle conflict openly and positively. It is clear from dealing with the multiple personae that have emerged in Karen's personality that the caretaker must be multiply engaged. Various personae have been furious at me and have attacked me vigorously in my attempts to support and assist Karen. I have had to accept these attacks and to challenge back without rejecting. Many times I have been a moderator of the conflict between the personae in Karen's personality and I have had to help her moderate conflict between others in her world who would overpower her because of her inability to help herself. Assisting her to be assertive, to set limits, and to moderate conflicts has been extremely important.

Since much of her experience has not separated conflict from violence, a major reeducation has been necessary. In helping persons develop a greater capacity to love themselves, God, and neighbor, as well as to contend for more egalitarian and just relationships in their world, a capacity for assertion and power is necessary. Values will always contend. It is important that the caretaker be cognizant of this and have ways of making the contention less harmful and more productive.

It is also essential in striving to increase love and justice to recognize that not all values may be harmonized. For example, it is not possible always for perpetrators and survivors to reconcile. Little if any reconciliation is possible if perpetrators are unwilling to accept accountability and to demonstrate true remorse and to participate in acts of genuine restitution. To ask a survivor to persist in seeking reconciliation with someone who continues to victimize them is to perpetuate lovelessness and injustice. This must be firmly and clearly stopped. Thus the ability to set and maintain boundaries between incompatible values is indispensable for assisting victims to increase love and make justice possible.

A particular responsibility of the pastoral caretaker is to help persons increase their love of God. Because human beings are multiply contextual and all consciousness is informed by our interactions with our world, our belief in God is contextually ambiguous. It is made up of both the positive and negative elements of our experience with significant others. It is mixed up also with our positive and negative feelings toward ourselves. Part of the pastoral counseling task is to help the persons rework their experiences of God so that they are more significant and appropriate in their lives. We see that in Karen there was initially lovelessness toward God, as expressed in indifference and void. As she experienced greater healing and affirmation in the pastoral psychotherapy process, the rich matrix of her life experience eventuated in a sensibility regarding divine activity that is transforming for her. To be sure, her relationship to God was ambiguous. At times she felt distressed because she could not communicate this to me, or act effectively in accordance with it. Yet, on the whole, she found in God a power for sustenance and healing. This is an ongoing resource for her, which on the whole continues to positively affect her life.

A central question that requires a pastoral response is, "How is God's love to be related to the injustice I am experiencing?" That is, "If God is permitting or perpetrating these circumstances which I experience as unjust, is not God really loveless rather than loving?" I vividly recall a student, several years ago, struggling with this question. Renee was a widow, left with three children adopted by her and her late husband. Her husband had taken his life after years of painful struggling with depression. Renee knew that she wanted to be a minister in order to assist persons with their suffering and to help them struggle with their faith in the midst of life's circumstances. However, she also recognized how angry she was at God for "creating a world in which the only option for relief to suffering persons is taking their life." She wanted to come to terms with a God who apparently was unable to create a better world. She was puzzled and angry that there were not more positive options available to God and humans so that persons did not have to harm themselves and others to be liberated from intolerable circumstances.

She struggled with contending values. She was in a transactional impasse in her faith, occasioned by these conflicting values and her loss of her husband. How could a good, all-powerful God allow unjust suffering? She concluded that God could not be held responsible for the unjust and unloving acts perpetrated upon and by her late husband. She had experienced too much love from God in her life to let injustice overcome it. She incorporated a process theological view to help her resolve her spiritual impasse. She said, "I do not believe that it was God's will or activity which led to my husband's death. God cannot control everything that happens, since everyone in the world has some responsibility for what they do. I now know that God's heart was broken just like mine was at my husband's death and that God has received my husband graciously.

God will strengthen my children and me to learn from this and to overcome it in ways that can help others."

Renee came to a new view of God that enabled her to love God and accommodate injustice in the world without ascribing injustice and lovelessness to God. Not all persons would take the same theological journey as Renee in order to relate their faith in God to the lovelessness and injustice they have experienced. However, it is important for the pastoral caretaker to understand the *theological* dimension of crises in persons' lives and help them address it forthrightly and openly. To ignore it or to settle for premature solutions is to further estrange individuals from God, themselves, and their neighbors. It is therefore important that at some point in the caretaking process, the caretaker introduce the question, "How does what you believe or think about God address the situation you are now challenged to resolve?" It may take some time for this question to be responded to significantly. However, asking it with respect and seriousness allows persons to begin to work on it and provides a pastoral framework for caretaking.

INCREASING ECOLOGICAL PARTNERSHIP THROUGH THE MINISTRY OF CARE

The biblical and theological concept of shalom unifies concern for the increase of love, justice, and harmony within and between persons, and between persons and the natural order. It is an inclusive concept that links social justice and personal welfare with God's relationship to nature. It can hardly be doubted that the most significant need for harmonizing contending values is between humanity and nature. The ecological movement has shown that our human patterns of consumption, agriculture, industrialization, and national defense function as a death-grip on the life of our planet. We have inherited models of domination that interpret nature as inert and subordinate. Nature is understood as a resource for human fulfillment, quite apart from its own viability and integrity. Various ecological movements have helped us understand the threat to all of life, including our own, which results from this conceptualization.

The ministry of care does not normally directly promote ecological partnership. In some ways, the incorporation of this concept into a theory of pastoral care and counseling has an add-on quality. Certainly in the course of this book it has not been possible to develop this conceptualization adequately. Nonetheless, the inability to look at microsystemic dimensions of the ecological crisis continues to perpetuate that crisis. Therefore it is necessary, at least at the conceptual level, to recognize that the ministry of care needs to derive from and extend to care of the earth, however indirectly. Further, it must be recognized that our ecological disarray is perpetrated by individuals and families. It has negative consequences for them on both the short and long term. The pastoral caretaker has a responsibility to help persons and families examine their life-style in terms of its ecological consequences, as well as its possibilities for increasing neighbor-love and promoting justice. In fact, these three come together in a responsible theory of care. It is also important that the pastoral caretaker assist with the formulation of guidelines in harmonizing contending values between respect for the integrity of creation and the need to draw upon natural resources for human welfare and fulfillment.

The ministry of care provides opportunities to assist persons to examine their life-styles and the values underlying them. I recall a crisis in a family in a congregation I once served. This congregation had a number of people who worked in a nuclear arms industry. One of the adolescent children of a nuclear worker became very depressed and outraged because of his family's reliance upon the nuclear arms industry for its security and prosperity. He made life extremely uncomfortable for the family and a great deal of stress eventuated.

At first the adults in the family did not want to consider issues of science, nuclear energy, and national security as essentially religious. They understood these as being self-evidently moral and understood religion as applying only to their personal and family lives. They were upset with their son for defining these in religious and moral terms. They were uncomfortable with my backing him on this score and were at first chary of allowing me to provide pastoral care to them. Since a number of other families in the congregation were struggling with similar matters, we inaugurated an adult class on the relationship of Christianity to science, followed by a class on Christian interpretation and response to nuclear energy and nuclear warfare. These ran simultaneously with ongoing pastoral support to the family in crisis.

Over the course of a year we all studied more about nuclear energy and the relation of Christian faith to natural science. We became better informed on these scores and established ways to talk about our deeply held differences on them. This inevitably led into discussions of patriotism and the relation of Christian faith to national security. After this process was finished it appeared that little change of basic outlooks took place for any of us. However, we were better able to talk with each other about these matters.

The family in crisis became less stressed and was better able to accommodate their diversity of opinion. They did not become estranged or emotionally cut off from each other. There was more respect for differences, though these differences continued to be held with deep feeling and with sharp exchanges of opinion. Some of the adult members of the congregation became less antagonized toward those who were protesting nuclear arms in the name of their faith. On the whole, this study process, which began in a family crisis, led to deeper engagement in the congregation and helped persons affirm differences without denigrating shalom between them.

It is becoming clearer that social justice and ecological partnership must be paired if there is to be shalom. The World Council of Churches is organizing much of its current study and mission under the topic of "Justice, Peace and the Integrity of Creation."[29] Ecofeminists have brought together into one conceptual and programmatic context a number of issues previously separated by the justice movement on the one hand and the ecological movement on the other. Charlene Spretnak says:

> The central insight of the complex linkage of the oppression of women and the oppression of nature is the common ground among ecofeminists, as are scores of concerns . . .: ecological wisdom, peace, justice, a new economics, ways in which humans might regain deep feelings of connectedness with the rest of the earth community, issues in reproductive technology and genetic engineering, organic agriculture, appropriate technology, an end to nuclear power and weapons, an end to the plunder by the multi-nationals and the plight of the third world, an end to the onslaught of nation-states against indigenous (Fourth World) peoples, and much more.[30]

The story of the murder of Chico Mendes, the organizer of latex tappers in Brazil, demonstrates how issues of life-style, social justice, and ecological responsibility cohere. Mendes was attempting to organize poor rubber tappers in order to resist the encroachment upon their livelihood and homes by large cattle ranchers who were clearing the forest for their own greed. The rubber tappers were made vulnerable by government policies and unjust practices of police and bureaucrats. For some months before his death it was clear that he was a marked man. He was shot to death in his backyard three days before Christmas, 1988.

His death brought to light the deep connections between social injustice and ecological disarray. In Brazil only 1 percent of the population owns half the arable land. It is estimated that about ten million landless peasants exist in Brazil, while a great deal of the land is unused for production. It is held for speculative purposes or to generate government subsidies and other fiscal incentives.[31] Further, clearing the rain forest land and converting it into "degraded pasture" is accomplished by a great deal of burning. The effect of this burning is global warming, depletion of the ozone layer, and the demise of Indian tribes evicted from the land.

The United States has been a supporter of these government policies and a beneficiary from other Latin American countries who have similarly put lush rain forests into production for beef and other exportable goods to sustain our life-style.

In this example we see that the death of Chico Mendes and the subsequent grief and consequences throughout his family system and social network were the result of policies related to social injustice and ecological rapaciousness. Pastoral care to the Mendes family would certainly require attention to these interlocking factors if it was to effectively increase love, justice, and ecological partnership.

Another example of the centrality of contending values is seen in the tension between ecological responsibility and human welfare. It turns out that an endangered tree in the Pacific Northwest may hold the promise of extended life for women with ovarian cancer. The Pacific yew tree contains an extract called taxol, which has been found to be effective in fighting cancer. Up to 30 percent of those treated with taxol have shown significantly favorable response. However, environmentalists fear that these slow-growing trees will be decimated by the demands for its substance. There is a large debate about whether to protect the tree or to utilize it for saving lives. The prospect is that, while a number of lives will be saved, there are not enough yew trees to meet the demand. Eventually the yew tree population will become extinct and there will only be a temporary antidote to cancer.[32]

Further, since there does not appear to be adequate taxol to treat all who might benefit from its properties, questions of just distribution become acute. Sally Thane Christensen, a thirty-eight-year-old Forest Service lawyer who has sought to blend conflicting values concerning the use of Forest Service land, has been selected for clinical trials on taxol to treat her ovarian cancer. She realizes the irony of this, given her history as a Forest Service lawyer. She is aware of her gratitude at being accepted for these tests. She is also aware of those who were not chosen: ". . . I watched the precious, clear fluid drip into my veins and prayed for it to kill the cancer that had ravished my body. I thought about the thousands of women who will die of cancer this year, who will not have my opportunity."[33] Christensen goes on to say that she believes that it is possible to preserve the yew tree while making its properties available for research and treatment of cancer. She concludes her thoughtful article:

> The yew may be prime habitat for spotted owls. It may be aesthetically appealing. But certainly its most critical property is its ability to treat a fatal disease. Given a choice between trees or people, people must prevail. No resource can be more valuable or more important than a human life. Ask my husband. Ask my two sons. Ask me.[34]

This compelling and stark assessment of contending values between nature and human welfare, and between humans who qualify for treatment and those who do not, requires a harmonizing characterized by shalom. Certainly any compassionate human being wants Sally Thane Christensen to survive, and all women and men with cancer to prevail. No compassionate, sensitive person wants to exploit unrenewable resources for human ends. Can these goals be blended as Christensen hopes? Apparently they can. Two large corporations have joined forces to blend these contending values in a more synchronistic and harmonious manner. The Weyerhauser Paper Company and Bristol Myers-Squibb Company have agreed to explore how large-scale greenhouse cultivation of yew trees might be developed. An individual who has spent his life studying how to reproduce trees is being delegated to lead this project. He was extremely pleased to be in a project that enabled him to relate his concern for ecological responsibility directly to human welfare. He said, "We're really tickled about being involved in this. It's not every day us tree growers get a chance to cure cancer."[35] This form of ecological partnership provides an example of how values that might be regarded as unalterably conflicted can, in principle if not in fact, be harmonized for mutual welfare at a variety of levels. There are economic, ecological, personal, professional, and familial benefits that can accrue from such partnerships. We can only hope that this substantial project will eventuate in specific advances throughout the psychosystemic milieu.

CONCLUSION

The struggle to harmonize contending values is central to the ministry of care. Persons seeking the ministry of care are often locked into transactional impasses and virulent power struggles about which values will predominate in their lives together. The ministry of care is also organized around particular values which, taken together, contend to promote greater harmony and intensity of experience characterized by shalom. Symptomatic crises based upon conflicting values provide occasion for the ministry of care to increase love toward self, God, and neighbor, to promote justice, and to increase ecological harmony. Strategies such as acceptance, conflict management, and conscientization are drawn upon to overcome alienation, oppression, and exploitation throughout the psychosystemic matrix. Creative transformation of contending values is essential for shalom to emerge. In the following chapter we will more fully explore the role of creativity in the ministry of care.

CHAPTER 8

RELEASING THE CAPTIVE: LIBERATING CREATIVITY THROUGH THE MINISTRY OF CARE

Creativity is the imaginative use of the materials at hand.
Natalie Sleeth[1]

Unbind him, and let him go.
Jesus (John 11:44)

DEFINING CONTEXTUAL CREATIVITY

For change to be possible there must be creativity. Otherwise the world and its multiple subsystems would be static, mired in duration and repetition. Persons in symptomatic crises would have no fundamental basis for hope in a meaningful future and altered circumstances. Yet, given the reality of enduring organizational structures, creative possibilities are not unlimited. All change must take into consideration the realities of the past as well as present circumstances. Thus, change in an individual, the larger system, and in the relationships between persons and systems is characterized by *relative* freedom or creativity.

This capacity for reconfiguring the psychosystemic matrix is what I have termed "contextual creativity."[2] Contextual creativity is the polar opposite of contextual organization. Contextual creativity is the dimension of the system that connects present structures to new possibilities. Contextual creativity is the locus of the appetitive and intentional dimensions of life. When joined with bi-polar power, it constitutes the basis for change. When joined with values, it constitutes the basis for strategic change in the interest of redemptive justice, increased love, and ecological partnership.

Systemic creativity is contextual insofar as it takes into account the enduring influence of the massive realities impinging upon the present moment. Systemic creativity is novel inasmuch as it contributes to the reconfiguration of the power arrangements, value orientations, and transactional patterns dominating the past and present. Contextual creativity appears as the capacity for observing ego and self-transcendence in individuals. In social and cultural terms, it is the impulse to reform and revolution. In the family context, contextual creativity is the basis for responsiveness to internal forces as well as external influences. It is the basis by which families both become adaptive as well as symptomatic, inasmuch as creative influences based upon internal and external forces may have positive or negative outcomes in the world.

The basis for creative contextuality lies in God's agency as liberator and lure to creative advance. In both process and liberation theologies God is on the side of an enlivened world. God is opposed to the evil of triviality and discord in which persons are dead before their time as a result of adverse patterns of relatedness in the world. In liberation terms, God seeks to free the captive from oppression and subordination and restructure living arrangements in terms of mutual faithfulness and covenant-keeping. The agenda of God is always in the interest of novel and creative advances of life over death, love over lovelessness, and justice over injustice.

The pastoral caretaker and the caretaking community are in strategic positions to be a recipient of God's contextually created activity, as well as to mediate and discover this creativity through the ministry of care. One expression of contextual creativity in the context of the ministry of care is rethinking care in both prophetic and pastoral terms. As indicated in the Introduction,[3] both prophets and pastoral caretakers, if they are to be faithful to their Judaic and Christian heritage, comprise a unity of individual and social perspectives. There is identification with the plight and symptoms of God's people, as well as a novel interpretation and response to this plight.

Thus, in responding to symptomatic crises in the ministry of care, the pastoral caretaker has continuity with the prophetic voice of the Old Testament. Both look beyond the particular individuals and symptoms to the larger social, cultural, and historical circumstances accounting for the crisis. Both anticipate that their efforts will contribute to a new heaven and a new earth as well as a transformed individuality and just humanity. Nature shall rejoice and benefit as well from these dramatic events in the contextually creative activity of God in partnership with God's caretakers.

DIAGNOSING VITIATED CREATIVITY

If every entity, person, and system must have some capacity for creatively affecting its world, including its own identity and function, a symptomatic crisis occurs when no creative options are apparent, or where there is no power to carry out the options at one's disposal. Lack of contextual creativity reflects a transactional impasse and a stagnant, homeostatic organizational structure. Persons seeking pastoral care under these conditions often express a sense of futility and meaninglessness: they see no viable way out. Their creativity and the power to act upon it are vitiated. There are three particularly common symptoms emerging in pastoral caretaking by which vitiated creativity may be diagnosed. These are discounted creativity, paralyzed creativity, and underground creativity.

Discounted creativity occurs when the efforts of persons or systems are negated or opposed. In the case of Joan, Mike, and Little Mikey, the creative options available are limited and negated by one another. To be sure, this family is contextually creative, on the one hand, in its attempts to maintain itself and delegate child care. On the other hand, the chaotic arrangements lead all to feel frustrated and opposed by one another. Joan's attempts to creatively balance autonomy and belonging are particularly discounted by her husband and parents. Other common forms of discounting creativity are double-binding, triangling, and maintaining hidden loyalties.

In the case of Ron, discussed earlier, the young businessman whose marriage was in crisis because he was overly involved in family of origin dynamics, we see the consequences of a lifelong pattern of having his creativity discounted. At first his father discounted his and his brothers' creativity, criticizing their attempts to use their power on behalf of their own aspirations and values. This discounting was introjected by Ron and his brothers and has continued to operate apart from the direct activity of their father. Maintaining the internalized voice of the father perpetuates a self-discounting that is extremely costly in terms of depression, frustration, and low self-esteem. The social consequences are that Ron and his brothers discount the creativity of others as well, as reflected particularly in Ron's relationship with his spouse. Until recently he has repudiated her efforts to improve their relationship, as well as discounted her achievements in her profession.

Until this pattern was identified and modified, it has operated to maintain an ongoing crisis in their lives. As Ron has been able to move away from a position of double-binding and to confront the hidden loyalties to his father's expectations, his capacity to celebrate rather than discount his own creativity and that of others has increased. He has removed himself from the stabilizing position between his father and his older brother. Consequently, he has experienced an increase in creative energy to live his life and achieve greater business success.

Paralyzed creativity exists when persons are either unaware of their capacities to uniquely respond to their environments or lack the agential power by which to respond on the basis of what they know. There may not be current active opposition and discounting; the paralysis may exist because of discounting in the past. That is, whether for current or past reasons, persons are unable to appropriate their creativity on their own behalf and to act consistently in accordance with it.

Karen, the multiply-molested woman we have discussed, was for years unaware of her artistic creativity. At times her therapy and her capacity to produce art were blocked because of painful emotional material. This paralysis led her to consider suicide. Her creativity was paralyzed, though there was no active discounting of it by anyone in her world at the time. During these occasions her anxiety and depression increased to alarming proportions. It was necessary to reassure her that she had creative gifts as an artist and that her art in fact had received positive critical acclaim and had earned her a modest living. At these times we found ways for her to thematize her current impasse in an artistic manner. Such creative breakthroughs helped her to feel less paralyzed and to make a novel advance in her self-understanding and social functioning.

Another example of how creativity becomes paralyzed is found in the hidden loyalties connected with unresolved grief. Persons or family systems who have not accommodated the loss of a significant member by active grief work are often paralyzed in their capacity to move forward creatively. Through projective bonding with the lost person energy is displaced and diffused. In her book, *Death in the Family,*[4] Lily Pincus discusses in insightful detail how the death of a significant member in the family can impede the capacity of each member to move forward. At a recent conference for parish ministers, a case was presented in which a female parishioner had decided to leave her husband and raise her two daughters alone. Upon exploration, the minister discovered that she had no specific complaints about her husband's inadequacy. He did not want the marriage to end, and was deeply aggrieved that he was being separated from his family in this manner.

Further inquiry on the part of the minister revealed that the mother had grown up in a family of two daughters parented by a single mother. Her father had died at an early age. She was convinced that children did not need a father in the home in order to thrive. She believed that her daughters would do better in a single-parent family similar to the one in which she was raised. Her mother encouraged this course of action. Throughout her life her mother had told her and her sister negative things about their father, stating that, "We are all better off without him."

She had not recognized her grief at the loss of her father in her life. It became clear that she also had identified with her mother's valuation of her father. In the counseling she recognized also that she was feeling pressure to care for her increasingly demanding mother whose health was failing. Her pastor recognized that the unresolved grief about her father's death, and the ongoing overattachment to her mother's image of parenting, contributed to crises in her current marriage and family. At the time this case was reported, the female parishioner was only beginning to see these dynamics and take account of them. Through the guidance of her pastor she began to realize more clearly the depth of her conflict. She began to recognize that given these unrecognized internal messages, which linked her to her father's death and her mother's attitudes toward her father, she had little basis for succeeding in a marriage and as a co-parent of her children. In fact, to succeed was to be disloyal to her identification with her mother. Such projective bonding functioned to paralyze her creativity and to dissipate her energies in relation to her marital and parental commitments.

Another manner in which creativity is paralyzed is through denial of anger and rage. Persons who have been wounded or who are in chronically subordinated positions are filled with rage. The rage scares them because they are afraid it will either destroy the oppressor or result in further injury at the hands of the dominating party. Mothers of sons in particular are paralyzed because of their anger. On the one hand they are dependent upon their sons (and husbands) for their welfare and cannot easily jeopardize that position in a sexist society. They suppress their anger and amplify the affectionate feelings they have in order to maintain their position, as untenable as it may be. On the other hand, they are enraged at this dependency and its cost to them, which paralyzes their capacity to love more deeply and to become more autonomous and mutual in their relatedness.[5] On a similar note, analysis of the high level of violence in the North American black community against itself suggests that this is displaced rage and aggression against the white society for its ongoing racism and oppression of blacks.[6] The depression, displaced aggression, and overaccommodating behaviors of subordinated groups all are evidence of paralyzed creativity. This has significant costs to individuals, subgroups, and to the culture as a whole.

In addition to discounted and paralyzed creativity, there is the possibility of *underground creativity*. When creativity has been discounted and becomes paralyzed it often goes into hiding. It is out of awareness and inaccessible to individuals and the system. It may operate unconsciously or in a surreptitious manner without opportunity for affirmation, accountability, and conscious intentionality. It is less effective as a consequence. Its options are more limited than they would be if they were more consciously available. In spite of Karen's increasing capacity to celebrate and disclose her creativity more consistently, it is still necessary for much of it to function underground. She keeps many of her artistic productions in a bank vault, hidden from her parents and the larger public. These productions are simply too emotionally powerful to share; they leave her with the terror of being exposed. On the few occasions when she has shared them with others, they have been responded to positively. However, when she directly thematizes her experience of abuse in graphic detail, she becomes extremely anxious and needs to hide or destroy these productions. The multiple personae in her psyche also function to discount and keep her creativity underground. While it is quite amazing that this creativity exists in the first place given the massiveness of her wounding, it is tragic that it is so disjunctive from her conscious and typical functioning.

A striking example of an individual whose creativity was discounted, paralyzed, and underground emerged from a student chaplain's verbatim a few years ago. On routine visits in the hospital, he encountered a middle-aged, male lawyer, Mr. Tyler, who was in the hospital for suspicion of having a heart attack. Mr. Tyler was set to go home later in the day. The interview is as follows:

C-1:   Hello, my name is Peter. I'm with the chaplain's office. How are you today?

P-1:   Hi, (he shakes hands) good to see you. I'm about to get out of here, how is the golf out there?

C-2:   I couldn't tell you about that, what were you in here for?

P-2:   They thought I'd had a heart attack. (He is indignant.) Hell, I'm in better shape than any of them. I'm in as good a shape as I was in the Marines, maybe better!

C-3:   What happened to make them think you had a heart attack?

P-3:   I had a bad pain in my chest. (Pause.) My wife worries about me. Do you want some coffee? (Indicates the coffee he has.)

C-4:   No thanks. Your wife worries about you?

P-4:   Yeah, she thinks I'm not taking care of myself. She's always after me to slow down and quit smoking. I smoke a pack-and-a-half a day. But I don't want to live forever, when people are old and in pain I think that euthanasia is a good alternative. Are you sure you don't want some coffee? (I shake my head.) I drink between thirty and thirty-five cups a day. (I raise my eyebrows and he laughs.) I drink two six-packs of beer a day and I'm a firm Roman Catholic, what do you think about that!

C-5:   It sounds like you work pretty hard.

P-5:   (The laughter ceases abruptly.) I'm a trial lawyer. I used to be a cop, and then I went to work for the D.A.'s office. (He pauses and then says very seriously.) I prosecuted serial rapists. I had to quit, it was really getting to me.

C-6:   That sounds intense.

    (He proceeds to describe some cases and to express his anger at the system for allowing repeat offenses.)

185

P-6: Yeah. (Pause.) I've got to keep up. The opposition is always improving. I'm the only thing between those *!+#!* and the victims.

C-7: You feel that you are the only safety the victims have.

P-7: The opposition is always getting better (pause) if I don't keep up a lot of scum are going to get off. (He is much quieter.)

C-8: So you have to keep up with the competition. (He nods absently and there is a long pause.) Do you have kids?

P-8: Yes, I have two boys. When I get out today we are going to do something together. I don't get to spend as much time with them as I'd like.

C-9: Why do you drive yourself so hard? (He pauses and I cushion my question.) I don't want to be offensive, and if you'd rather not answer that's O.K. . .

P-9: (He shakes his head and continues to think.) Well I want a better home for my kids . . . and we have to do what we have to to get ahead. I have to start putting away a nest egg for retirement. (He is reflecting and then he suddenly turns to me.) Why do you push *yourself* so hard?

C-10: That's a good question. (A moderate pause.) I guess I'm convinced that if I don't do it, it won't get done.

P-10: There is always somebody else to do it. There are other chaplains aren't there? (I nod.) Well . . .

C-11: There are other lawyers too aren't there?

P-11: (He laughs openly.) Yeah, you're right about that! (A pause) Boy it looks like perfect golf weather out there.
(The encounter ends with small talk.)

We see that Mr. Tyler had very little creativity. He was locked into a mind-set that was highly precarious for him. He subordinated his tender side. His emotional side was dominated by his intellect and did not allow much creative energy to come forward. He seemed like a driven man rather than a man who was open to vital impulses of self-care and loving relatedness to his world. He obviously was not open to creative challenge by the chaplain at this time, and continued to live a life of high risk and denial of his mortality. His passion for justice conflicted with his capacity for self-care. Rather than being alive to the creative activity of God by which his life might be deepened and expanded, it is a narrow, canalized existence. It is largely repetitious with little novelty. For reasons that are unclear, based upon the data in the verbatim, he has settled for vitiated creativity rather than a vital engagement with himself and his world.

STRATEGIES FOR LIBERATING CREATIVITY

In my work I have found five approaches to identifying and releasing creativity. These include grief work, dream work, body work, faith work, and network.

In order to release creativity, many people need to do *grief work*. Grief work involves recognizing hidden attachments from the past and resolving these. Hidden attachments include the intentional identification with ideas, persons, and patterns of relatedness that no longer allow for a creative response to one's present situation and future opportunities. Since all of us are interrelated, and one of the marks of being created in the image of God is to be multiply attached, it follows that severing attachments is painful. There is tension between maintaining loyalty to the network in which God has called us to live and following God's lure to "make all things new."

It is instructive that the prophetic call to faithfulness includes lament over loss of dreams and real relationships, as well as involving courage to face a new future.[7] The Old Testament scholar, Walter Brueggemann, states in his book on the prophets, "I believe that the proper idiom for the prophet in cutting through the royal numbness and denial is the *language of grief*, the rhetoric that engages the community in mourning for a funeral that they do not want to admit. It is indeed their own funeral."[8] For Brueggemann the lament demonstrates that Israel is embedded in a covenant relationship and that loss of relatedness is a sacred matter. In the presence of the covenant-making God, faithful human action includes rage and protest, as well as grief and praise.[9]

In their work on grief and loss, Herbert Anderson and Kenneth Mitchell contend that in the Sermon on the Mount Jesus affirmed the desirability of actively, publicly, and emotionally expressing one's pain in the face of loss.[10] They wisely affirm that the reason that those who grieve openly will be comforted is that they *can* be comforted because their pain is available to the community and to God for solace. Thus the refusal to grieve not only blocks creativity within one's own being, it also distorts the relationship persons have with God, neighbor, and the larger covenantal community.

The importance of recognizing hidden grief in the ministry of care became central for me many years ago as a result of a workshop conducted in Princeton, New Jersey by Norman Paul, a psychiatrist on the faculty at Harvard University. Paul conducted a day-long workshop for psychotherapists on the relation of grief to marital and family distress. By means of lectures, role play, and videotaped presentations of his work, he dramatically demonstrated the manner in which unrecognized grief debilitated one family's life. As I recall, the identified problem centered on an adolescent male who was in trouble with school and the law. All attempts to rehabilitate him failed. The family was in increasing pain and distress by his acting out and by their inability to either contain him or to contain their distress with each other as they reacted to his behavior. Larger gaps were created and revealed between the mother and the father, and between their other child whom I remember as a younger daughter. Paul took us through many failed attempts to break the impasses in the family. We all felt the pain and frustration in the family.

The breakthrough in the therapy came when the therapist, who · I believe was Paul, asked the father to talk more fully about his own father. It turns out that the paternal grandfather had died when the father of the treatment family was in his early adolescence. At the time, his father's death did not seem to be particularly significant to the father. Paul asked the father to describe what he remembered about the time of his father's death. The father began describing the color of the walls of the hospital. He began to weep as he recounted the day on which his father had died. Pretty soon he was sobbing. The pain that emerged became an active grieving in the presence of his own family. This softened the emotional tenor of the family system and drew them together.

As he began to become more comfortable with his loss and pain, the father was aware of how emotionally unavailable he had been to his wife and children. Indeed, he was aware of how emotionally unavailable he had been in all areas of his life since that period. He realized that his creative energy was paralyzed because it was invested in his father's grave, much like the mother of two daughters mentioned above. As he was able to make his grief more available to him, he was also able to receive comfort for his loss. Other energy began to become available to him for living his life and relating to his family: The relationships with his wife and children shifted significantly; the acting-out behaviors of the son diminished as his father connected more fully with him. Finally, the father was able to deal with the family problems from a position of strength and resiliency.

It is important for the pastoral caretaker to help persons experience their pain, even when it makes others in their family system more uncomfortable to do so. This is especially important when other attempts at boundary setting and problem solving have not been successful. Our culture denies the reality of pain and grief. It regards stoic discounting of pain as virtuous and isolates and denigrates those who show difficulty in resolving the loss of significant others. This is backwards and must be countered for creativity to emerge.

Another form of grief work that is necessary to link persons to the larger society is illustrated in the work of Joanna Rogers Macy.[11] Macy directs her book to help all of us come to terms with our paralyzed creativity resulting from our denied grief reaction to the nuclear threat that dominates life on earth. She believes that because we are open systems and emotionally connected to each other, the threat of nuclear destruction of our world has grievous personal consequences. The threat is so great that we have numbed ourselves to it rather than face it. We are silently and individually grieving, rather than experiencing our pain directly and finding new ways to be empowered through it.

Macy's book is an attempt to help us to face our connectedness and to work through the pain of grief that has been discounted by our denial and separative orientation to our world. In order for us to connect with our deeper love for one another and the intersystemic web that is our home and that "both cradles us and calls us to weave it further,"[12] we must face the reality of our pain and grief. She identifies five guidelines that delineate our process, whether we begin sequentially or not. Thus, to do grief work in relation to our personal and familial pain, or in relation to our larger systemic interexistence, several interconnected steps are necessary.[13]

First, Macy suggests that journal writing, open communication, and prayer are ways in which we can take the necessary step of acknowledging our pain. Second, we must "validate our pain for the world." By this she means we must not discount it as unhealthy or abnormal, but "honor it in ourselves and others," without trying to talk ourselves out of it prematurely with "words of cheer."

Third, it is important to experience the pain. She affirms that experiencing it will be healthy. It will not shatter or break us. Neither will we get stuck in the pain since we are open systems and can transform our pain by allowing it to flow through us. She suggests that "words, movement and sounds" are useful mechanisms for experiencing our pain and allowing it to flow more fully.

Fourth, Macy says we need to "move through the pain to its source." She asserts that the source is rooted in caring for the whole of humanity as well as for our own selves and for our own primary loved ones. Thus by being in touch with the symptomatic reactions of pain and grief, we move to a clearer awareness of our "interconnectedness with all beings." It is important that we allow words and images to emerge that give a thematic expression to this reality and to share them with others.

Finally, she suggests that it is essential to "experience the power of interconnectedness." To experience the power of interconnectedness it is vital to link emotionally to the "web of life" and "to all humanity." Though this involves an increase of trust and exposure of vulnerability to pain, paradoxically it does not leave us more debilitated, but results in a greater sense of "personal security and economy of effort."

I recall a student in one of my classes writing a reaction paper to Macy's book. She said that she was angry at the book at first, and felt that Macy's ideas were simplistic and faddish. She reluctantly read on since it was too late to set aside this book and find another in order to complete her assignment on time. As she finished the book, she said:

> I found myself moving from anger to a sense of tightness in my chest. I suddenly began crying. I could not explain why I was crying. But I was. I sank to the floor and lay on the rug. I felt it against my cheek. I began to sob. I do not know how long this lasted, but as I finished I suddenly felt stronger and surer. I had a surprising sense that I belonged in the world and that the world was a good place. I found that I wanted to protect the world and help preserve it. I felt sadness for those who were facing death when they wanted to live. I was surprised at the impact of this book on my life and suddenly knew that what Macy was saying was what I and all of us needed to hear.

Grief is a powerful discounter of creativity. As an instrument of death, rather than of life, unexpressed grief sends our creativity underground and leaves us less than fully alive. When faced, it allows us to creatively reconnect with ourselves and the world of which we are a part. It reveals the depth of our love and our drive for just relatedness. The pastoral caretaker can seldom go wrong exploring multiple losses and ongoing grief responses carried by careseekers into the helping relationship. Activating the sorrow connected with these griefs can be the basis for watering the shoots and seedlings from which new fertile life might be grown.

A second strategy for liberating creativity is *dream work*. Dream work refers to the efforts to identify and explore the meanings of dreams and imagery of careseekers. It also involves releasing power to act upon the energy revealed in the dreams so that persons' lives and social environments may be altered. In the context of this discussion, dreams refer to the mental functions of the unconscious of individuals, but extends also to hidden values and aspirations in families, society, and culture. Dream work therefore includes the attempt to uncover a variety of repressed mental energies and hidden values which, when activated, have the potential of creatively transforming individuals and their social world.

There is vast literature on dream work. Most of it relates to the intrapsychic dimension of dreams. In my pastoral work I have found it important to respond to several interlocking levels of dream material. First, it is important to recognize the correlation between the content of dreams and the reality in which persons live. The key pastoral question here is, "How does this dream material help you understand better what you are dealing with in your world?" Second, it is important to look at how dreams compensate for unpleasant realities and reveal how individuals wish things were. It functions to help resolve the gap between desire and reality. A third dimension of dreams is to provide symbolic expressions of cut-off dimensions of one's own self. Each element of a dream represents some aspect of a person's personality. When integrated and joined in a synergistic partnership, these elements may be the basis for more integrated and productive function. Finally, dreams may reveal novel or creative directionality of values in the person/world relationship, and provide the power for changing this relationship.

In pastoral work, all of these elements should be explored as constituting a whole rather than as mutually exclusive. The overall task of dream work is to find a strategic intervention by which a focused responsiveness on the part of the dreamer may be enhanced. Once this influence and responsiveness come together, there is a likelihood of change in behavior, consciousness, and the structural organizations in which persons live.

An example of dream work is seen in pastoral care with Stan, a Vietnam veteran. Stan was depressed and unable to function well in his marriage and business. He sought guidance from his priest because of a recurring dream. He dreamed that he was getting off the plane in Washington D.C. upon returning from his combat tour of duty in Vietnam. He was expecting to be greeted warmly by the crowd of citizens celebrating the end of the war. Instead, persons turned their faces away in disapproval and horror. He was left alone feeling naked and exposed.

Stan explored the meaning of this dream. At one level he recognized that he was treated with disdain in the same way our nation treated all veterans of the Vietnam war. The dream was a simple reflection of his actual experience. As he got more fully into the dream, he recognized that the dream also compensated his sense of moral superiority over other soldiers because he did not brutalize or exploit Vietnamese people when he was a soldier. He remembered his horror at fellow soldiers taking target practice at an elderly woman walking some distance along a dike in Vietnam. While at first he was outraged at their callousness, and helpless to prevent it, he also recognized that he had an inner sense of superiority at his marksmanship. He said, "I knew that I could have been the one to hit her with bullets if I'd allowed myself to shoot. It has been difficult for me to admit this, and to admit that I had pleasure in the knowledge." He recognized that he was also turning away from himself at the airport, rejecting the part of him that expected honor for his capacity as a soldier.

At another level, Stan realized that the dream revealed an internal conflict between the part of him that wanted to be celebrated for being a warrior, and the part of him that abhorred war. He could no longer project his own internal contending values onto his society or other soldiers. He had to face his own struggle and find a way to harmonize this dissonance. His priest was able to help him clarify this conflict. Stan was helped to use his dream energy to face the truth about himself, and to move into a more creative response to his world. This meant that he stopped undermining his achievements in school and work, became more cooperative with his wife in relation to their children, and joined an active peace network that allowed him to express his values more effectively in the larger environment. Further, he changed from Baptist Christianity in which he had felt there was no forgiveness or genuine community that supported persons in their moral failings, to the Roman Catholic tradition. In Roman Catholicism, Stan found confession and forgiveness to be meaningful. He discovered the communion of saints, which made him feel that "I am not alone in my struggles to follow God's will and to live the life of peacemaker that God calls us to live."

Stan enables us to see the relationship between grief work and dream work in moving from vitiated to vital creativity. He needed to grieve his failures and participation in the Vietnam war. His dream helped him see the depth of his pain and loss. This loss extended from his self-image to his relationship to his society and culture. It included his religion. It incorporated his relationship to his family. The deep woundedness he experienced revealed itself in his dreams, allowing him to face the pain and to move to new visions or relatedness that fit his personality and his coalescing values. From this he was able to join in a larger network, and to expand his faith work into more congruent patterns.

A third strategy for liberating creativity is *body work*. As we have seen in the chapter on the psychosystemic person, the body and psyche comprise an interactive unit. We gain access to each by way of the other. The body is the carrier of emotional life, as well as the foundation for our creativity and vitality. The body in turn is enlivened by our spiritual and emotional lives, including the way our values function in our personalities and behaviors. One way to release emotions and dreams is to access the body. Matters such as nutrition, rest, and the use of tobacco and other substances affect the creativity, or lack thereof, of the body. We have seen in the case of Mr. Tyler, the lawyer mentioned above, that his bodily life is precarious and underfunctioning. He is at extreme risk because he has neglected his body's vitality. His diet, life-style, and operating values have led him to abuse his body and thereby to vitiate his creative possibilities for living.

There are a variety of therapies that stimulate bodily functioning and emotional creativity. Bioenergetics, rolfing, and music therapy are common techniques. These resources are typically outside the framework of the pastoral caretaker, though they need to be recognized as important referral sources for people who are chronically stuck. They are sometimes helpful treatments of choice for individuals who need to recover from severe abuse and other forms of emotional blocking. At the same time, they can be important adjuncts to other forms of pastoral care and pastoral psychotherapy. Anne Wilson Schaef underscores the importance of body work for women whose bodies have been made into objects for male pleasure. Rekindling the vitality of the body in more direct terms can be a way for women to overcome the vitiated creativity that has resulted from the discounting of female bodily life in patriarchal society.[14]

More accessible modes of using body work in the context of the ministry of care have to do with teaching yoga, breathing, and increasing sensate focus. Eastern spirituality may be drawn upon by western Christians to help us connect more deeply with our spiritual centers and to overcome the split between body and mind. The dualisms of the West reflect an estrangement in the psychosystemic matrix that works against the unitive love of God. Encouraging fitness and exercise as well as responsible intake of food and other substances are also important ways of enabling persons to connect with their bodies in an enlivening manner. Encouraging sensual pleasuring in relationships of mutual care and responsibility are further manners in which the ministry of care can foster creativity through bodily experience.[15]

I recall a male physician who sought counseling to find a way "to have more fun in life." He was rather compulsive and emotionally reserved. He recognized that his life was limited. His spouse encouraged him to seek counseling in order that he "not become a couch potato and further squeeze the emotional life out of our marriage." Upon beginning the counseling process he stated, "Before I am able to have fun I have to know what it is. How do you define fun?" Beginning where the careseeker was, I defined fun as the "freely chosen activities from the conflict-free sphere of the ego which involved others in a playfully competitive but non-goal-achieving manner." Having established to our mutual satisfaction the definition of fun, we proceeded together to help him have it. It was clear that this rather cerebral individual was limited in sensuality and bodily vitality. As we explored what brought him pleasure (and conceptually established the relationship between pleasure and fun), we discovered that the sensual experience of liquid on his skin released his energy for conflict-free functioning in social environments. Thus, at parties the feeling of liquid on his lips and tongue in itself released his sense of humor and his capacity to relate to persons in a more playful manner. He found that taking a shower or having his wife pour water on him was erotically stimulating. Developing the tactile relationships to life helped him release a playful creativity in his social interactions and in his relation to the larger world. While this was an ongoing struggle for him, he did find that he was able to have fun and experience greater pleasure in life.

A fourth strategy for liberating creativity is *faith work*. Faith work refers to the explicit attention to persons' religious beliefs, practices, and experiences. It looks at what individuals regard as the spiritual centers of their life, and how these are thematized in their religious vocabulary and symbol systems. It includes exploration of what persons believe about God and how they have experienced God in their lives. It includes any conversion experiences or other transforming and illuminating experiences. It involves the exploration of their devotional practices in relation to prayer, worship, and Bible study. It encompasses the meaning of the sacraments and their developmental religious history. In my experience each of these areas constitutes a focus around which revolve many other areas of power, values, creativity, and transactions. They both exist as subsystems in their right, and reveal the meanings and relations of other subsystems throughout the psychosystemic matrix. Enabling persons to have a creative relationship to their faith, and find in their faith the basis for liberating creativity, is one of the most unique responsibilities entrusted to the ministry of care.[16]

I have mentioned that Karen, the multiply-abused woman who sought pastoral psychotherapy for her healing and recovery, has connected profoundly with an experience of God that is assisting her recovery process. Through the persona she has called Christopher, she has discovered a vital, enlivening God who is enabling her to creatively transform her experience and make it more available for the healing of others. Stan, the veteran discussed above, found that he was under judgment in the light of his faith and needed to find a faith that helped him rework his grief and loss as well as implement his dreams related to peacemaking. His faith work led him to a new understanding of forgiveness and religious community, which also eventuated in finding a more vital religious affiliation. In both of these cases, the work of faith was an energizing component of the dream work and grief work that needed to be done for creativity to be liberated.

During an internship in a general hospital the importance of faith work became especially clear and meaningful to me. I was a seminary student visiting on a regular basis a late-middle-aged, Lutheran minister who was dying of a rare blood disease. I remember at that point in my life I was into Rogerian nondirective listening. I found that after a short time, Pastor Edwards became impatient with such an approach and insisted that I encounter him more authentically as one person to another. Thus I tried to combine listening with speaking, and made an attempt to stay engaged with someone who both intimidated me and touched me with his pain and openness about it. During the weeks in which I saw him on a one-on-one basis, he shared the gratification of having a rich ministry and a meaningful family. He also shared how guilty he felt that he did not spend more time with his sons as they were growing up. He believed that he let the demands of his calling to ministry override his responsibilities as a father and husband. He felt he had betrayed his family for the sake of ministry. He expressed a lot of guilt about this.

In the course of our conversations he shared his disappointment that his body had betrayed him. He also felt guilty that he perhaps had neglected his body by his overcommitment to work. There was anger along with his guilt. He recognized that it was too late to do anything about it. It became clear that he also needed blood transfusions on a regular basis in order to sustain his life. He felt embarrassed about this need, and was not sure how to ask for blood from beyond his family. He was also feeling that the family's financial resources were being burdened by his need for blood.

I found myself responding to him in two ways. First, I organized a blood drive among several congregations of his faith group. People were glad to provide blood for him, and he received it gratefully. Pastor Edwards and I interpreted this as a positive experience of the church as the Body of Christ and the communion of saints taking action to care for its members in need. Second, I asked if I could bring communion to him. He was eager to have me do this. I suggested that we invite his family so that they could have communion as a family. He was surprised by this. He said that it never occurred to him to have communion with the family when he was a minister.

His wife and sons gathered with him at an agreed-upon time. As I was leading us through the communion service, I found myself inspired to say something as follows: "We are reminded that Jesus gave us the sacrament of communion on the night in which he was betrayed, before the hour of his death. Communion is born in betrayal. It was used as an example of love to connect Jesus with his disciples and to point them to a future together. We are asked to do this as the body of Christ, in remembrance of Him, and with the hope of a meaningful future together. As we take of the blood and the body of Christ, it is important for us to recognize that the blood of other Christians has also been shared to extend your life together. They are here with us both symbolically and literally. It is also important to recognize that we take this sacrament in the context of betrayal. Jesus was betrayed by those closest to him. His body betrayed him on the cross on which he died. At one point he felt betrayed and abandoned by God and cried out for God to receive him in this betrayal and abandonment. As you receive this sacrament be reminded therefore that we do this in the context not only of betrayal but of belonging, of failure and forgiveness, of death and new life. Receive the bread and the wine in remembrance of the Jesus who also knew betrayal. He is here too."

We completed the communion service. It was meaningful to all of us. We felt surprisingly connected and deeply touched. As the weeks went on before Pastor Edwards' death, we had communion on several other occasions. All of us talked about this first time and its impact upon us. Pastor Edwards said with tears in his eyes, "The communion service helped my family and me talk more deeply afterwards about how we failed each other and how much we loved each other. It particularly helped me talk to my oldest son who is preparing for ministry. I asked his forgiveness for not being available to him and expressed my hope that he would not repeat this pattern with his family. He forgave me with tears and said that he loved me and would try to be the kind of minister that would make me proud. Thank you for asking members of the church to provide blood. This has meant a great deal to me. It was hard for me to ask and to receive this, but I am deeply grateful that you did this and that people responded. I feel loved."

For me this was a transforming experience of ministry. This experience helped me understand that the sacramental life of our faith does more than label what is happening in our lives. It actually brings about the very realities to which our faith points. The ministry of care in this sacramental context enabled creativity to be released and vital life to be experienced. It helped persons connect in a deeper love of self, neighbor, and God. It was a strategic intervention that promoted a focused responsiveness and new depth of healing in the face of death.

This form of faith work enabled persons to deal with their bodily lives in more tangible ways, to express their failures and dreams in relation to each other, and to express and release the grief that was keeping a vital creativity from emerging. It came as an inspiration in the actual carrying out of the pastoral work, rather than as a calculated strategic response. I was grasped by the power of the insight of the communion service to thematize the transactions and conflicting values at work in the family. I no longer felt like a little boy learning techniques by which to conduct a grown-up ministry. I came to think of myself as an adult peer with people whom I came to love and who ministered to me as well as I to them.

The final strategy for liberating creativity is to help persons *network*. Network refers to coalition building. It involves a replacement of destructive triangles with positive alliances. It recognizes the deep interconnections that are structured into reality and the desirability of transactional effectiveness. When vital networking occurs, creativity is renewed. It becomes possible then for creativity to be recognized and active. Its consequences can be celebrated openly, rather than being discounted or driven underground and paralyzed.

A pastoral counseling colleague of mine discovered the importance of networking in his own personal and professional development. He recounted that on the day of his birth in Holland during World War II, two teenage sons of their minister were shot to death. The pastor's sons were in the Dutch underground and were found in hiding on Roger's family's farm where they were killed by the Nazis. My colleague said that the stress on his family was heightened by their father's imprisonment as a suspected member of the Dutch underground. Roger was quickly baptized by the minister since it was not clear whether the Germans would allow him and his family to live as a result of their possible collusion with the underground. The family was allowed to live and later emigrated to America. Roger experienced great difficulty in being raised as an immigrant, and being the youngest son in his family.

Later in life Roger had a professional crisis when a pastoral counseling center he was directing was closed for financial reasons. This was a shameful experience for him, raising for him again the sense that he was inadequate and did not belong. He recognized that to some extent he was scapegoated in the process of his center's closing, which was not unlike his early family position of being the carrier and container of the family's rage in order for it to function. As he worked in therapy and supervision on these matters, he became aware that his life-experiences had made him chronically anxious. He handled this anxiety by becoming scattered, angry, and overfunctioning. He also isolated himself. He believed that it was best "to keep your mouth shut if you hope to survive and to not trust people who would eventually betray and injure you." This was essentially his mode of functioning when his center failed.

As he worked through the center's closing and the need to rebuild his professional life, he found himself reconnecting with his family of origin. At age forty-three, he returned to Holland with his two sisters and three brothers. They went to celebrate the 150th anniversary of the church in which they had been baptized. During this celebration two women came up to him and asked his name. After hearing it one of them said to him, "You were born February 11, 1944! Do you know how I know?" He replied, remembering the story of his birth, "Yes I do. Your two brothers were killed that day!"

This experience helped him recognize that he was part of a long heritage, rather than an isolated individual in a foreign country. It also helped him recognize some of the basis for his anxiety and its expression in anger, isolation, and overfunctioning. Rather than seeing himself only as an isolated immigrant, he recognized that he was a part of a network that had continued socially and psychologically quite apart from his presence. To be sure, the network was united and maintained in a common concern for justice and freedom in opposition to the occupation of the Nazis. But it also connected him through baptism to the larger Dutch heritage and to the Christian tradition.

This experience was instrumental in helping Roger recognize his broader connections. He identified it as a time that helped him better connect his feminine and masculine selves, intrapsychically speaking. He also recognized the need to develop a pastoral counseling center in which responsibility for success was shared rather than solely placed on his shoulders. He allowed himself to trust his colleagues in ministry by exposing a greater extent of his vulnerability. He was able to lean on his wife's support and trust it more fully through this time of personal and professional crisis.

As a consequence of these dimensions of networking, Roger found a vital and creative relationship with God. He found that by facing his anxiety with courage, a new sense of God's power and presence were opened to him. He reconnected to his seminary studies of Paul Tillich's concept of "courage to be" and "new being in Christ." He found that he was able to let go of angry and isolated overfunctioning, and to take better care of his own person. He reconnected with his body and improved his diet and exercise patterns. He took more time for recreation. He distinguished between family and professional life in a more positive manner. In time, his efforts became more effective and his rewards greater. His income and professional esteem have increased. Rather than discount it and let it be discounted by others because of his immigrant status, he is now able to celebrate his achievement. His creativity is active, rather than paralyzed or undermined by himself and others. He is able to be more visibly up front in his activities, rather than keeping them underground for fear of ridicule or destruction. He is proud of his heritage and able to own it with a sense of courage.

Another example of where the ministry of care can release creativity through strategic networking is in coalescing family resources for the care of elderly parents. In an earlier chapter I discussed the importance of not letting the care of elderly parents fall on only one or two of the family members. To do so becomes disruptive and leads the family to an inadequate capacity to provide nurture for its members. Further, when persons are facing terminal situations or other crises, extended network care is essential.

The family of Pastor Edwards mentioned above is an example of the need for the communion of saints to provide tangible physical resources during crises. The ministry of care in this context drew upon these resources, as well as upon the network of resources in the spiritual heritage of the church as mediated through Scripture, liturgy, and sacrament. A fuller example of a network model of care is developed in the following section. It is important to note, however, that in a psychosystem's view, networking does not diminish individual resources but increases them. Creativity is a function of a rich interplay of multiply-connected persons, institutions, and perspectives. The fuller the network, the fuller the creativity. Diversity of resources creates fuller living. Life is diminished by chronic sameness and predictability.

A CREATIVE MODEL OF CONTEXTUAL CARE

The concept of network can be expanded to undergird a practical model of ministry for caring. Such a model has been long established in California: the San Francisco Network Ministries. Not only a creative example of ministry, it is also an attempt to show how those whose creativity has been discounted, paralyzed, or driven underground by the larger structures of our society can experience a measure of God's love as they work for justice and vital creativity in their circumstances.

The San Francisco Network Ministries began in 1972. Glenda Hope, a Presbyterian minister, and her husband, Scott, founded a house-church in their home. Initially the house-church was concerned about the number of young adults in San Francisco who were without resources to assist with their physical, spiritual, and emotional needs. The San Francisco Young Adult Network was formed to help meet these needs. From the beginning a number of resources, places, and groups, as well as other services for people aged twenty through forty in the area, were mobilized. There were house-churches at various locations in the city, resident hotel visits, Bible study classes with downtown women, and a coffeehouse.

The overarching goal of the San Francisco Young Adult Network was "to work with young adults for their empowerment: mental, spiritual, emotional, political, economic."[17] The San Francisco Young Adult Network saw social justice as well as personal renewal as integrally related to the message of the Gospel."[18]

Early in the ministry, the Young Adult Network was connected with larger social organizations. It affiliated with the Third World Fund, which provided money to community organizations promoting social change. From this alliance the Genesis Church and Ecumenical Center emerged. This organization helps fund persons who are dedicated to overcome "racial and cultural chauvinism, class privilege and economic exploitation."[19]

In addition, the Young Adult Ministry for a time was responsible for revitalizing the Seventh Avenue Presbyterian Church. This congregation had become nonviable. Through the efforts of the Young Adult Network it was gradually brought back "into a vital ministry in the city."[20] The church became a center of creative ministry.

After a time the coffee house became located within the church facility itself and the congregation became involved and supportive of the various projects of the network. The joint ministry with Seventh Avenue included: Sunday Worship, House Churches, Retreats and "Pilgrim Days," a senior citizens' center, choir, a church community night on Fridays (quarterly). "Extended family" groups for discussing world issues, Sunday concerts, tutoring (Indochinese), Seventh Avenue Women's Association, a Wednesday night gathering called "The Art of Conversation," where topics were discussed ranging from philosophy, psychology, literature, political issues, educational issues, and so on; and the publication of the Network Journal. The goals of the network blended with the activities of the church and something new was created that enhanced the original vision of both partners.

In 1982 these ministries added a creative approach to seminary education named "The Network Center for the Study of Christian Ministry." This offers students from nearby seminaries an opportunity to study for academic credit in a program that addresses the "spiritual/psychological life, growth and discipline of students and the Christian communities in which they serve."[21] In addition to bringing together their academic work with the community setting, this program helped students develop analytical skills for working with "the personal and political realities of the life context of the students and those with whom they minister."[22] It was during this period that the Young Adult Network changed its name to The San Francisco Network Ministries.

At this point, in late 1982 the network ministries changed their focus to work on the "plight of the poor and homeless throughout the country and especially in San Francisco." They are particularly focusing on their work on the Tenderloin area of San Francisco, which houses a number of wealthy persons as well as elderly and homeless. They have joined with the central city shelter network to help alleviate the conditions of street people on both a short-term and long-term basis. The network ministry has expanded to include the St. Clair Hotel Ministries, the Tenderloin Elder Friends, the San Francisco Young Adult Network, the Tenderloin AIDS Network, the Tenderloin Ministry, and Women Emerging.[23]

In addition to this creative networking in order to reach out with care to those who are the least and lost among us, there is a creative restructuring of ministry identity and staff relationships. Thornton writes:

> Their communal self-understanding is evidenced by the way they organize their working life together. There is no distinction in salary, each person be they secretary, ordained clergy or lay staff person earns the same amount.

(Of note, too, salaries are of a minimum amount; not much left for "extras" beyond the basic necessities of life.) Titles of those who work with a Network are de-emphasized. There is a strong belief in the "priesthood of all believers." Whoever participates in the work of the Network, whether it is paid staff, volunteer, people from the community; all are treated as equals and "part of the family."[24]

In addition to the restructuring of the context of care, the community of care, and the objects of care, Thornton points out that the San Francisco Network Ministries reconceptualizes the means of care. The pastoral function of sustaining, as practiced by the San Francisco Network Ministries, is best understood as solidarity. Reconciliation is reinterpreted as justice. Guiding is understood as empowerment. Healing is understood as the hope of restoration of wholeness for all of creation.[25] This restructuring of the functions and means of care is another way of saying that the goal of ministry is to increase love of self, God, and neighbor, to promote justice, and to work for ecological partnership. Thornton believes that this interpretation of network caring is an alternative to the shepherd perspective of "tender and solicitous care." Instead it is "the way of the suffering righteous one," which is expressed in "a strong sense and communal understanding of service."[26] The role of the followers of the suffering righteous one in the community is that of "servant of compassion and justice."[27]

In his book, *The Spirit and the Forms of Love*, Daniel Day Williams argues the provocative thesis that divine love has a history in the world.[28] By this, Williams means that God's love is diverse and takes strategic formation in response to the actual realities in the human situation. We see in the San Francisco Network Ministries an example of the creative form the ministry of care can take when ordered by a vision of the interrelatedness of all things and God's creative immersion in the symptomatic situations of persons. To be sure, more traditional congregational models also were creative in their time and provide important contemporary avenues for celebrating and enhancing contextual creativity. The professional model of specialized pastoral care and counseling also continues to be contextually creative in relation to its social location. No single ministry or form of ministry can be adequate for all situations, especially if the world is understood in its diversity and multiplicity. But the San Francisco Network Ministries should receive serious consideration as the normative form of ministry required for today's world. It will be important for pastoral theologians providing and writing about pastoral care and counseling to continue to find ways to learn from this and other models as we evaluate and develop contextually creative formats of care.

CONCLUSION

Since it is rooted in the creativity of God who loves the world in novel ways, the ministry of care is also to be understood as the creative liberation of vitiated creativity. In place of discounted creativity, it promotes celebrated creativity. It substitutes active creativity for paralyzed creativity. Visible creativity supplants underground creativity. Through this novel and transforming activity of God in partnership with the ministry of care, power relations are changed, organizations are modified, values are harmonized, and transactional impasses are resolved. The consequence for the social order as well as for the structure of personal selfhood is significant. To these realities we now turn as we explore the response of the ministry of care to impaired structures of being.

CHAPTER 9

REBUILDING THE COVENANTAL FRAME: CHANGING STRUCTURES THROUGH THE MINISTRY OF CARE

The aim is to transform reality: To bring about a radical systemic change of the material reality of injustice, to replace injustice with right relationship, the shalom of peace and justice for the whole of creation.

Jane Carey Peck and Jeanne Gallo[1]

THE CREATION-COVENANTAL MATRIX

The ministry of care in a psychosystemic perspective affirms the reality of the world in which care takes place. Rather than finding healing on an otherworldly plane, or in the privatized inner space of individuals and their primary loved ones, the pastoral caretaker responds to pain in the context of one's entire network of relationships. Drawing upon the positive affirmations of creation and covenant delineated in the Old Testament materials, the ministry of care affirms that the quality of the structures of our communal and natural environments has severe consequences for individual and social life.

Yoder discusses how Psalm 89 links the concept of justice to God's role as Creator.[2] God establishes a moral universe characterized by unity and justice through which relationships are ordered. God's power as Creator is inherently linked to God's being as just. Because God is just, God has the right to be the King of Israel. Further, as liberator from oppression, God demonstrates God's power as deliverer from structures of oppression. As Creator and liberator, God is covenant-giver. The purpose of covenant is to regulate relationships and to bring about shalom by delineating the mutual responsibilities of all parties.[3] According to McBride, the covenantal community is required to seek justice, to promote individual and collective well-being, and to maintain the sanctity of life.[4] Thus, early biblical faith establishes a creation/covenant matrix that is the responsibility of the whole community in partnership with God.

These themes of creative partnership and covenantal responsibility ordered by justice and shalom are echoed in contemporary feminist concerns. Jane Carey Peck and Jeanne Gallo state that "feminists might . . . characterize justice, peace, and the integrity of creation as 'right relationship for the whole creation' seeing the three terms as mutually inclusive and constitutive of the good society, the common-wealth of God.'"[5] They go on to state more fully the criteria by which the link between justice, creation, and covenantal mutuality are discerned:

> Many feminists understand justice as right relationship, with God, oneself, other human beings, and the rest of creation, as evidenced by: mutuality—affecting and being affected positively by others; equality—equal worth and dignity as humans; autonomy within relationality; inclusivity; desire for relationship; caring; responsibility to each other for basic human rights assessed in terms of basic necessities of life and the power to act and affect one's own reality.[6]

Peck and Gallo argue that the creation/covenantal matrix is impaired when it is characterized by "wrong relationships of domination, exploitation, and dehumanization."[7] They believe that until women are treated with respect, mutuality, and care the structure of creation will continue to be denigrated because it, too, is identified as female and exploited accordingly. They particularly examine the need to correct the variety of injustices perpetrated upon women, especially those that keep women in poverty and other powerless positions.

Drawing upon these and other materials, a psychosystemic approach to the ministry of care affirms the importance of the structures of creation and covenant. And while these structures are in process and need to be revised in accordance with their capacity to increase love, justice, and ecological partnership, they are always to be preserved and modified. The psychosystemic approach that I am taking sees a potentially creative interaction between present structures and future possibilities. When symptomatic behavior emerges, there are always structural difficulties accounting for it. Attention to the repair, maintenance, and modification of structures is essential for enhancing individual life and creating a viable social and natural order. Walter Brueggemann, an influential contempo-rary Old Testament scholar, argues that the Old Testament depicts a bi-polar relationship between maintaining the structures of being and modifying them in the light of embracing pain that calls the past into question and points to new modes of relatedness and self-understanding.[8] A psychosystemic approach to pain, like Brueggemann, acknowledges the need to affirm structures as well as to replace them in the light of new possibilities. A psychosystemic approach seeks to develop organizational contexts most fitting for well-being at all levels throughout the creation-covenantal matrix.

DIAGNOSING ORGANIZATIONAL IMPAIRMENT

Symptoms reveal a crisis in the organizational structure or fabric of existence in which the individual or affected group resides. Structural family therapists, and feminist and liberation theologians, have greatly helped us to understand the large extent to which "function follows form," as well as the other way around.[9] This means that personal distress emerges from impairments in the larger order in which individuals live, and is not finally accounted for by internal and individual dynamics. For example, in the case of Joan, Mike, and Little Mikey, Joan's distress is partially a function of an impaired marital and parental structure. Joan and her husband have not effectively insulated themselves as a couple and as parents from the needs of her parents and from the larger worlds they inhabit. Neither have they worked out their own mechanisms for handling conflict, intimacy, and the shared tasks of marriage and parenthood. The marital structure is impaired, leaving them open to pain, anger, guilt, and confusion as individuals.

Organizational impairment, religiously understood, can be regarded as a tear in the creation/covenantal frame. The concept of covenant points to a bonded mutual agreement to live within an enduring framework of meaning, identification, limitation, and accountability. Tearing the covenantal frame involves rupturing internal and external boundaries that identify and protect the parties of the covenant, disordering the accountabilities and limitations necessary to maintain the covenantal frame, and generating a runaway system that experiences a crisis in meaning.

1. Inadequate boundaries are one central characteristic of an impaired organizational structure, or a torn creation/covenantal frame. Every system and subsystem needs boundaries to define and maintain itself. These boundaries are internal and external. Internally, they clarify the subsystems; externally, they identify the system and regulate its interactions with other systems. Boundaries may be permeable, impermeable, or absent. When they are absent, there is great danger of invasion and possession by other entities. Enmeshment, bondage, or even death may result. When boundaries are rigid or impermeable there is protection from invasion, but the end result may be boredom, suffocation, isolation, malnutrition, and death. Permeable or open boundaries, characterized by flexibility and volition, are generally most desirable. These allow for interchange without enmeshment and invasion on the one hand, or stagnation and isolation on the other.

In the case of Joan and Mike, it is quite clear that there are multiply inadequate boundaries. Rather than having clear and permeable boundaries, this family structure is enmeshed or fused, with little real difference between the members. This makes it very difficult for any kind of individuated selfhood to emerge; the family system is stabilized around keeping its members chaotically enmeshed and, paradoxically, isolated and disengaged from genuinely loving communion. More optimal boundaries would involve a clearer alliance between the adult couple as parents. Their marital relationship would have a life of its own apart from their responsibility as parents. Mikey and Joan's parents would not play so major a role in Joan's and Mike's marital and parental roles. This would free Mikey to be a little boy, with clarity about who his parents are, and would enable Joan and Mike to work out their problems with less interference from her parents. Such a covenantal framework would be more positive for all of them, at least in this culture.

Further analysis of this case, however, reveals that there are inadequate boundaries at the levels of society, culture, and nature, which must also be taken into account. At the social and cultural level, Joan has organized herself to succeed in the business world, but feels chaotically enmeshed and out of control in her personal, interpersonal, and familial world. It is likely that her overinvestment in work, resulting partially from pressures in her family, as well as from her relative precariousness as a woman in a male-dominated work force, contributes to maintaining her underfunctioning in her familial and personal arena. Her husband supports her success in the world of professional work because it reinforces his own underfunctioning in this area. It provides resources for his support, the means for him to speculate and gamble, and a mechanism by which he contributes to maintaining the chaos in the family system. Because of the ruptured boundaries between the social fabric and the family, Joan remains overburdened, Mike chaotic, and Mikey neglected. All are emotionally undernourished and deprived of appropriate economic and spiritual gratification.

At the larger cultural level, males have often been seen as warriors and adventurers, protecting the honor and virtue of women and children who, in turn, are expected to support and adore them. Hence, Joan's parents and husband are angry with her for not playing her part in living out these cultural expectations, further rupturing the covenantal structure of meaning and accountability, which should otherwise be expected to stabilize and nurture these persons.

We do not know Mike's war experience or early family history; we can only speculate how these might contribute to his present attitudes and behaviors. It is clear that Joan's father was frequently absent from the home due to his military obligations, and expected obedience and adoration when he was home. Joan reports that there was a great deal of violence in her family, and one crisis after another. She said that her early role was to reduce family tension and to support her overwhelmed mother. She denied her own needs in order to stabilize others. She became a parentified child very early. She was also a key player in her parents' struggle to maintain their relationship and family in the face of contending social and cultural obligations. Part of her present difficulty, and the basis for symptomatic behavior in the system, is occasioned by her unwillingness to continue suppressing her own needs in order to mitigate the chaos generated by the social and cultural expectations influencing the life-style of the other members of her family. As she has begun to set limits and establish more appropriate boundaries, the system has gone into greater distress.

There are two areas in which natural biological elements combine with cultural factors to play a role in rupturing the boundaries in this family. Mikey's loss of consciousness, which is suspected to be the consequence of physical abuse by the father, has played a big part in separating Mikey from living with his parents and increasing the tension in the larger family system and between the family and larger systems. A child protection team investigated the possibility of abuse, without filing charges. Mike's greater biological strength, coupled with Mikey's relatively greater vulnerability, has led to a dangerous situation and to family instability.

The second area where nature impacts this systemic structure is Joan's fertility and Mike's sexual exploitation of her body. Joan is afraid of having more children; Mike wants more children. She is afraid of any kind of birth control, aside from the diaphragm. He hides the diaphragm or secretly pokes holes in it. He tells her later that he has done this and promises not to do it again. He forces her to have sexual relationships with him when she is unwilling. Much of the pastoral and therapeutic work is directed at helping Joan put a stop to these behaviors, and to hold Mike legally accountable for this marital rape. Unfortunately, at the time of this writing, she was unable to exercise many of the options available to her.

It is evident that sexual and biological differences play an enormous factor in relation to the organized personal and social structure of their life together. The threat and actual fact of physical danger and abuse both reflect and contribute to serious organizational impairment. Attempts to confront these issues have thrown the system into crisis, which may eventuate in structural growth and change or result in retrenchment or disengagement.

2. Disordered hierarchies are also indicative of organizational impairment, indicating a tear in the creation/covenantal framework. One of the characteristics of systems is focused accountability, which is sometimes organized hierarchically. The concept of hierarchy in the context of this book does not refer to normative values, persons, or roles, but to functions and concentrations of influence. Thus, to say that a family must be organized hierarchically does not mean that father

must be head of the household, mother secondary, and children third, and so on. Rather it means that there must be age-appropriate differentiation of power and influence; there should be parents whose roles differ from those of children, but who have parity with respect to one another. Optimally, parents need to be in charge of the decisions and children free to be children, in charge of those decisions appropriate to their developmental level in the larger social and cultural milieu in which they are being reared. Thus, accountabilities should be characterized by clarity, order, responsiveness, and replaceability. Problems occur in a system when accountabilities are disordered. Accountabilities and hierarchies are disordered when they are unclear, unresponsive, and irreplaceable.

When authority and power are unclear, hidden, or denied, chaos and pain may result in the system. Neurosis is a good example of this at the individual level. Neurotic symptoms mask hidden power relationships: something covert is in charge, in spite of overt ego intentions and aspirations grounded in the ego ideal and superego. The individual defends against whatever unconscious forces are driving the person, with resulting symptomatic behavior and painful emotion. When the ego is able to regain influence through incorporation of these unacceptable hidden influences, these other forces influencing the self are made overt. They become accountable to the ego and subject to modification.

In families and social systems it is common for those in power to hide or deny—and sometimes displace—their power. Failure to act is one way of acting powerfully while denying one's power. Becoming ill, dysfunctional, overwhelmed, or emotionally reactive often clothes power in the disguise of vulnerability. When adults parentify children they simultaneously deny their own power and authority as parents while using their influence powerfully to control and restrict the character of the child's self-understanding and behavioral roles.[10] Unacknowledged conflict between those who are most powerful in the system not only hides power and power struggles, it sets the stage for inducting those with less power into this conflict as either hidden allies or active enemies to one another.

Sibling rivalry is largely accounted for by these dynamics: siblings unconsciously identify with the hidden struggle of one parent against the other and act this out against the sibling who has identified with the other parent. Hidden romantic alliances between boss and employee, or parent and child are also covert organizations of power. In such circumstances, there is a level of hidden influence operative that is impervious to public scrutiny. No matter how vehemently denied, it mightily shapes what happens in the social system.

Another form of hiding accountability is to scapegoat individuals within the system, rather than to hold the whole system accountable for its activities. Such scapegoating and stereotyping—usually of the most powerless or the most threatening individuals or subgroups—overly personalizes and displaces responsibility. Thus, in the case of Joan and Mike, Joan is targeted as the problem by the system. This keeps her as well as the larger system from recognizing the roles of marital dysfunction, parental conflict, and transgenerational influences in keeping the situation symptomatic.

A second indicator of a disordered accountability is lack of responsiveness. The current form of the psychosystemic matrix becomes self-perpetuating and self-justifying, ordering all reactions in the light of its dominant position, values, and ideology. In our sexist society, for example, males dominate hierarchically and define reality in terms of the "white male system," as Anne Wilson Schaef describes it.[11] This means that women's perspectives and aspirations to share power are discounted and undermined; their view of reality has little or no positive shaping influence upon those in control of the dominant system. The boundaries become destructively rigid, rendering the system impervious to internal and external influence. For women, the personal cost of such rigidity is depression, rage, low self-esteem, and the like.[12] For men, the consequences are anxiety, isolation, and emotional cut-off.[13] Denial mechanisms must work overtime to maintain this system. Those seeking to make it more responsive are subject to even greater risk.

A third indicator of disordered accountability is the presence of irreplaceable hierarchies. Healthy systems are open systems, and change in relation to external and internal influence. Hierarchical arrangements useful in one situation may be inappropriate for another. Hierarchies must be temporary and replaceable if they are to be most optimal. Temporary expressions of power differences are necessary for systems to maintain themselves and to meet specific mutually agreed upon ends. But they must be accountable and capable of dissolution. Change and richness of experience require change and modification of existing arrangements. For change to occur, there must be built-in mechanisms for replacing the hierarchical arrangements and moving to new forms.

Persons voluntarily enter, to their great benefit, a variety of temporary hierarchical relationships. Relationships between student-teacher, client-professional, parishioner-minister, citizen-government, and employee-employer provide examples that come easily to mind. In all of these cases, there is the potential of perpetrating negative patterns, as well as overcoming them through temporary arrangements for limited purposes. When accountabilities for hierarchies become disordered, such as in oppressive situations, totalitarian governments, and dysfunctional families, the hierarchical status is often regarded as permanent (and sometimes as divinely ordained, to boot), rather than temporary.

Disordered accountabilities are pervasive and they constitute a great challenge for pastoral caretaking. The power arrangements in Joan and Mike's family need to become more responsive. Their permanence has contributed to an impaired family structure that is in a runaway crisis. Thus, Joan's attempts to change her situation vis-à-vis Mike and Mikey are regarded by her family and her husband as a violation of divine order that requires women to have enduring secondary status in the family hierarchy. Pastoral psychotherapy is helping them to find more appropriate accountability patterns for their lives.

3. A runaway system is the third characteristic of an impaired organizational structure, or torn covenantal framework. "Runaway" is a cybernetic term used in family systems to indicate that the normal processes of maintaining order and regulating communication are no longer intact.[14] The system is out of control; deviancy-amplifying interactions are increasing and the system is in acute crisis. The system is in danger of entering chaos, turbulence, and destruction. Boundaries no longer contain, or contain so oppressively that the pain is intolerable and the structure itself becomes threatened. Accountabilities and hierarchies become so disordered that the system itself is in jeopardy. Self-correcting mechanisms no longer work to bring the system to its earlier level of functioning; it must change or end. It is often during runaways that the family or system is forced to interact with systems at the next level in the psychosystemic matrix: individuals in runaway often seek help from their families; families from the wider society; nations from other nations, and so on. Runaways, therefore, provide the occasion for new relationships, change, and transformation. However, they may also become stabilized at an acute level of "symptomatic redundancy" and continue to injure each party in the system.

Joan and Mike's family went into runaway around Mike's abuse of little Mikey. This forced them to reach out to her family of origin, which both stabilized the symptoms and reduced the acute dangers. They also reached out for pastoral and psychotherapeutic help, which is enabling them to consider more planned and controlled change. The system is quite unstable, however, and threatens to go into runaway at any time. Such a runaway may be extremely destructive—resulting in death or severe psychological disturbance for one or more of the members—or it may lead to a transformed system.

Runaways occur throughout the social order; a runaway in one subsystem may potentially disrupt the interactions in another subsystem. They occur when the conditions maintaining a system have changed and the adaptive mechanisms are not adequate to adjust the system to the new conditions. At the societal and cultural level, the 1960s in the United States were characterized by runaway: the existing intergenerational patterns, dominant values regarding race, gender, war, and patriotism, and assumptions about obedience to authority were severely challenged at all levels of society. The system went into acute crisis. Its deviancy-regulating mechanisms were inadequate to return the system to the status quo. As a consequence, new freedoms and opportunities developed and the system changed. The recent phenomenon of Jesse Jackson's emergence as a black leader in the Democratic party, and the new political power of American blacks, witness to the permanence of some of the changes resulting from these earlier runaways.

STRATEGIES OF INTERVENTION

A major goal of the ministry of care is to move from contextual impairment to contextual integrity. As we have seen,[15] contextual integrity means that the structures comprising the system are intact and endure in a manner that protects the system from internal and external threat. This means that internal and external boundaries should be clear and flexible without too much openness or too much rigidity. It also means that accountabilities within the system are clear and neither unfocused nor disordered. Finally, it means that the transactional processes within the system, and between the system and other entities, are predictable and ordered rather than out of control in a threatening and runaway manner.

1. Strategies for restructuring inadequate boundaries. Because boundaries protect from further harm, it is extremely important for the caretaker to assist persons to block out injuring forces and to be open to positive influences. A simple technique for closing persons and systems to destructive influences is to teach them how to say no and to set limits.

I remember an example from the work of Virginia Satir. A teenager in the family was having trouble setting limits on his grandmother's over-solicitous concern. The grandmother did not respond to overt attempts to stop this behavior. Satir told the family that no one ever dropped dead by saying or hearing the word "no." She then suggested that the next time the grandmother tried to force him to eat, the teenager should say, "Thank you, Grandmother, for thinking about me." Satir advised him to continue eating what he himself wanted to eat. Satir said, "and Grandmother will feel valued, and she will not control you."[16] Normally, overtly setting limits and refusing unwanted activities is adequate. However, as in the case indicated above, sometimes a more indirect approach is necessary.

When there is marital and family conflict, it is extremely necessary to strengthen the boundaries between the marital and parental dyad. Often parents fight about how to discipline children or how to care for a symptomatic child in order to avoid distress in the marital arena. It is important to help parents understand that they might be doing this and to help them to identify and separate marital problems from their responsibility to cooperate as parents. It is especially important for ministers to help persons who are divorcing, or who have divorced, to learn to cooperate as parents even while they are in disagreement about their marriage and have disengaged from it. Helping persons to fight more effectively as a marital dyad, while cooperating more effectively in the parental dyad, is one important strategy for developing more adequate boundaries in the family.

Another place where the minister can provide assistance in restructuring boundaries is during premarital guidance. It is important that there be adequate generational boundaries between the individuals seeking marriage and their respective families of origin. It is often at this time, as well as at subsequent birth and baptism of children, that family of origin dynamics become acute. Parents make claims on their children and on their children's commitments that are sometimes inappropriate. Persons seeking to establish their own households are often ambivalent, and become overly reliant on their family of origin. Sometimes hidden loyalties and unrecognized attachment to one or both parents complicates their commitment to their marital partner. Discussing these matters openly can be quite helpful in assisting parents and children to maintain generational boundaries.

At a recent conference, a local minister presented a case for consultation. The daughter of divorced parents was seeking premarital guidance. Her mother, also a member of the congregation, opposed the marriage. The minister had the mother come to see him alone. He said to the mother, "It is time for your daughter to choose her own way in life and to have her husband become her primary partner. I know this will be hard for both of you. If you want her to succeed in marriage, you will let her make this decision and support her in it. You will also need to find other sources of support for yourself while you and your daughter renegotiate your relationship with each other as adult women." The minister reported that the mother took this advice to heart and began to support her daughter.

Shortly afterward, the daughter's father came into the picture after a long hiatus. He too opposed the marriage. He would not respond to the minister's attempts to consult with him and his daughter. The minister suggested that his parishioner seek her grandmother's help and support for the marriage. Her grandmother was not a member of the congregation, and had had a rocky history with her son. However, the grandmother was glad to assist her granddaughter and intervene with her son on her granddaughter's behalf. Shortly thereafter the father did support the marriage and took part in the ceremony.

In this intervention, the minister was quite successful in strengthening the transgenerational boundaries in the family, opening some and closing others. He helped improve the communication processes in the family, and enabled the daughter to secure her parents' and grandmother's support for this major developmental stage in her life. He freed each person to do their own work and to better individuate as persons, while simultaneously developing more appropriate connections with one another. There appears to be an increase of love as a consequence.

Since all relations are transactional and reciprocal, it is very important that all parties have a role in boundary setting and boundary management. The pastor has many opportunities for educational guidance on these matters. One important arena for preventive care is in relation to sexuality and dating. It is important that women know that they have a right to maintain the integrity of their bodies, and to see that the boundaries they set in their relationships are respected. Many young children and adolescent girls in particular need assistance in knowing that they have the right to say no to unwanted touching. They also need some help in learning techniques in saying no and protecting themselves against those who do not understand that no means no.

At the same time, it is very important that we educate boys and young men to respect the limits set by girls and women. It is not uncommon for males to persist in spite of limits, and even to interpret a "no" as a challenge. Also, when females change their minds about behavior, there is no warrant for males to persist in the behavior that is no longer desired by the female. It is extremely important that the church take leadership in these areas as a part of maintaining our commitment to the viability of God's creation of our bodies as good, and to the conviction that our sexuality should be ruled by just practices that lead to the increase of love rather than to exploitation and domination.

2. Strategies for differentiating clear accountabilities. A second pastoral strategy to promote contextual integrity is to help persons and systems to differentiate clear accountabilities. Differentiating accountabilities involves clarifying proper responsibility, and working to make the structure more responsive and flexible. Clarifying accountabilities involves bringing to light what is happening so that persons are no longer victimized or paralyzed by improper self-blame. And though change in operative accountabilities may not be immediate there is usually an easing of symptomatic reactions. It is important to underscore that changing accountabilities parallels changing power arrangements and restructuring boundaries. Thus, when an underfunctioning adult, such as Mike, is held accountable for his underfunctioning and pressured to at least take responsibility for the consequences of his passive behavior, the power equation shifts. Also, whether he changes or not, he is asked to draw a line between irresponsible childish behavior, which undermines his marital and parental responsibilities, and to function more appropriately in these roles.

One technique for accomplishing clarity about accountabilities is reframing. Reframing a situation enables those who are victimized by the power of others to gain power, as well as to neutralize the unaccountable behaviors of others. I recall a supervisory session in which a supervisor helped clarify power dynamics in relation to a male counselor and his female client. The supervisee repeatedly referred to the client as "attractive" and "seductive." He obviously regarded these as problematic behaviors on the part of the woman. His attitude and diagnosis clearly put him in a superior relationship to her. The supervisor skillfully asked him about his own reactions to her. At first he said that he was angry at her and disliked her because she used her attractiveness and seductiveness to manipulate him. He owned up to feeling angry and frightened, but still identified her behaviors as the fundamental problem. The supervisor continued to explore his reactions, asking if he had felt any attraction to her and any inclinations toward an intimate relationship with her. He finally admitted that he did find her attractive and had "fantasies toward seducing her." By these admissions he became accountable for his own responses and no longer defined the accountability for the relationship solely in terms of his perceptions about her. He became more empathic and open to her, and was able to more productively explore with her her own experiences of fulfillment and disappointment in relationships.

Other ways to neutralize power centers, in addition to clarifying accountabilities through reinterpretation and reframing, includes coalition building, isolation of power centers, and direct confrontation. Since I have spoken of these techniques in earlier sections[17] I will not elaborate them here. It is important to remember that unaccountable power is a systems function rather than purely an individual matter. Consequently there needs to be systemic action by which to neutralize and restructure accountabilities. Building coalitions to confront intractable and unresponsive power is very effective. It is especially important for family members who have been sexually abused to find resources by which to confront their abuser as a condition for a healing process and for restructuring family power dynamics. This confrontation usually comes at the end of a long-term psychotherapy process and is normally required for proper accountability to take place. Once confrontation has occurred, accountability in the form of repentance, restitution, and remorse can be genuine. These religious values can have significant meaning once justice is established through uncovering and modifying hidden accountabilities in the system.

Another way of differentiating accountabilities is to uncover secrets. Secrets impair organizational structures by eradicating essential cross-generational boundaries and establishing hidden loyalties. Because they are hidden, the power that is attached to the secret and to the role of persons carrying the secret is unaccountable and nonresponsive. The consequences are enormously destructive for the system and the persons within it. For example, I recall a family with an anorexic daughter. The mother was closely allied with the daughter against the father. The father seemed to be overly critical of the daughter. It was difficult for the parents to have a clear working alliance together as parents in relation to the daughter. There was not a strong generational boundary between the daughter and her parents. The system was in runaway.

Through the course of pastoral psychotherapy, it became clear that the daughter was carrying secret knowledge of the father's affair with a colleague. She felt that bringing this affair to light would make her father even more antagonized toward her. She was also afraid that it would lead the parents to divorce and she would be responsible. If the parents divorced, she felt that she would lose her mother as an ally and be bereft of parents. She was greatly relieved when the father's affair came to light on other grounds. The parents were helped to develop a coalition of consistent parenting in relation to their daughter, while they confronted their troubled marriage on its own terms. Genuine reconciliation took place as the result of this therapy. The parents were able to rebuild their marriage. The husband was able to end his affair responsibly. The daughter felt less conflicted in relation to her parents. Her eating disorder came under control. Her school and social functioning increased. There was genuine forgiveness at all levels.

It is very important for the pastoral caregiver not to confuse confidentiality with collusion and secret-keeping. To do so means that the pastoral caretaker can no longer be a resource in helping the family differentiate accountabilities and repair impaired structures. It is crucial that pastoral caregivers challenge secret-keeping among their parishioners. The relationship of confidentiality means that we provide a protected place in which to help persons find the strength and capacity to confront their spouses with the truth and work through its meaning for their lives. If they are unwilling or unable to do so, it is important for us to not reveal the secrets but to at least let others know that we have received confidential material that indicates that there are secrets in the family that need to be confronted for further help to occur.[18] It then becomes the responsibility of others to handle the reality of secrets in their own way. When they are able to do so, contractual pastoral caretaking can resume.[19]

A third strategy by which to differentiate accountabilities is to renegotiate rules. As power centers are clarified and neutralized, and secrets are brought to light, it becomes important for the rules of accountability to be clarified and to be renegotiated along more mutually responsible lines. Usually this involves persons sharing responsibility rather than it being hierarchically or unevenly concentrated. As we saw in the case of the supervision of the pastoral counselor, the accountability for sexual feelings in psychotherapy became more mutually defined. Neutralizing the dominant-subordinate power arrangement that kept the female client in a disadvantaged position also led to the capacity for fruitful exploration of her experiences of intimacy and sexuality.

In my pastoral work with families, a presenting issue has commonly been an acting-out child. Not infrequently, this acting out has taken the form of petty stealing. Upon exploration, it has always turned out that while the young person is accountable for his or her stealing, others in the family also had to take accountability for what they were stealing from the child and the family as a whole. As accountability for family behavior became clearer and family secrets were uncovered, it was revealed that the child felt robbed by one or both of the parents. There was inevitably hidden marital discord, and one or the other parent was overinvolved, while the other was underinvolved in parenting. Specifically, one child said, "Dad is never home and Mom has gone back to work so I never see her anymore. I can't get what I want from you, so I'm taking it any way I can." It turned out that the father was furious at the mother for going back to work, and the mother had for a long time been depressed at her inability to involve her husband more consistently in her life and in co-parenting the children. Each felt robbed by the other.

The rules were negotiated once these dynamics came to light. The parents decided that they did want to remain married and to strengthen their relationship. They also found a more suitable pattern of being with the children and maintaining the integrity of the family unit as a whole. This meant that they said no to certain expectations on their career, and especially on the heavy involvement in their very active congregation. The stealing stopped and symptomatic behavior in the family diminished. In this case there was systemic clarity about accountability for what was happening, as well as responsiveness to the need for shared responsibility. Accountability was strengthened and power arrangements were modified. There was a subsequent increase of love and a sense of justice in the family.

3. Strategies for responding to runaway systems. The third overall strategy for moving from contextual impairment to contextual integrity is to replace runaway systems with regularized transactions. Runaway systems are characterized by chaotic and self-perpetuating transactional patterns. These patterns are not accountable to the values and appropriate boundaries in the system. Conflict normally escalates exponentially during runaways. It is necessary for the pastoral caretaker to be a buffer during this time, and to absorb much of the conflict and thereby neutralize it. The pastoral caretaker must find ways to help persons control the crisis and manage their anxiety. Providing appropriate reassurance, promise of faithful participation, referral to other help, and encouragement to move into support groups helps neutralize chaotic and runaway systems.

On a more strategic level, the pastoral caretaker may engage in conflict management. Conflict management enables persons to normalize the reality of contending values and struggles over power, boundaries, and the creative possibilities facing families. To help persons and systems manage conflict adeptly, the pastoral caretaker must be able to support and challenge each member in the system, and each interacting subsystem. Usually the process of conflict negotiation proceeds from escalation, to polarization, to resolution, to transformation. The pastoral caretaker needs to allow this process to occur rather than attempting to gain premature closure. He or she must stay in contact with each party and not become a principal on any side unless invited to do so by mutually acceptable rules. And while reconciliation and transformation are usually the ultimate goals for the pastoral caretaker, he or she must recognize that premature closure is not synonymous with reconciliation and transformation. Therefore, the ability to stand the stress of unresolved conflict is an important skill that needs to become natural for pastoral caretakers.

Escalation and unbalancing are sometimes necessary strategies for moving conflict to a negotiable resolution. Escalation and unbalancing should not take the form of immoral or illegal behaviors, but they might be otherwise outrageous and problematic. For example, I recall the pastoral caretaker who was trying to help a sixteen-year-old member of his youth group say no to his mother's expectations that he sleep with her. She was frightened of being alone since she had a recent cancer operation. The young man's parents were divorced, and his siblings were out of the home. He was becoming increasingly discomfited at having to sleep with his mother. He wanted to return to his own room but did not know how to confront her.

The pastoral caretaker wondered if he could find a way to have his mother reject him since he could not effectively confront her or extricate himself directly. He could not think of any ways. His minister suggested that he begin wetting the bed. He laughed at this idea, but rejected it. The pastor suggested that he begin tossing and turning and not sleeping, creating such a ruckus that his mother would be so disturbed as to ask him to leave. He didn't like that idea either. The minister suggested that he take a glass of water or soda to bed and spill it on a regular basis. That idea was also rejected. Finally, the pastor said, "I simply don't know what to tell you." The young man replied, "After hearing all these crazy ideas, it seems to me I might just tell her no, that I won't sleep with her anymore." That is exactly what he did. The prospect of an absurd escalation led the young man to take responsibility for his own behaviors, and to put appropriate boundaries and regularize the transactions between him and his mother.

A second strategy for reducing runaway systems and regularizing transactions is intersystemic assessment. The pastoral caretaker is located in a larger matrix. The school system, courts, social services, medical profession, and the psychotherapeutic community are some of the larger systems most commonly impinging upon the pastoral caretaking role.[20] It is not uncommon for these systems to become misallied and to compound problems of symptomatic persons. In her groundbreaking book, *Families and Larger Systems*, Evan Imber-Black shows how important it is for the helper to be aware of the consequences of larger systems for helping families.[21] These systems, while positive in their intent, often function to overwhelm the family's boundaries, to perpetuate undifferentiated accountabilities, and to keep the system in a runaway mode. It is very important that the pastoral caretaker not blame any individual in the family, or the family alone, for its ongoing crises without assessing the impact of larger systems upon these individuals and their families.

Imber-Black provides a compelling example of a systems impact on families. She described the Moore family, which consisted of a mother, Caroline; father, Alan; a daughter, Sandra; and another daughter, Ellen. Sandra was twelve, Ellen eight. Sandra was diagnosed as anorexic and then presented for family treatment. It turned out that Sandra had a congenital heart defect. She was not actually anorexic, but did have unusual eating habits that worried her mother. Caroline had primary responsibility for Sandra's care, including frequent medical visits for the heart condition. Alan had a more distant role, and reassured his wife who had considerable fears about Sandra's welfare. Ellen was regarded by the family as a "very good girl, who will eat anything."[22]

It is clear that there was a rift in the parental dyad. Caroline was overanxious and Alan underanxious about the problem. While Caroline and Sandra struggled daily over their problems, Alan withdrew, covertly supporting Sandra against her mother. Thus there was a transgenerational boundary problem. Caroline's mother was Caroline's ally, and agreed that the problem was big. Alan's mother believed that the problem was small, and sided with Alan. There was a difference between Caroline and Alan, and their parents, with respect to outside help. Caroline's side of the family sought outside help regularly, while Alan's did not. There were clear triadic patterns between Sandra and her extended family. Sandra, like her mother, had difficulty in stating her own preferences.

There were several interesting connections with helpers as well. It came out that "the professional network completely mirrored the family constellation." A dietitian agreed with Caroline and her mother that this was a life-threatening situation needing immediate attention. Sandra's physician and her father agreed that the situation was not that serious, and would correct itself if left alone. "Each position encouraged an exacerbation of the other position. A pattern of escalating complementarity pervaded the family-professional system. As one side minimized the problem, the other side maximized the problem. The system was paralyzed."[23] There was no harmonizing these contending values and power struggles.

Another therapist was brought in who proceeded to treat the family in the light of intersystemic and "multiple-helpers" involvement. The therapist took the stance of neutrality, rather than offering a solution as in the past: "the therapist maintained a stance of openness and curiosity in the relational domain but refused to be drawn into the alliance patterns."[24] This neutrality put the parents on the same level and neutralized their conflict about seeking outside help. In addition, the therapist framed all interventions in terms of "experiments or information gathering, rather than as proposed solutions."[25] In addition, the therapist asked the parents to take turns being in charge of Sandra's eating, rather than trying to resolve their differences. This had the effect of equalizing the parental responsibility, involving Alan, and distancing the mother to some extent. Another intervention involved asking the family to bring a meal to the therapy session and to reframe the meaning of eating from health and illness to "having favorites."[26] Moving the process of eating into a more relaxed and conflict-free environment helped normalize and regularize their transactions.

This case situation is beyond the expertise of most pastoral caregivers. It does however illustrate the necessity of recognizing the impact of larger systems in maintaining symptomatic behavior. There needs to be adequate boundaries between, and strategic responses to, these systems for positive change to occur. The minister's role in referral, challenge, and support becomes crucial in cases like these. It is also important to recognize that the caretaking system and the religious culture constitute larger systems impinging upon individuals and families and the other systems to which they belong. The way persons relate to helpers in the larger system will largely be affected by their religious values and orientation. It is therefore very important that pastoral caretakers be aware of the negative and positive dimensions of their participation in the caretaking enterprise where other helpers are also involved.

MINISTRY TO A GAY FAMILY

Working with gay persons and their families provides acute opportunity for the pastoral caretaker to help replace contextual impairment with contextual integrity. Once families become aware that a member is lesbian or gay, it is very difficult to maintain boundaries, accountabilities, and regularized transactions. There are enormous tears in the covenantal framework of these families, and issues of love and justice become acute. It is very important that the pastoral caretaker provide appropriate moral assessment to these situations, and to help persons delineate adequate accountabilities. And while I recognize that there is much debate and disagreement in the religious communities about the ethical status of homosexuality, I believe that a psychosystems approach, informed by theories of strategic love and redemptive justice, offers a productive approach.[27]

A Pentecostal minister presented to his pastoral psychotherapist supervisor a case with which he was working in pastoral psychotherapy. Reverend Jones was working with the Baker family. Daryl Baker was in his late thirties. Mary Baker, his wife, was in her mid-thirties. They had a son, John, who was fifteen and a son, David, who was eleven. It had come to light that Daryl was in a homosexual affair with a college student. Daryl was very conflicted about this, but believed that he was probably gay and wanted to leave the family. However, he was unable to make up his mind about this and vacillated for several months. Mrs. Baker was terrified at losing her husband, but afraid of AIDS on the one hand, and disgusted with the possibility of her husband's homosexuality on the other. She also felt betrayed and abandoned, and that she was a failure as a woman. They kept the information about Mr. Baker's homosexuality from their children. They said the marriage was in trouble because they could not get along and they were considering ending it. The older son sided with his father and wanted to live with him. The younger son sided with his mother and felt the need to protect her.

There was deep concern on the part of the family and the counselor that the father's homosexuality would become known to the congregation. They were afraid that the conservative congregation would reject them. The father felt very guilty about his homosexuality, believing that he was under the judgment of God for it. At the same time he was sure that he was gay and was struggling to decide whether to affirm his gay life-style or to try to change it. The Pentecostal pastor was quite anxious in conducting this pastoral psychotherapy for fear that his attempts to help Mr. Baker sort out his sexual orientation would be construed as condoning ungodly behavior. At the same time, the Pentecostal pastor disagreed with his tradition and believed that full acceptance of homosexuality was more in keeping with the Christian witness. His attempts to introduce this approach in the family therapy were initially opposed by both Mr. and Mrs. Baker. The supervisor disclosed that his own orientation to homosexuality was full acceptance.[28] He helped the minister manage his anxiety in relation to his tradition so that he could be emotionally and pastorally available to this family and each member within it.

As the pastoral psychotherapy progressed, the Bakers decided to divorce. Mrs. Baker became more autonomous and less dependent upon Mr. Baker for emotional support and financial sustenance. She began to date, even having sexual relationships with a lover. Though she felt guilty about this in the light of her religious tradition, she also felt liberated and excited about the possibilities for having more gratifying relationships with a male partner. Mr. Baker left his college student lover and found a man with whom he was more compatible. They began exploring the possibilities of their relationship. And while he did not come to full acceptance of his homosexuality, he said, "I believe that God understands and forgives me for this condition. I therefore am choosing to affirm it knowing that God also accepts me even though what I am doing is less than what He desires for me."

Another dimension of the therapy was to help the parents develop more cooperation in relation to their children. They discontinued triangulating the children between them, and were more mutually available to them in both disciplinary and supportive roles. They no longer allowed their sons to play them off against each other and to maintain hidden cross-generational alliances. The family system calmed down and began to act more positively. The oldest son lived with his father, the younger with his mother. There was regular exchange of information and advice regarding the parenting of the children.

A crisis emerged when John inadvertently found out that his father was gay. He reported feeling disgusted and angry. He did not want to see his father again and wanted to move back with his mother. In the psychotherapy, John was able to verbalize this to his father and his father to accept it. Mrs. Baker was present and was able to validate her son's shock. She shared how her own initial response was similar. She was also able to offer him support. She expressed the hope that he would some day come to understand homosexuality in different terms and to be positively related to his father, as she had been able to do. He was reassured that he was not necessarily gay because his father was gay. Common myths about homosexuality were confronted at this time, and the pastoral psychotherapist helped John and his family normalize the homosexuality. They agreed that John's father would not go to commonly frequented social environments with his lover for fear of John and/or his friends seeing him. They also agreed not to tell the youngest son for fear that he would not keep it confidential. Through this intervention, John was able to find a way to stay in relation with his father, including remaining in his father's home.

Later, as parental cooperation increased and the family became more adjusted to the divorce and to the father's homosexuality, they were able to share with David the truth about Mr. Baker's gay life-style. David was able to receive this with family support, and to keep it confidential from his friends and other persons. He did not have a strong aversive reaction to the news.

With guidance from the pastoral psychotherapist, the family decided not to disclose to their congregation and their local minister the reality of the homosexuality. They were having enough difficulty feeling accepted in their religious community as a divorced couple. They did maintain continuity with their heritage, though the father found another congregation to attend. The pastoral psychotherapist decided not to insist that the congregation and minister be notified about this, though there was some reluctance on his part to maintain these boundaries between the larger religious system and the family. He construed other ways to engage the congregation and his tradition in a reassessment of their orientation to gay and lesbian life-styles. He believed that he could use his strategic position in his denomination for educational purposes. He also felt that he could be an advocate in other public ways for a more tolerant approach to homosexuality.

It is clear that many intervention strategies were at work to assist this family to move from impaired organizational structures to structures of integrity. Though the marital dyad needed to be disengaged, the family structure was maintained with respect to parenting children. Transactional impasses were resolved and more open communications took place. There were fewer runaways in the system. John's behavior became more normal and his acting out in school and church ceased. Both parents became more emotionally available to their sons and to each other, even as they became more independent in relation to other adult partners. The father was able to take accountability for his life-style and to seek the family's forgiveness for the pain that his secret life had caused them.

The pastoral counselor was able to help them recognize that the secret in the family was partially perpetrated by a homophobic and heterosexist culture, including the religious community to which they were committed. Thus they could see that while the accountabilities for the homosexual life-style were ultimately the father's, its presence was not a matter of his choice. Further, they recognized that his early need to keep his behavior secret had as much to do with the larger society as with the father's own moral failure. This reduced improper self-blame.

In addition, the family built new coalitions and alliances. The functional accountabilities of the family became more open, flexible, and realistic. There was an increase in mutual respect. The mother's disadvantaged position by virtue of a sexist culture was identified, and countervailing measures developed for her to gain more autonomy and economic viability. Through pastoral psychotherapy there was clearly an increase of love and justice eventuating from these strategic interventions and from the focused responsiveness of the family individually and collectively.

CONCLUSION

The world is a matrix of relationships. There are many modes and structures in which relatedness occurs. These modes mediate qualities of being, and have both positive and negative outcomes with respect to love, justice, and ecological partnership. The ministry of care seeks to overcome structural impairment reflected in inadequate boundaries, disordered accountabilities, and runaway systems. Pastoral caretaking seeks to increase contextual integrity by developing intact boundaries, clear accountabilities, and reliable transactional patterns within the system and between the system and its larger network. When successful, pastoral caretaking promotes growth and contextual creativity, harmonized values, and optimal power arrangements. The way this all comes together can be seen in the following chapter in the case of a congregation that is seeking to overcome its impairment by a pastor who abused his power by sexual means.

CHAPTER 10

RESTORATIVE AND LIBERATING CARE: HEALING A CONGREGATION

A rich and mature experience is one in which such feelings as pain and joy, hope and fear, anger and penitence all coexist in a complex whole rather than one in which they simply displace each other.

John B. Cobb, Jr.[1]

THE CONGREGATION'S CRISIS

This chapter recounts and interprets one congregation's struggles to recover from the discovery that its highly regarded married male minister had been sexually involved with several female members of the congregation over an extended period of his ministry.[2] Psychosystems categories are drawn upon to interpret the symptomatic crisis and intervention strategies necessary for a transformative recovery of a congregation. The purpose is to illuminate how a psychosystemic approach may be applied directly to the world beyond that of individuals and families. The qualitative connection between persons and their larger worlds is dramatically apparent in this situation.

The Suburban Mennonite Church is a small, activist congregation of the Mennonite Church.[3] It is located in a middle-class suburb near a nuclear bomb factory. It has been noted for its peace activism. Its membership is made up of largely college-educated persons from the professional class. It has a wide range of ages, but most of the adults are from thirty-five to fifty-five. There are a variety of programs by which to educate believers and to inform activists. The congregation has inspired a strong loyalty. There is a strong connecting network. It is a covenant-like community, deeply committed to promote justice, to enhance individual and collective well-being, and to preserve the sanctity of life.

There are several identifiable phases involved in the congregation's movement from crisis to resolution. It has been difficult to determine a precise chronology and to select the most relevant facts from a variety of conflicting accounts. However, the congregation has not raised questions of fact in responding to my accounting.

The *precursor-secret phase* is largely reconstructed retrospectively, in the light of subsequently remembered and discovered facts. The minister and the congregation had been in fellowship for over twenty years. The minister was a widely known leader in the church and community. He was particularly noted for his creativity in congregational leadership and for his courageous peace activism. He was an influential model of radical discipleship. He mixed a charismatic personal style with facilitative leadership in the congregation. Members of the congregation found him sensitive and available in their personal crises, offering support as well as decisive assessments about which course of actions would be best for them. At the same time, he affirmed the obligation of people to make their own decisions, even if these were in tension with conventional wisdom. He easily evoked confidence in his pastoral leadership and elicited personal trust so that a number of people readily confided in him. He knew a great deal about the intimate personal lives of his parishioners.

The congregation had a clear identity and took itself very seriously, in the best sense of that word. It saw itself as uniquely faithful to the Anabaptist tradition and conceived its mission to be a peacemaking and justice-seeking church. New members were welcome. Because of the nature of the congregation and its minister, there were strong disagreements at times about how the church should interpret and live out its ministry. For example, some wanted more commitment to community living; others wanted a broader program and more emphasis upon improving the facilities. In spite of a strong covert lay hierarchy and these differences of opinion, the congregation usually followed the vision of the minister, in whose person many of their own convictions were expressed. This congregation had a lot to be justifiably proud of; it had a heritage, an ethos, and a mission to protect and to further. In psychosystemic terms, there was a positive relationship between contextual integrity and contextual creativity. Transactional processes were effective. Contending values were harmonized or accommodated. Power seemed to be open and accountable. Efforts to increase love, justice, and ecological responsibility were sustained and effective.

From time to time since 1974 there were rumors that the minister had "inappropriate relationships" with certain female parishioners. These rumors were not pursued. A year or so before the sexual abuse of power came to light, there was some concern over the state of the minister's marriage and some financial assistance was provided for marital counseling. There was also concern that the minister appeared to be dating a single woman in the congregation. The romantic overtones of their public interactions were troubling to some, but little was done to confront this until other allegations came to light. The systemic impetus toward homeostasis predominated in spite of increasing dissonances.

During the *discovery-chaos phase,* beginning in the fall of 1986, a female member of the congregation confided to a study group that a year earlier the minister had made sexual advances to her when they were alone in a house on a work trip. During a back-rub, which was suggested by him, he began fondling her breasts. She was shocked and asked him to stop. It took nearly a year to make this public. When she told the study group, some thought it should be confronted as sexual abuse on the part of the minister. Others thought she was overreacting and that it should basically be forgotten. The group finally decided that the deacons should know and that the minister should be confronted. Through escalating symptoms, the congregational system began to enter a crisis centering around contending values, power imbalances, and creativity versus impairment.

The chronology here is conflicting and incomplete. But it appears that something like the following happened. Individuals in the group were assigned to inform each of the deacons of the allegations. On the basis of Jesus' directive to confront an offender personally, the deacons asked the woman to confront the minister herself and to arrange a meeting with him and the deacons. This turned out badly, since the minister was angry and the woman felt more vulnerable.[4] Subsequently, a meeting was arranged with the woman, the study group, the deacons, and the minister. The minister was confronted publicly at this time. He denied that he had done anything wrong and became very emotional. He said that he was being victimized by this process. The results were inconclusive, emotions were high, and people were quite conflicted about what to do next. The crisis had now become acute and the system was on the verge of a runaway.

The deacons continued deliberating about how to proceed, since some members of the study group insisted that further victimization was taking place and they were very angry. The minister was angry, feeling he was being falsely accused, and victimized by this process. Others were angry that "the women" (a term used to designate a group of both males and females who were identified with the needs of those who survived the minister's victimization) were overreacting and taking out on the minister their hostility toward male authority. In the meantime, one woman in the study group and at least one deacon was informed that another woman in the congregation was being sexually abused by the minister in her counseling with him. She, however, was not ready to have this become public (partly because of how badly she thought the minister and deacons were handling the relatively less shocking case that had already come to light, and partly because the deacons told her not to bring it to light since they had enough information already). A number of other people in the congregation knew of these cases on a private, secret-keeping basis, while a larger number of members of the congregation were in the dark about any of these allegations. There was no real distinction between confidentiality and secret-keeping in this system over these matters.

After a month or so, a congregational meeting was held to consider how to respond to the minister. This was very difficult, since some of the deacons wanted to be "over this whole thing," while some members of the congregation had no idea anything was amiss. The congregational meeting was skewed by the minister offering his resignation earlier in the day. He admitted general improprieties and asked forgiveness. Action was delayed for two weeks, in accordance with church polity. There was much pain and conflict in the church during the period that followed. Some thought the minister's remorse was not genuine. Some thought the women were overreacting to his behavior. They believed that his accuser was partially responsible for what happened. There was conflict over whether to accept his resignation, or to request it. The congregation was acutely symptomatic by now.

The *awareness-polarization phase* began at the congregational meeting two weeks later when a well-respected female parishioner disclosed that the minister some years earlier had sexualized their relationship when she was receiving pastoral counseling from him. She disclosed that there had been "intimate sexual caressing" as a "regular occurrence" in her counseling. She said that this "clearly included gratification of sexual appetite which I knew then and now was appropriate only to your wife and required an agreement to secrecy." She broke it off. She shared that consequently she was deeply depressed and considered the possibility of suicide. Her statement, which had high credibility, galvanized the congregation into further awareness of the nature of the abuse and focused the congregation's response toward the minister. The minister's relationship to the church was terminated, with pay effective for five months.[5] His pastoral duties would not include preaching or counseling. There was a sincere beginning attempt to hold him accountable, though he took little or no public responsibility about the specific charges.

In the next several months, there was ongoing conflict and pain. The minister was allowed to use his office for other ministerial work, which caused further distress to both the public and still hidden survivors. He was finally asked to vacate the premises. This caused further conflict. A few members of the church burned all his office furniture. The burning was regarded by some as a hopeful purging. For others it was an ungodly act of violence and vengeance.

The conflict escalated to triangle in other persons and larger systems. The current associate minister was torn in many directions: she was criticized by those who wanted her to speak more forcefully on behalf of the victims, she was attacked by those who wanted her to speak more positively on behalf of the healing process that had already taken place, and she was the target of anger from those who wanted her to be more positive toward her victimized senior minister. There was anger at the denomination for doing very little, other than offering general support. There was a great deal of pain and anger toward the congregation's former associate minister and her congregation, who took in the minister and let him perform pastoral duties. Multiple interlocking triangles and hidden alliances operated at this time.

In addition, there were many hidden transactions. A number of individuals confronted the minister privately. They did not reveal this publicly because they did not want to give fuel to the anger and pain that was so dominant. It was stated by at least two people that the minister admitted his behavior, and indicated that something similar may have taken place with up to a total of twelve women over the years. There was general agreement among those who talked to him privately that the minister was neither genuinely repentant nor remorseful, in spite of general public apologies and requests for forgiveness. In private, he indicated to a number of people that he did not think that he had really done anything wrong. He was cited as saying, "There is nothing wrong with this; this is a higher form of spiritual love and those who do not understand it are not as spiritually advanced." He was also quoted as saying, "I don't see anything wrong with this and I hope it happens again."

In an attempt to gain clarity and to further resolution, the congregation sponsored four study groups during this period. One studied David Augsburger's book on forgiveness.[6] Another studied Marie Fortune's work on abuse.[7] Another studied consensual decision-making processes. Another began to work to develop an official chronology and information packet to hand out to those seeking information and help. In addition, the congregation hired two specialists in sexual abuse to help those who wanted to process their feelings in a support group. A weekend retreat was also led by this team.

Unfortunately, these attempts to gain awareness and clarity tended to solidify the polarization that was emerging between those primarily identified with the survivors, the minister, and the congregation as a whole. Those studying forgiveness were believed to be colluding with the minister in avoiding accountability. Those studying the Fortune material were seen as holding on to anger and vengeance too long. Those interested in consensual decision making were regarded as prematurely moving toward closure, without recognizing the depth of the wounded-ness that remained. There was little harmonizing of the contending values dominating the congregational system. Much blaming was occurring and transactions were at a severe impasse.

In the spring, awareness and polarization increased simultaneously when the victim who had secretly come forth in the fall shared her story at a congregational meeting. She described in some detail the sexual activity that took place in the minister's office during counseling over a seven-year period. She described how hard it was for her to stop it and how badly she felt about it. She felt positively that she had found enough agential power to stop it. She wanted to share her story to help people understand, as well as to gain support for herself. And while she did feel support by some, overall she felt further victimized by attitudes of denial, blame, and puzzlement about why she didn't stop it earlier. Some members of the congregation were angry that this should come out since the minister's abuse had already been dealt with. Others reported that this was the last straw in their judgment about the former minister. They believed that if he would do this with someone so vulnerable and not recognize the inappropriateness of it, he should not be in ministry.

During the remainder of the first year several other important events took place, which both increased awareness and intensified polarization. There was a major conflict between those writing the official accounting and a woman who wrote an article for publication that criticized the self-congratulatory tone of the congregation.[8] She thought the congregation did not recognize enough its ongoing denial and its secondary victimization of the women. In turn, many members of the church criticized her for not taking part in the healing opportunities of the church, and regarded her as a trouble-making leader of the "victim-identified fringe group." Second, while the regional Mennonite Conference was generally supportive of the congregation's steps toward healing and began processes that eventually led to the revocation of the credentials of the offending minister, at the same time it decided not to contribute to the congregation's therapy fund for the victims for fear that this would be admitting liability. Third, a number of the members of the congregation left the church either because they did not think it did enough to confront the minister and gain justice for the victims, or because it victimized the minister and generally overreacted to this issue all around.

The *recovery-rebuilding phase* blends with the earlier phases, though it is also arrested to some extent because of some of the dynamics of the prior phases. In the light of the events detailed above, the deacons and the official interpretation group, among others, realized that more attention needed to be paid to maintaining and nurturing the congregation's ongoing life. They affirmed that the abuse was only one issue among others, and that in spite of mistakes it was being handled properly. Positive corrective mechanisms began to emerge within the system. New leadership and stronger governance structures were appearing. A new permanent ministry team was being planned (and subsequently inaugurated). There was a great deal of behind-the-scenes individual work: friendship, small groups, and ongoing conversation among many members of the congregation. Though a number of persons had left the church, and a few had joined or were considering joining, there was a solid core of persons committed to holding on and rebuilding. There was a kind of pride that they had survived something so awful, and an underlying belief that those who were still hurt or angry would eventually gain further healing. The congregation realized that there had been a severe diminishment of morale, leadership, vision, self-esteem, and energy for outreach. It knew it had survived a severe vocational malaise. It also affirmed the strength, creativity, and resiliency that emerged from openly seeing-through the trauma.

It was at this point that I entered the picture. Because of what I had learned about them, I expected the recovery-rebuilding phase to be more advanced. I found, however, that in spite of real healing and resolution there was still considerable underground pain and conflict and that their healing process was at an impasse. The issues I have already identified festered beneath the surface, and clearly emerged through the interview process. Specifically, there was still struggle about how to relate to the former minister and debate about whether and to what extent genuine healing had occurred. There seemed to be considerable tentativeness and uncertainty about the congregation's vision for the future. While there had been true recovery and healing, there was ongoing diminishment and dissipation of energies. The rebuilding process was making them keenly aware of what has been lost, and the depth of trauma from which they were slowly recovering. Perhaps another phase, understood as a resolution-transformation phase, has yet to appear, but not enough time and effort have passed to bring this about.[9]

PSYCHOSYSTEMIC ANALYSIS

There were four polar tensions around which the dynamics of the congregation at each stage can be interpreted. Each tension reflects one or more central psychosystemic concepts.

The first tension was the struggle between focusing upon the pain and loss in the congregation, versus giving primary attention to the congregation's strength and resiliency. Some members of the congregation emphasized how much pain there was and how this pain needed to be faced and worked through. Others thought that there was too much emphasis upon pain and that the strengths and healing processes ought to be more emphasized. In the discovery-chaos and awareness-polarization stages there was extreme disagreement on this, to the extent that victims felt revictimized by the congregation's emphasis upon its strengths, while others were unhappy or left because they thought that the congregation was making too much out of the whole thing. These and other values continued to clash well into the recovery-rebuilding phase. Psychosystemically, the core issue is a power struggle between contextual creativity and contextual organization.

One particularly noteworthy dynamic revealed the depth of organizational impairment. The pervasiveness of multiple shame-driven "shoulds" underlies the polarities of pain versus strength, but also plays a part in all of the other polarities. To overcome the deep sense of shame felt by individuals and the congregation as a unit, various parties were demanding of one another particular behaviors and attitudes that they regarded as necessary for re-establishing the loss of esteem.[10] This led to increased power struggles. One former member told me that he was ashamed of his church; he left because it no longer expressed the unique Mennonite spirit of reconciliation and radical discipleship. The survivors and those identified with them expressed ongoing shame because the congregation blamed them or asked them to heal at a faster rate. In opposition, they believed that the congregation should have made justice and accountability a greater priority than healing or forgiveness. Members of the congregation said that they felt exposed and shamed in front of other Mennonite churches which seemed happy that they finally were being brought down. They believed that the Conference should have done more to support them. Others have said to the victims, in effect, "We have done a lot to help you heal; now you should not make us feel further shame by continuing to be so weak." Or, "We really have this behind us; do not make us feel more shame by reminding us how vulnerable we have been and how much we have lost. You should put it behind you too!" These shame-driven shoulds revealed disordered accountabilities and victimizing power arrangements. They became most virulent in the awareness-polarization phase, but persisted into the recovery-rebuilding phase.

The second fundamental tension was between the tendency to individualize and polarize on the one hand, and to organize and communalize on the other. This congregation, in the free-church Anabaptist tradition, put a great deal of emphasis upon individual responsibility and the doctrine of the "priesthood of all believers." Contextual creativity is generally valued over contextual integrity in this tradition. Organizational structures are underemphasized to begin with, and they tended to become relatively weak over the years of this highly powerful minister's tenure in the congregation.

Strong-willed and strong-minded individuals dominated what was supposed to be a communal process. In the initial stress of discovery, the study group, the deacons, and other strong individuals carried the major responsibility for confronting the allegations. The church council, the moderator, and the congregation were basically left out, further complicating the organizational dynamics. Information was spotty, and largely by hearsay. Transactional messages were tangled and double-binding. Roles, rules, and responsibilities were confused and disparate. Boundaries were ruptured or unclear. For example, one of the survivors was instructed by the deacons to go alone as an individual to confront the minister rather than developing a communally devised due-process structure to protect her, the minister, and the congregation. Many individuals confronted the minister and supported the survivors on an individual, private basis, but did not share this with others who sometimes misperceived their actions (or lack of actions) as avoidance and denial of the issues. The study groups and the consultants were developed on a largely volunteer basis. The Conference minister was supportive, but there were few intact structures of communication and consultation between the congregation and the Conference.

In addition to this individualization, it became clear from the beginning that the community had become polarized into three groups. As noted earlier, there were those who projectively bonded with the victims and sought justice. Second, there were those who projectively bonded with the minister and wanted him to be accountable on the one hand, and not victimized on the other. The third group consisted of those who projectively bonded with the congregation itself and did not want this situation to divide it or diminish its ministry. By these means, conflicting values became structured into the organizational context. They maintained power imbalances and contributed to vitiated creativity for many individuals and for the system as a whole.

Much of the work required of the congregation was to develop communal and organizational structures to regularize this event as a part of its life and to process it with strength as a unified community. Overcoming the individualization has been complicated by the fragmentation into polarized groups, each of whom regarded the other through anger and shame-driven shoulds. These tensions were most acute during the awareness-polarization phase, but still exist and are finally being openly addressed in the early recovery-rebuilding phase.

The third set of dynamics consisted of the tension between the need for forgiveness and reconciliation on the one hand, and accountability and justice-making on the other. From the beginning the crisis was a crisis of contending values. A number of people said something like, "This is no big deal; the victims should forgive and forget." This was experienced by survivors and survivor-identified persons as cheap grace: as forgiveness without accountability, remorse, or restitution. It was forgiveness without justice. They emphasized that the minister and the congregation had to confess their sin against the victims if true healing, including forgiveness and reconciliation, were to become possible. This struggle became polarized into the three groups identified earlier, and expressed itself in tensions between the study group on forgiveness and the study group on abuse of the pastor's role. When the minister was confronted about his behavior he was upset and claimed to be a victim of the anger of women. Some members of the church identified his pain as the pain of abuse, while others identified it as the pain of accountability. The need to clarify power accountabilities was paramount at this time. Because of intractable power arrangements, fueled by sexism, it was impossible to do so.[11]

The tension between the values of forgiveness and justice was exacerbated (especially in the discovery-chaos stage) by the congregation's difficulty in knowing how to name the problem. Early on, there was a wide range of opinion: some saw this as adultery and/or affairs between consenting adults, others as sexual indiscretion or inappropriate touching, others as abuse of power, others as sexual abuse, others as seduction on the part of the women, and so on. There was great feeling about this, and the feeling fueled the shame, polarization, assessment of moral responsibility, and the nature of the appropriate response. To its credit, the congregation came to identify the events as an abuse of the role and power of the pastoral office by the pastor's inducting parishioners into a sexualized relationship in the name of ministry.[12] As part of its recovery and rebuilding, it is now revisiting how to seek meaningful justice for the victims/survivors (including forgiveness for its own secondary-victimization of them), and to develop appropriate lines of accountability and restitution from the minister.

Fourth, there was strong polar tension between contemporizing versus remembering and hoping. Some people were not able to consider celebrating the past or building for the future because of the pain of the present. Being locked into a polarized group, which was expecting something from others, made it impossible for them to feel good about the past or to hope for the future. Others said that too much emphasis was placed upon the here-and-now in a kind of tyranny of emotional reactivity, rather than appreciating enough their heritage and working to fulfill their mission. Unfortunately, in the awareness-polarization phase, this tension became acute and led to transactional impasses. Those working toward the future and celebrating the past, felt angry and put-upon by those who could not move beyond the single issue of the abuse. The latter group thought that the congregation was denying its pain and history by trying to get beyond it, rather than finding a way to normalize and carry it into its future as a part of its past. These contending values resulted in vitiated creativity and disordered accountability. They were indicators of projective bonding and destructive triangling. Severe double standards prevailed. The result was a vocational malaise.

Finally, there was tension along the axis of moral responsibility versus legal liability. Moral responsibility emphasizes accountability, justice-making, and due process on the part of the religious community for the victims as well as for the alleged offending minister. It includes attention to the way in which the congregation and the larger denominational structures respond to the allegations and to the victims. Legal liability refers to the civil or criminal responsibility of these parties to one another.

Specters of lawsuits or criminal charges brought intersystemic boundary issues to the forefront, increasing power struggles within the congregation. For example, one prominent leader left the congregation in part because he feared a lawsuit by either the victims or the minister for lack of due process. Some members of the congregation were further angered at the Conference's withdrawal of a promise to provide financial assistance to the survivors because legal counsel for the Conference reportedly thought that such assistance would be admitting liability for the offense. Moral responsibility of the denomination to the victims/survivors was in this case impeded by an overly sensitive fear of legal liability. To my knowledge there were no actual threats of lawsuits in this case, but potential threats have clearly contributed to the rupturing of the covenantal framework of Suburban Mennonite Church.

In conclusion, Suburban Mennonite Church has been structurally impaired at multiple levels. Its internal and external boundaries have been ruptured. There is fusion and enmeshment, on the one hand, and isolation and emotional cut-off, on the other. The accountabilities for the abuse and its aftermath are unclear and disordered. The system has been in acute runaway. At some points it was not clear whether it would survive. Power has been seriously imbalanced, functioning in a victimizing and chaotic manner; there has been little cooperative and accountable power. Power struggles have centered in conflict over which values would predominate in their communal life and who would control the mechanisms for responding to the crisis. The search for love and justice paradoxically led to enmity and further domination and marginalization of the survivors. The vitality of this creative congregation and many of its multi-talented members has been discounted and paralyzed. Much has gone underground. There have been many transactional impasses, expressed in frozen roles, tangled messages, and disagreement about the rules by which the crisis would be handled. It has been difficult to identify strategic interventions by which love might be increased and justice become redemptive. The preoccupation with the need to increase love and justice in its own ranks has inhibited the congregation's ability to further its mission to promote the sanctity of life and ecological partnership through its opposition to the nuclear bomb plant nearby. Much has been lost, and the struggle to rebuild continues.

TOWARD FURTHER TRANSFORMATION

This congregation inspired me with its courage and its ability to name and share its pain. The bonds of commitment to the church and one another were deep; people who left still had strong feelings toward the church and many of its members. The particular strengths of the members of the congregation in relation to their recovery process were many: They agreed to face and work through rather than deny or avoid their experience; there was individual courage to confront and support all parties, as well as corporate agreement to study and understand their experience, and to help others learn from it; they suspended the minister from pastoral duties pending further investigation, and later requested (or accepted) his resignation when it became clear that his ministry was not viable; there has been an ongoing resolve to remain out of fellowship with him pending genuine accountability on his part; they established a fund to help restore the victims, and they retained consultants to study the church and to help it work through its trauma; the congregation has rebuilt its leadership structure, and is determined to survive and overcome. Members have contributed to helping their Conference build policies for responding to similar allegations in other churches. In all these respects, they have responded strategically to their crisis in a contextually creative manner.

The congregation has made some mistakes as well. It failed to request written charges from the survivors. The deacons, the original study group, and strong individuals were too responsible for the flow of information and the mode of response; other structures were over-looked, negated, or bypassed. They did not set up a due process procedure early enough, and the consultants they hired were not invited to be centrally involved in shaping a comprehensive response of the church. They were only available on an elective basis to individual members who chose to work with them. There was not a clearly identified survivors' support and advocacy group, nor regularized structures of support for the minister during the investigation.

There was great disagreement in naming the problem, which led to intense conflict and disagreement over who was responsible, and for what. This contributed to secondary victimization by the congregation, and to the polarization and individualization that subsequently took place. There was confusion about the relationship of accountability to forgiveness, and no mechanism for regulating communication and information. The Conference was basically ineffectual in providing support and guidance, leading to further scapegoating of the survivors and a sense of abandonment by many of the parishioners. At the price of suppressing painful feelings and issues, there was a premature desire to move on. There has been a tendency to "blame the victims" for not healing faster, for "holding on too long." There has been no clear way to process the grief over the loss of the minister and to express the legitimate appreciation many have of his ministry. Nor has there been a way to grieve the loss of the members who left. Hidden loyalties and emotional cut-off persists. There is no long-term structure to normalize this event as an ongoing part of the congregation's history: too much energy has been focused prematurely upon "getting it behind us and moving on."

The ministry of care from a psychosystems viewpoint seeks to promote organizational integrity and transactional effectiveness. It works to enhance synergistic power arrangements and to actualize harmonious value orientations. It strives to help symptomatic situations discover a vital creativity by which an increase in love, justice, and ecological partnership might come about. In the case of Suburban Mennonite Church, for the recovery and rebuilding phase to move from paralyzed to vital creativity a focused responsiveness to four specific strategies is necessary.

First, for greater organizational integrity to emerge, there must be communal action to incorporate this event and its ongoing effects into the liturgical and official life of the congregation. Though much healing has indeed taken place, there is an ongoing tendency to disown the pain and the truth of the tragedy in the congregation's history. Instead, it must be defined as a part of who the congregation is, not as something to get over as though it never happened. Cobb is correct. The context with the greatest integrity is the context that can vitally contain the most contrast. "A rich and mature experience is one in which such feelings as pain and joy, hope and fear, anger and penitence all coexist in a complex whole rather than one in which they simply displace each other."[13] In order to incorporate the experience of abuse into their life in a more vital way, it would be desirable to have an annual worship service focusing upon confession, remorse, and hope. This will do much to stop the hidden power of cut-off feelings and discounted realities. Naming the congregation in its write-ups will also help break the denial process and release latent internal healing resources. It will also make it possible for further assistance to arise from the external environment, as well as to help other congregations better face similar situations in their own ranks.

Second, for values to become harmonized, there must be corporate expression of appreciation for the survivors and a primary commitment to seeking justice on their behalf. This will help resolve the polarization discussed above, and will help the congregation reconnect with its historic commitment to justice-making in the public arena. Such networking and "faithworking" can produce vitality and renewed vision. It is crucial that the congregation affirm the survivors for breaking the silence and to be clear that they were *not* responsible for the minister's offense. The congregation must clarify accountabilities and neutralize the abuses of power by confessing its own sin of secondary victimization. It must support the development of agential power on the part of the survivors by seeking their guidance about how best to help them with their recovery process. Above all, it is important to stop discounting the survivors' agential power and active creativity by asking them to heal at the congregation's pace. The survivors must be supported as partners and affirmed in their healing process, feeling the congregation's cooperation rather than coercion.

Third, for there to be increased contextual vitality and ongoing recovery, an intentional and comprehensive corporate healing plan needs to be established. Transactions dare not remain at the present level of impasse. Roles, messages, and rules need continual modification. There are three dimensions to developing an intentional plan for recovery. First, there needs to be an ongoing invitation for people openly to share thoughts, feelings, hearsay information, and opinions at the monthly Church Council meeting. This should be built into the meeting for at least a three-year period. By putting it here, the congregation would be saying that this healing process is central rather than peripheral to its life. It also gives people time to come forward at their own pace. Finally, it undercuts the rumor, gossip, and secret alliances that have built up in the congregation.

The second dimension is a congregation-wide workshop on the sexual abuse of power, to be required of all current leaders and officers. Such a workshop can help pull together information and focus understanding. By requiring all officers to attend, it can help build a more united leadership and undercut some of the residual polarization in the congregation.

The third dimension is to actively contact all who left the church to find out why they left and seek to gain a reconciled closure. Such an approach will help resolve grief, dissolve hidden loyalties, and minister to those who left with unattended wounds.

Fourth, for redemptive justice to emerge there need to be corporate guidelines for requesting genuine accountability from the offending minister. This requires a letter to him from the congregation stating that they have appreciated his leadership and grieve the situation under which he left. There needs to be a clear statement that he is responsible for breaking the integrity of the pastoral relationship by sexualizing his ministry to the survivors and that he must make public acknowledgment of this offense and his full responsibility for it. He must also provide evidence of genuine remorse for the pain his actions caused others and provide evidence of repentance or fundamental change. There must also be meaningful and realistic restitution to the victims and to the congregation for the emotional and financial costs incurred by his actions. When these things have taken place—through a liaison committee, and with no direct contact with the survivors without their permission—then the background work for a reconciled relationship to the congregation will be in place.

It is important that the congregation commit to these steps serially. Its tendency has been to debate the merits of the fourth step, rather than to begin with the earlier steps. To do so gives too much power to the offending minister and perpetuates the tensions of the polarities outlined above. Beginning with the first step and proceeding accordingly will lead the congregation to the place where it can effectively respond to the explicit justice-seeking dimensions of the fourth stage.

CONCLUSION

Suburban Mennonite Church has implemented all of these strategic recommendations. Informal reports have indicated that they have been helpful. The offending minister has not responded to calls for accountability. All the survivors have left the congregation. Persons who have left have been contacted and there is greater closure. The church has gained new membership and has reengaged its outreach mission, though to a lesser degree than before the crisis. The new pastoral leadership is established and accepted, and there has been broader lay leadership. The congregation has shared its identity and its story with others. Though its losses are grievous, there is genuine hope for a stronger congregation in the future. There is greater organizational integrity, more shared power, and an increasing synchronicity of values. Transactional processes are more positive and there is a greater sense of vitality in the church.

The ministry of care, when informed by the prophets and contemporary liberation theologies and family systems thought, provides resources to increase love, justice, and ecological partnership throughout the creation and covenantal matrix. This model of care offers resources for helping congregations such as Suburban Mennonite Church recover individually and corporately from its experience of sexual abuse by a beloved pastor. It offers perspectives to help individuals gain power in relation to their own symptomatic situations. It assists couples and families to maintain their commitments and to find fulfillment in their relationships. Its concepts and methodologies also have relevance for the interplay of individuals, families, and congregations with the larger systems with which they interact. Its scope ranges from the cup of cold water given to individuals in desperate straits, to making a new heaven and a new earth. Psychosystemic care seeks no less than the joyful transformation of persons and worlds, and of the interplay between them.

DIAGNOSTIC OUTLINE

Symptom	*Goal*
Contextual Impairment	Contextual Integrity
Inadequate boundaries	Intact boundaries
Disordered hierarchies	Accountable hierarchies
Runaway systems	Reliable feedback
Power Imbalances	Synergistic Power
Victimizing/chaotic power	Cooperative power
Unaccountable/intractable	Accountable/flexible
Exclusive/inaccessible	Shared/accessible
Destructive Value Conflicts	Synchronized Value Outlooks
Lovelessness/enmity	Love/partnership
Toward self	With self
estrangement	reconciliation
denigration	affirmation
domination	sharing
Toward neighbor	With neighbor
enmeshment/isolation	participation
double standard	single standard
vocational malaise	focused concern

Toward God	With God
indifference	trust
idolatry	faith
despair	hope
Injustice	Justice
Domination	Liberation
Marginalization	Participation
Abuse	Nurture
Ecological exploitation	Ecological partnership
Humanocentrism	Ecocentrism
Economic Determination	Economic planning
Acquisitiveness/greed	Relinquishment and sharing
Vitiated Creativity	Vital Creativity
Discounted creativity	Celebrated creativity
Paralyzed creativity	Active creativity
Underground creativity	Visible creativity
Transactional Impasses	Transactional Effectiveness
Frozen roles	Flexible roles
Collusion	Interdependent
Scapegoating	Shared Responsibility
Triangulating	Differentiating
Tangled messages	Energizing messages
Avoid conflict	Affirm conflict
Double-binding	Non-binding
"You" messages	"I" messages
Disparate Rules	Congruent rules
Covert rules	Overt rules
Oppositional stance	Cooperative stance
Imposed rules	Negotiated rules

NOTES

INTRODUCTION

1. Harry James Cargas and Bernard Lee, eds., *Religious Experience and Process Theology* (New York: Paulist Press, 1976), p. xiv.

2. John Patton, *Pastoral Counseling: A Ministry of the Church* (Nashville: Abingdon Press, 1983), pp. 117-18.

3. *Knight, Death and the Devil* can be found in H. W. Janson, *History of Art* (Englewood Cliffs, N.J.: Prentice-Hall, 1964), p. 391. Picasso's *Three Musicians* is the 1926 edition. It is on display in the Metropolitan Museum of Art in New York City.

4. See Beverly W. Harrison, *Making the Connections: Essays in Feminist Social Ethics* (Boston: Beacon Press, 1985); Anne Wilson Schaef, *Women's Reality: An Emerging Female System in White Male Society* (New York: Harper & Row, 1986); Jean Baker Miller, M.D., *Toward a New Psychology of Women* (Boston: Beacon Press, 1977); and Archie Smith, Jr., *The Relational Self: Ethics and Therapy from a Black Church Perspective* (Nashville: Abingdon Press, 1982). For an overview of ethical analyses and responses to the culture of dominance and subordination, see Dana W. Wilbanks, "Church as Sign and Agent of Transformation," presented at the Ecumenical Symposium on the Church's Public Role: Retrospect and Prospect, Princeton Theological Seminary, September 1990.

5. Archie Smith (*The Relational Self*) and Charlotte and Howard Clinebell have incorporated these perspectives in print. See Charlotte H. Clinebell, *Counseling for Liberation* (Philadelphia: Fortress Press, 1976); Howard Clinebell, *Basic Types of Pastoral Care & Counseling: Resources for the Ministry of Healing and Growth* (Nashville: Abingdon Press, 1984). Bonny Dillon and Gail Unterberger have written dissertations related to these themes. To date, their work has not appeared in print. Bonny K. Dillon, "Contributions of Selected Feminist Theologians and Feminist Psychoanalytic Theorists to Pastoral Psychotherapy" (Ph.D. diss., Southern Baptist Theological Seminary, 1987); Gail Unterberger, "Through the Lens of Feminine Psychology and Feminine Theology: A Theoretical Model for Pastoral Counseling" (Ph.D. diss., School of Theology at Claremont, 1990).

6. The recipients of care shall be referred to as careseekers in the remainder of this book. The preferred term would be "parishioners," but religious care is provided to many nonparishioners, or outside the parish context altogether. The common terms, "client," or,

"patient," are problematic because neither adequately reflects the historic covenantal relationship between believers, and between the minister and his or her "charges." Likewise, the technical term, "shepherding," is not adequate inasmuch as it is archaic. Further, it would be infelicitous to refer to persons seeking care from a "shepherd" as "sheep." And while the term, "careseeker," does not grasp the covenantal elements of the heritage, neither does it distort them by ordering them from an archaic perspective or from nonreligious perspectives such as medicine or the larger contemporary professional paradigm.

7. On March 12, 1991, the United States Judiciary Committee reported that the United States "is the most violent nation on earth." The report indicated that Americans rob, rape, and kill each other at a rate that surpasses every other country that keeps these statistics. It is increasingly likely that Americans will be victims of violence. Since 1960 the population has grown 41 percent, while violent crime has increased 516 percent. About 200 persons are victimized each hour in the U.S. today, compared to 35 in 1960. *The Denver Post*, March 13, 1991.

8. See Howard J. Clinebell, Jr., *Basic Types of Pastoral Care and Counseling* and William Hulme, *Pastoral Care Come of Age* (Nashville, Abingdon Press, 1970).

9. Robert N. Bellah et al., *Habits of the Heart: Individualism and Commitment in American Life* (New York: Harper & Row, 1985).

10. This will be developed more fully below. See also Larry Kent Graham, "Prophetic Pastoral Caretaking: A Psychosystemic Approach to Symptomatology," *Journal of Psychology and Christianity* 8, no. 1 (1989): 49-60.

11. Professor Karen Lebacqz of the Pacific School of Religion in Berkeley, California, gave a wonderful address on this subject, titled "How Do We Act?," at the AAPC convention in Portland, Oregon, 1988. It has not been published.

12. The characteristics of a unique pastoral perspective, or pastoral perspectives, on the ministry of care have yet to be fully identified or consensually validated. The recently published *Dictionary of Pastoral Care and Counseling*, ed. Rodney J. Hunter (Nashville: Abingdon Press, 1990) both reveals this fermentation, and begins to overcome it. See Rodney J. Hunter, "What Is Pastoral Theology? Insights from Eight Years of Shepherding the *Dictionary of Pastoral Care and Counseling*," *Journal of Pastoral Theology* 1, (Summer, 1991): 35-52.

13. See David W. Augsburger, *Pastoral Counseling Across Cultures* (Philadelphia: The Westminster Press, 1986), p. 31.

14. The classical tasks of healing, sustaining, guiding, and reconciling are discussed in William A. Clebsch and Charles R. Jaekel, *Pastoral Care in Historical Perspective* (New York: Harper & Row, 1964); and Seward Hiltner, *Preface to Pastoral Theology* (New York: Abingdon Press, 1958). For attention to the prophetic dimensions, see Edward P. Wimberly and Anne S. Wimberly, *Liberation and Human Wholeness: The Conversion Experiences of Black People in Slavery and Freedom* (Nashville: Abingdon Press, 1986); Smith, *The Relational Self*; and Graham, "Prophetic Pastoral Caretaking."

15. My understanding of pastoral theology grows most directly out of the work of Seward Hiltner, particularly his *Preface to Pastoral Theology* (Abingdon Press, 1959). In Hiltner's view, pastoral theology draws theological conclusions and develops theory and practice for ministry from reflecting upon the process of shepherding in the light of "cognate secular knowledge." I agree with Hiltner's view that pastoral theology is a subdiscipline within practical theology, which, in turn, is a branch of theology.

16. Don S. Browning's *Religious Ethics and Pastoral Care* (Philadelphia: Fortress Press, 1983); and his *The Moral Context of Pastoral Care* (Philadelphia: Westminster Press, 1976); and Howard Clinebell's *Basic Types of Pastoral Care and Counseling*, have contributed to bringing personal and social ethical perspectives more clearly into the theory and practice of pastoral care and counseling. Their contributions have been of great importance in the field, and of help to me. However, neither of them writes as a pastoral theologian in the way I am thinking of the term, and neither draws upon systemic perspectives in the way I attempt in this book. Roger Fallot, "On Narcissism and Post-Narcissism: Psychology and Theology in Context," *Pastoral Psychology* 33 (Summer 1985): 255-66, has drawn upon systemic resources to introduce cultural resources into pastoral theology and to interpret narcissism from a pastoral-theological perspective.

17. Nancy Chodorow, *The Reproduction of Mothering: Psychoanalysis and the Sociology of Gender* (Berkeley: University of California Press, 1978); and Joanna Rogers Macy, *Despair and Personal Power in the Nuclear Age* (Philadelphia: New Society Publishing, 1983).

18. Pastoral care and counseling/psychotherapy and pastoral theology have most consistently relied upon psychoanalytic and humanistic-existentialist personality theories and psychotherapies for this part of their work. In their original development, these theories were concerned with the impact of social reality on psychological function and with the implications of their viewpoints for social change. However, for a variety of reasons, the social dimensions of these approaches have been neglected in favor of intrapsychic and interpersonal emphases. For a fuller discussion of the social history of personality theory, see Philip Rieff, *The Triumph of the Therapeutic* (New York: Harper & Row, 1966); Russell Jacoby, *Repression of Psychoanalysis: Otto Fenichel and the Political Freudians* (New York: Basic Books, 1983); Sherry Turkel, *Psychoanalytic Politics: Freud's French Revolution* (New York: Basic Books, 1978); and Robert Bellah and others, *Habits of the Heart.*

19. Rebecca S. Chopp, *The Praxis of Suffering: An Interpretation of Liberation and Political Theology* (New York: Orbis Books, 1986); and D. L. Petersen, "Introduction: Ways of Thinking About Israel's Prophets," in *Prophecy in Israel: Search for Identity*, ed. D. L. Petersen (Philadelphia: Fortress Press, 1987).

1. TRANSFORMING CARE

1. Martin Buber, *Between I and Thou* (New York: Charles Scribner's Sons, 1959), p. 63.

2. The works of Reinhold Niebuhr were influential representatives of this point of view in theology. See Reinhold Niebuhr, *Moral Man and Immoral Society* (New York: Charles Scribner's Sons, 1932) and *The Nature and Destiny of Man*, vol. I (New York: Charles Scribner's Sons, 1964), pp. 55-60. The self-actualization theories of Carl Rogers, *On Becoming a Person* (Boston: Houghton Mifflin, 1961), were psychological influences.

3. It commonly takes up to seven attempts for women to leave violent situations. For a fuller discussion of pastoral care in these circumstances, see Rita Lou Clarke, *Pastoral Care of Battered Women* (Philadelphia: The Westminster Press, 1986).

4. For a description of individual egoism as an ethical stance, see Don S. Browning, *Religious Ethics and Pastoral Care*, Theology and Pastoral Care (Philadelphia: Fortress Press, 1983). For a description of expressive individualism, see Robert N. Bellah et al, *Habits of the Heart: Individualism and Commitment in American Life* (New York: Harper & Row, 1985).

5. See Carole Gilligan, *In a Different Voice: Psychological Theory and Women's Development* (Cambridge, Mass.: Harvard University Press, 1982) and her discussion of this point. In her feminist-based ethics, she argues against the views in masculine-dominated personality theory that selfhood proceeds from autonomy to relationship, as in the case of Erikson. A feminist reading of psychology understands persons to be innately rather than sequentially relational.

6. Derald Wing Sue, "Eliminating Cultural Oppression in Counseling: Toward a General Theory," *Journal of Counseling Psychology* 25, no. 5 (1978): 419-28.

7. Ibid., p. 419.

8. Ibid., p. 422.

9. Ibid.

10. Ibid., p. 425.

11. I have already referred to the works of Bellah, Turkle, and Rieff. In addition, see Christopher Lasch, *The Culture of Narcissism: American Life in the Age of Diminishing Expectations* (New York: Warner Books, 1979); and Seymour L. Halleck, *The Politics of Therapy* (New York: Science House, 1971).

12. See E. Brooks Holifield, *A History of Pastoral Care in America: From Salvation to Self-Realization* (Nashville: Abingdon Press, 1983).

13. See Browning, *Religious Ethics and Pastoral Care;* see also Don S. Browning, *The Moral Context of Pastoral Care* (Philadelphia: Westminster Press, 1976).

14. Gaylord Noyce, "Has Ministry's Nerve Been Cut by the Pastoral Counseling Movement?" *The Christian Century* 95 (February 1978): 103-6.

15. See Gordon E. Jackson, *Pastoral Care and Process Theology* (Washington, D.C.: University Press of America, 1983).

16. See James N. Lapsley, Jr., *Salvation and Health: The Interlocking Processes of Life* (Philadelphia: Westminster, 1972).

17. See John Patton and Brian H. Childs, *Christian Marriage and Family: Caring for Our Generations* (Nashville: Abingdon Press, 1988).

18. See Charles V. Gerkin, *The Living Human Document: Re-Visioning Pastoral Counseling in a Hermeneutical Mode* (Nashville: Abingdon Press, 1984). See also his *Widening the Horizons: Pastoral Responses to a Fragmented Society* (Philadelphia: Westminster, 1986).

19. See Archie Smith, Jr., *The Relational Self: Ethics and Therapy from a Black Church Perspective* (Nashville: Abingdon Press, 1982).

20. Howard J. Clinebell, Jr., "Toward Envisioning the Future of Pastoral Counseling and AAPC," *The Journal of Pastoral Care* 37, no. 3 (1983): 189ff.

21. See Howard J. Clinebell, Jr., *Basic Types of Pastoral Care and Counseling: Resources for the Ministry of Healing and Growth,* 2nd ed. (Nashville: Abingdon Press, 1986).

22. Ibid., p. 29.

23. Some thinkers use the concept of "hierarchy" to describe this feature of systems. I have tried to avoid this term as much as possible because of its close relationship to the domination and subordination paradigm. However, I also believe that hierarchies may appropriately exist without functioning oppressively. See Chapter 9 for a fuller discussion of this idea.

24. The concept of reciprocal interaction does not imply equal responsibility for what happens in a system. Since systems are organized differentially, there are varying degrees of power, which implies varying levels of responsibility. This is especially important to recognize in cases of physical and sexual abuse, in order not to wrongly blame victims and protect perpetrators from accountability.

25. Seward Hiltner, more than anyone, tried to locate the function of caring within a larger view of ministry, but he did not fully spell out what he meant by ministry and its larger purposes. Though he brilliantly saw the interconnections between the communicating, organizing, and shepherding functions of ministry—and how the shepherding function was a reciprocal partner and contributor to other branches of theology—he did not similarly relate the functions of ministry, and particularly the shepherding function, to a self-conscious view of the larger purposes of ministry. As a consequence, Hiltner and some of his students have contributed to an increasing isolation of pastoral caretaking from the larger purposes of ministry. This is ironic, since Hiltner was always a vociferous opponent of those who wanted to make pastoral care and pastoral counseling special branches of ministry. It seems to me that his argument would have been strengthened had he based it on a fuller theory of ministry.

More than strictly theological influences were at work to keep pastoral caretaking separate from general ministry. The strong reliance upon personality sciences and secular modes of helping were initially opposed by theological educators and church officials, and utilized by pastoral caretaking specialists as a basis for rejecting or reinterpreting ministry itself. Practitioners became increasingly estranged from the church, and in some cases still are. During the secularization of specialized ministry in the 1960s and 1970s, there was little sustained need to develop a theory of pastoral care that related itself to a general theory of ministry. Emphasis upon new linguistic expressions of faith, new settings for ministry, being a "man for others" and following the agenda of the world rather than imposing our own, and generally rejecting the tradition as oppressive and anomalous worked against constructing a positive basis for ministry in general and pastoral caretaking in particular.

There has been a swing back to re-examine and broaden the theological foundations of ministry and pastoral caretaking. Paul Pruyser, John Patton, Don Browning and Thomas Oden have all pointed in this direction, and have made beginning attempts. However, none of these persons has defined ministry as I have, and none has drawn upon systemic perspectives to the degree that I have. See Paul Pruyser, *The Minister as Diagnostician: Personal Problems in Pastoral Perspective* (Philadelphia: Westminster, 1976); John Patton, *From Ministry to Theology* (1990); Thomas Oden, *Pastoral Theology: Essentials for Ministry* (San

Francisco: Harper & Row, 1983); and Don Browning's two books, *Religious Ethics and Pastoral Care* and *The Moral Context of Pastoral Care.*

26. H. Richard Niebuhr, *The Purpose of the Church and Its Ministry: Reflection on the Aims of Theological Education,* in collaboration with Daniel Day Williams and James M. Gustafson (New York: Harper, 1956).

27. See the work of D. Preman Niles, *Resisting the Threats to Life* (Geneva, Switzerland: WCC Publications, 1989). The World Council of Churches has recently devoted much attention to the theme of justice, peace, and the integrity of creation in an edition of *The Ecumenical Review* 41, no. 4 (1989).

28. Paul Tillich particularly underscores this dimension. See *Love Power and Justice: Ontological Analyses and Ethical Applications* (New York: Oxford University Press, 1954); and *The Shaking of the Foundations: Sermons* (New York: C. Scribner's Sons, 1948), especially the homily, "You Are Accepted," pp. 153-64.

29. Daniel Day Williams points to this quality of love. I also find it implicit in process and liberation theologies. See Williams, *The Spirit and the Forms of Love* (New York: Harper & Row, 1968).

30. This is largely a feminist-based interpretation, inasmuch as it emphasizes right relationships rather than equal rights or principles of fairness. See Jane Cary Peck and Jeanne Gallo, "JPIC: A Critique from a Feminist Perspective," *The Ecumenical Review* 41, no. 4 (October 1989): 573-81.

31. On the relationship of justice to peace, see Peck and Gallo, "JPIC: A Critique," 573-81; George E. Tinker, "The Integrity of Creation: Restoring Trinitarian Balance," *The Ecumenical Review* 41, no. 4 (October 1989): 527-536; and Perry Yoder, *Shalom: The Bible's Word for Salvation, Justice and Peace* (Newton, Kans.: Faith and Life Press, 1987).

32. The concept "integrity of creation" is utilized in the World Council of Churches to galvanize worldwide efforts on behalf of the earth. The term has been criticized for its static connotations, minimizing the co-creative nature of the human-world partnership. For this reason, I prefer the term "ecological partnership" to denote the mutually-enhancing and transforming potential that exists between humans and their environment.

33. Indeed, the tragic case of the murder of Chico Mendes, a Brazilian rubber-tapper, indicates the inherent connection between love, justice, and the quality of the environment. See Alex Shoumatof, *The World Is Burning* (Boston: Little, Brown & Co., 1990).

34. See Harvey Sindima, "Community of Life," *The Ecumenical Review* 41, no. 4 (October 1989): 537-51.

35. Pastoral care has been the generic term for any caring ministry to persons, as well as the term for the temporary specialized care provided to careseekers. Pastoral counseling and pastoral psychotherapy have been regarded as specialized pastoral care services provided on a longer-term basis to careseekers. It is a debatable point whether there is any difference between what is provided in pastoral counseling and pastoral psychotherapy, or whether political and symbolic issues underlie the distinction. For the purposes of this book, the terms are used interchangeably to refer to the long-term contractual arrangement between the pastoral caretaker and the careseeker that exists in order to remove or resolve intractable problems of living on the part of the careseeker(s).

In order to minimize some of the linguistic confusion connected with the various uses of the terms related to the ministry of care, in the pages that follow I will use the generic terms, "pastoral caretaking," "caretaking" and/or "the ministry of care" to refer to any direct service to suffering persons, without reference to the context of ministry in which such service occurs. This will replace the generic term "pastoral care," and the generic hybrid, "pastoral care and counseling." When it is important to refer to the specific sub-specialty or ministry discipline in which caretaking occurs, it shall be designated either as "pastoral care" or as "pastoral counseling/psychotherapy."

36. See Smith, *The Relational Self*; Miriam Greenspan, *A New Approach to Women and Therapy* (New York: McGraw-Hill Book Co., 1983); and Paolo Freire, *Pedagogy of the Oppressed,* trans. Myra Bergman Ramos (New York: Continuum, 1983).

37. See Alfred North Whitehead, *Adventures of Ideas* (New York: The Macmillan Co., 1933); and Jackson, *Pastoral Care and Process Theology,* pp. 99-121.

2. A PSYCHOSYSTEMIC VIEW OF THE WORLD

1. H. Richard Niebuhr, *The Meaning of Revelation* (New York: Macmillan, 1941), p. 52.
2. See John B. Cobb, Jr., "The Political Implications of Whitehead's Philosophy," in *Process Philosophy and Social Thought,* ed. J. B. Cobb, Jr., and W. W. Schroeder (Chicago: Center for the Scientific Study of Religion, 1981).
3. John B. Cobb, Jr. and David Ray Griffin, *Process Theology: An Introductory Exposition* (Philadelphia: Westminster Press, 1976), p. 23.
4. Alfred North Whitehead, *Process and Reality* (New York: Macmillan Co., 1929), p. 521.
5. Delwin Brown, *To Set at Liberty: Christian Faith and Human Freedom* (New York: Maryknoll, 1981), p. 24.
6. Cobb and Griffin, *Process Theology,* p. 82.
7. Because of its submicroscopic nature, the actual entity is not drawn on the chart on p. 54.
8. Erik Erikson's work on the psychosocial development of trust versus mistrust demonstrates this interaction quite well. See his *Childhood and Society* (New York: Norton, 1950).
9. Heidi Hartman, "The Family as the Locus of Gender, Class and Political Struggle: The Example of Housework," *Signs: Journal of Women in Culture and Society* 6, no. 3 (1981): 366-94; Donna Hodgins Berardo, Constance L. Shehan, and Gerald R. Leslie, "A Residue of Tradition: Jobs, Careers, and Spouses' Time in Housework," *Journal of Marriage and Family* 49 (May 1987): 381-90.
10. See chapter 3.
11. The epic study of "children in crisis" by Robert Coles traces the differential effects of one's social setting upon self-esteem, attitudes toward the world, values and life-styles, family organization, religious beliefs, and political commitments. See also Coles, *The Spiritual Lives of Children* (Boston: Houghton Mifflin, 1990).
12. Niebuhr, *The Meaning of Revelation,* p. 52.
13. Paul Rabinow is helpful in distinguishing society and culture. See Paul Rabinow "Humanism as Nihilism: The Bracketing of Truth and Seriousness in American Cultural Anthropology," in *Social Sciences as Moral Inquiry,* ed. Norma Haan, Robert Bellah, and Paul Rabinow (New York: Columbia University, 1983).
14. Pamela D. Couture has written an insightful book on the impact of public policy on pastoral care. See *Blessed Are the Poor? Women's Poverty, Family Policy, and Practical Theology* (Nashville: Abingdon Press, 1991).
15. See above chapter 1, pp. 32-38.
16. Sigmund Freud and Ernest Becker build strong arguments that the threat of death profoundly shapes our personal, cultural, and religious lives. And, while I am less inclined to reduce character and culture to defensive reactions to finitude, there can be little doubt about its impact on these realities. See Sigmund Freud, *The Future of an Illusion,* trans. and ed. James Strachey (New York: Norton, 1975); and Ernest Becker, *The Denial of Death* (New York: Free Press, 1973).
17. See literature from ecofeminists to detail the relationship between patriarchal culture and responses to nature: Ynestra King, *Rocking the Ship of State: Toward a Feminist Peace Politics* (Boulder, Colo.: Westview Press, 1989); Teal Willoughby, "Mother Earth: Ecofeminism from a Jungian Perspective" (Ph.D. diss., Iliff School of Theology and the University of Denver, 1990).
18. See Brown, *To Set at Liberty.*
19. David Ray Griffin provides an insightful discussion of bi-polar power in *God, Power and Evil: A Process Theodicy* (Philadelphia: Westminster, 1976). See also Bernard Loomer's classic essay on two types of relational power for an application of the concept of bi-polar power to human interactions: Bernard Loomer, "Two Conceptions of Power," *Process Studies* 6, no. 1 (Spring 1976): 30. See also chapter 3, pp. 81-83, below.
20. Phyllis Chesler's *Women and Madness* (Garden City, N.Y.: Doubleday, 1972) is an

insightful discussion of the triple-bind women are in relative to power: if they represent only receptive power they are less than what is regarded as healthy for mature humans; if they become depressed as a consequence of their social situation, they are regarded as ill; if they defy their social situation, they are deviant.

21. I am greatly influenced by feminist family therapists who believe that traditional family therapy has a sexist bias with respect to power arrangements between men and women. My analysis of power reconstructs family therapy to take account of patriarchal biases. I have been especially informed by Monic McGoldrick et al., eds., *Women in Families: A Framework for Family Therapy* (New York: W. W. Norton & Company, 1989) and Marianne Walters et al., eds., *The Invisible Web: Gender Patterns in Family Relationships* (New York: Guilford Press, 1988).

22. This aphorism has been attributed to Ludwig Feuerbach, the nineteenth-century philosopher.

23. Gordon Jackson's discussion of God as an "ally" in the pastoral care process is quite helpful on this point. Gordon Jackson, *Pastoral Care and Process Theology* (Washington, D.C.: University Press of America, 1983), pp. 56, 189.

3. THE INDIVIDUAL IN CARE

1. Karl Barth, *Church Dogmatics,* vol. 3, no. 24, authorized trans. G. T. Thomson (Edinburgh: T. & T. Clark, 1961), p. 248.

2. Malcolm X, *The Autobiography of Malcolm X* (New York: Grove Press, 1965), p. 164.

3. I am using the concepts self, psyche, and soul interchangeably at this point. Distinctions will be clarified below.

4. Sigmund Freud, *Group Psychology and the Analysis of the Ego,* trans. and ed. James Strachey (New York: W. W. Norton & Company, Inc., 1959), p. 61.

5. Ibid.

6. Reinhold Niebuhr, *Moral Man and Immoral Society* (New York, N.Y.: Charles Scribner's Sons, 1960), p. xii.

7. Reinhold Niebuhr, *The Nature and Destiny of Man,* vol. I (New York, N.Y.: Charles Scribner's Sons, 1964), pp. 55-60.

8. See Catherine Keller, *From a Broken Web: Separation, Sexism, and Self* (Boston: Beacon Press, 1986), for an illuminating discussion of the separative motif as a dominant interpretation of selfhood in Western religion, mythology, psychology, and culture. She contrasts this with a connective self, which she finds latent in certain psychologies and dominant in feminist reconstruction of the meaning of selfhood.

9. Robert Bellah et al., *Habits of the Heart: Individualism and Community in American Life* (New York, N.Y.: Harper & Row, 1985), p. 139.

10. Ibid., p. 141.

11. John B. Cobb, Jr. and David Ray Griffin, *Process Theology: An Introductory Exposition* (Philadelphia: Westminster Press, 1976), p. 82.

12. Wilhelm Reich, *Character Analysis* (New York: Orgone Institute Press, 1949), pp. 67-77.

13. See Ernest Becker, *The Denial of Death* (New York: Free Press, 1973).

14. Salvador Minuchin, Bernice L. Rosman, Lester Baker, *Psychosomatic Families: Anorexia Nervosa in Context* (Cambridge: Harvard University Press, 1978), pp. 23-52.

15. See Mark Pilisuk and Susan Hillier Parks, *The Healing Web: Social Networks and Human Survival* (Hanover and London: University Press of New England, 1986).

16. Ibid., p. 44. See also the work of J. K. Kiecolt-Glaser et al., "Stress and the Transformation of Lymphocytes by Epstein-Barr Virus," *Journal of Behavioral Medicine* 7 (1) (1984): 1-12.

17. Pilisuk and Parks, *The Healing Web,* pp. 41ff.

18. I am indebted to A. J. van den Blink of Colgate Rochester Divinity School for this phrase. Van den Blink was a senior colleague in my Ph.D. program and my clinical supervisor in family therapy training at Trinity Counseling Service in Princeton, New

Jersey. He coined the phrase "multiply conjoined" in his excellent dissertation, "The Helping Response: A Study and Critique of Family Therapy with Suggested Implications for Theological Anthropology" (Ph.D. diss., Princeton Theological Seminary, 1972).

19. See Malcolm Malz, *Psychocybernetics* (New York: Simon and Schuster, 1960).

20. *The Collected Works of C. G. Jung: The Structure and Dynamics of the Psyche,* ed. Gerald Adler et al., trans. R. F. Hull, Bollingen Series 20 (Princeton: Princeton University Press, 1960), pp. 254ff; and C. G. Jung, *Aion,* Bollingen Series 20 (Princeton: Princeton University Press, 1960), p. 254.

21. Jung, *Structure and Dynamics of the Psyche,* p. 152.

22. Charles Hampden-Turner, *Maps of the Mind: Charts and Concepts of the Mind and Its Labyrinths* (New York: Macmillan, 1981), p. 94.

23. For a brief, but illuminating discussion of family secrets, see Edwin H. Friedman, *Generation to Generation: Family Process in Church and Synagogue* (New York: Guilford Press, 1985), pp. 52-54.

24. Personal communication with George E. Tinker, Ph.D., Associate Professor of Cross-Cultural Ministries, Iliff School of Theology, Denver, Colorado.

25. The genius of the psychoanalytic tradition, in my mind, lies precisely in its contributions to this question. Concepts such as primary and secondary process, psychosexual and psychosocial development, introjection, projection, internalization, reaction formation, repression, sublimation, transference, fixation, regression, and the like, are fundamentally transactional categories that attempt to delineate the psyche's relationship to itself as well as its relationship to the world in which it lives. These and other terms, point to the dynamic interplay and mutual influence between the structures of the person and between the person and the world. Indeed, the very concept of "psychodynamics" underscores the reality of tension, balance, and interconnections between all of these elements. The psychosystemic view of this book builds on this dynamic interplay, but puts it into a less mechanistic, reductionistic, and separative framework than is generally characteristic of the psychoanalytic tradition.

26. The discussion that follows is based upon Fred Pine, *Developmental Theory and Clinical Process* (New Haven, Conn.: Yale University Press, 1985). See especially chapter 9, "Formation, Expansion and Vulnerability of the Self Experience."

27. T. B. Brazelton,"Mother-Infant Reciprocity" presented at Albert Einstein College of Medicine, New York. N.Y., Cited in Pine, *Developmental Theory and Clinical Process,* p. 115.

28. See Nancy Chodorow, *The Reproduction of Mothering: Psychoanalysis and the Sociology of Gender* (Berkeley: University of California Press, 1978).

29. See Anne Wilson Schaef, *Women's Reality: An Emerging Female System in White Male Society* (New York: Harper & Row, 1986).

30. Loomer's classic distinctions between linear and relational power stand behind this discussion. Linear power is agential power, without the balance of receptive power. My concept of bi-polar power is akin to his interpretation of relational power. Bernard Loomer, "Two Conceptions of Power," *Process Studies,* vol. 6, no. 1 (Spring 1976): 30.

31. We have already examined this in the section on transactional processes in human development. It is also clear that adults who become agents of sexual and domestic violence were typically receptors of this kind of parental power when they were younger. It is very clear in these cases that agency and receptivity are interconnected.

32. Joanna Rogers Macy argues that all of us in the First World are in unconscious despair because we have repressed our rage and helplessness in the face of the threat of nuclear destruction, and that new energy for life comes when we can regain contact with our latent agential powers. See Joanna Rogers Macy, *Despair and Personal Power in the Nuclear Age* (Philadelphia: New Society Publishing, 1983).

33. It is important to underscore that personal power is not the same as privacy. Privacy means withdrawal from the public realm. It includes shutting down or severely constricting one's receptivity and agency in relation to the public arena, while focusing upon the primary world of family, friends, and one's own selfhood. Personal power in the fullest sense involves persons as agents and receptors in all of the structures impacting their being. In my work as pastor and therapist, and my observation as a citizen, those who equate personal power with

privacy paradoxically end up more powerless and victimized by those who exercise (usually agential) power in the public arena.

34. It has always struck me as tragic how a person's agency and receptivity at one level in the system may be loving, generous, open, and even self-sacrificing, while this same person may be demonically brutal toward others when acting as agents of other structures in their systemic universe. One thinks of the loving father, son, and husband who serves as a sadistic torturer of the fathers, sons, and husbands of those marked as enemies of the state or nation.

35. C. Robert Mesle, "Aesthetic Value and Relational Power: An Essay on Personhood" in *Process Studies*, 13, no. 1 (Spring 1983): 59-70.

36. Jerome Frank argues persuasively that all psychotherapy is a process of helping demoralized persons—those whose personal moral and value orientations no longer fit the reality of their worlds—redevelop meaningful value orientations as a foundational condition for personal integration and meaningful behavior. Indeed, he contends that psychotherapy is not morally neutral as it sometimes pretends, but is itself a powerful context in which particular values and moral orientations are brought about through processes of indoctrination, socialization, and persuasion. See Jerome Frank, *Persuasion and Healing: A Comparative Study of Psychotherapy*, rev. ed. (New York: Schocken, 1974).

37. Indeed, it is a major strategy of the oppressor and victimizer to regulate the terms of the discourse and define the values by which human worth and behavior is to be measured. Persons who are overcome by this system of oppression are valued as inferior, weak, or lazy; those who defy it or attempt to change it in some way are valued as misguided, unintelligent, immature, criminal, sick, or treasonous. By so controlling the basis for defining and valuing which human attitudes, roles, and behaviors will be approved or rewarded in the organized structure of oppression, the oppressor uses power coercively to regulate the character of the transactions allowed in the system, and to keep the oppressed in the role of receptor rather than sharing in the creation of values that define the conditions of their own existence. See Phyllis Chesler, *Women and Madness* (Garden City, N.Y.: Doubleday, 1972); Schaef, *Women's Reality;* and Paolo Freire, *Pedagogy of the Oppressed,* trans. Myra Bergman Ramos (New York: Continuum, 1983).

38. Jung, *Aion*, p. 61; and C. G. Jung, *The Portable Jung*, ed. Joseph Campbell (New York: Penguin Books, 1971), pp. 273-300.

39. James N. Lapsley, Jr. uses the concept of personhood to articulate qualitative human becoming in the formation of the personality. He draws upon ego psychology and process theology in developing his views. See James N. Lapsley, *Salvation and Health: The Interlocking Processes of Life* (Philadelphia: Westminster Press, 1972).

40. Loomer, "Two Conceptions of Power," p. 30.

41. It is commonly asserted that Gandhi and King were not as enlightened and heroic in some of their personal relationships as they were in the moral and political arenas which they influenced so dramatically. In the view of psychosystems analysis, it is regrettable that there was not more consistency, but the lack of value congruence at one level does not necessarily negate the positive contributions at another. Since the subsystems in which one lives have relative autonomy, consistency is unlikely, and not always possible or desirable. Certainly, in these cases, however, working for a more just social order would not be inconsistent with transforming problematic personal relationships.

42. Jung, *Structure and Dynamics of the Psyche*, pp. 51, 223.

4. SYMPTOMS, CRISES, AND CHANGE

1. Stephen Crane, "The Blue Hotel," in *The Arbor House Treasury of Great Western Stories*, ed. Martin H. Greenberg and Bill Pronzini (New York: Arbor House, 1982), p. 71.

2. "Eyes on the Prize" (Alexandria, Va.: Blackside, Inc., 1989), PBS video.

3. See James N. Lapsley, Jr., *Salvation and Health: The Interlocking Processes of Life* (Philadelphia: Westminster Press, 1972). See also Issues: discussion papers on issues arising out of the life and work of the World Council of Churches in preparation for its Sixth Assembly, Vancouver, Canada, July 24 to August 10, 1983. Geneva: World Council of

Churches Publication, 1982. See especially Issue Paper Number 4, "Healing and Sharing Life in Community."

4. The work of Ernest Becker is quite helpful on this score. Drawing upon Kierkegaard, Otto Rank, and, to a lesser extent, Freud, he argues that our exploitation of nature as well as all our cultural accomplishments stem from our largely denied terror at our finitude and death. While he does not go so far as to suggest that psychotherapy can in itself resolve this terror, he does suggest that becoming aware of this on a personal and cultural level may reduce the cost we bear in our life-styles and relationships to one another and nature. See Ernest Becker, *The Denial of Death* (New York: Free Press, 1973), and *Escape from Evil* (New York: Free Press, 1975).

5. See above, chapter 3, p. 85.

6. See Miriam Greenspan, *A New Approach to Women and Therapy* (New York: McGraw-Hill Book Co., 1983); and Phyllis Chesler, *Women and Madness* (Garden City, N.Y.: Doubleday, 1972).

7. For a very illuminating discussion of these dynamics, see Jay Haley, *Strategies of Psychotherapy* (New York: Grune and Stratton, 1963).

5. OPENING EARS TO HEAR

1. Sophocles, *Oedipux Rex* in *Tragedy: Play, Theory and Criticism* by Richard Levin (New York: Harcourt, Brace & World, Inc., 1960), p. 3.

2. See Appendix for a diagnostic overview.

3. James Lynch's first well-known book was *The Broken Heart: The Medical Consequences of Loneliness* (New York: Basic Books, 1977). Also see his *The Language of the Heart: The Body's Basic Response to Human Dialogue* (New York: Basic Books, 1985); James J. Lynch et al., "The Effect of Status on Blood Pressure During Verbal Communication," *Journal of Behavioral Medicine* 5, no. 2 (1982): 165-72; James J. Lynch et al., "The Effects of Talking on the Blood Pressure of Hypertensive and Normotensive Individuals," *Psychosomatic Medicine* 43, no. 1 (February 1981): 25-33; and James J. Lynch et al., "Human Speech and Blood Pressure," *The Journal of Nervous and Mental Disease* 168, no. 9 (1980): 526-34.

4. Stuart A. Plummer, "Thoughts Regarding the Meaning of Death," *The Journal of Pastoral Care* 21, no. 1 (March 1967): 29-30.

5. See Donald Capps, *Reframing: A New Method in Pastoral Care* (Minneapolis: Fortress Press, 1990) for a captivating discussion of a variety of ways of using paradox and reframing in pastoral care.

6. See David Kantor and William Lehr, *Inside the Family: Toward a Theory of Family Process* (San Francisco: Jossey-Bass, 1975).

6. DETHRONING THE DEMONIC

1. Jean Baker Miller, *Toward a New Psychology of Women* (Boston: Beacon Press, 1976), p. 17.

2. Dana W. Wilbanks and Ronald H. Stone, *Presbyterians and Peacemaking: Are We Now Called to Resistance?* (New York: Advisory Council on Church and Society, Presbyterian Church, U.S.A., 1985), pp. 16-18.

3. Archie Smith, unpublished lecture delivered at the AAPC Annual Convention, Portland, Oregon, April 1988.

4. See Rollo May, *Love and Will* (New York: Norton, 1969).

5. See Appendix for diagnostic overview. I supervised this pastor briefly.

6. See Murray Bowen, *Family Therapy in Clinical Practice* (New York: Jason Aronson, 1978).

7. Miller, *Toward a New Psychology*, p. 122.

8. See Frantz Fanon, *The Wretched of the Earth*, trans. Constance Farrington (New York: Grove Press, 1968).

9. Mark Pilisuk and Susan Hillier Parks, *The Healing Web: Social Networks and Human Survival* (Hanover and London: University Press of New England, 1986); and Pamela D. Couture, *Blessed Are the Poor? Women's Poverty, Family Policy, and Practical Theology* (Nashville: Abingdon Press, 1991).

10. For a discussion of these issues, see Marianne Riché, "The Systemic Feminist," *The Family Therapy Networker* (May-June 1984): 43-44; and Rachel T. Hare-Mustin, "A Feminist Approach to Family Therapy," *Family Process* 17 (June 1978): 181-94. Marie Fortune, an expert in sexual and domestic violence, reported in personal conversation that many liberal males and feminist women oppose her strong stance regarding the necessity of recognizing the power differentials between careseekers and caretakers. Failure to recognize this differential and to take account of it morally and professionally is to run extreme dangers of further victimizing the vulnerable. For there to be genuine mutuality of consent, there must also be genuine mutuality of power.

11. See above, pp. 99f.

12. These terms are common in the field. See A. J. van den Blink, "The Helping Response: A Study and Critique of Family Therapy with Suggested Implications for Theological Anthropology" (Ph.D. diss., Princeton Theological Seminary, 1972). I am indebted to van den Blink for introducing me to these concepts. The development that follows is largely my own. I highly recommend van den Blink's dissertation as an example of linking theology and ethics to family systems thought and pastoral care.

13. A fuller description of the case of Karen can be found in Larry Kent Graham, "Care of Persons, Care of Worlds: Discovering the Prophetic in the Ministry of Care to Suffering Persons," *Pastoral Psychology* 40, no. 1 (1991).

14. See Malcolm X, *The Autobiography of Malcolm X* (New York: Grove Press, 1965).

15. Jean Baker Miller, *Toward a New Psychology of Women* (Boston: Beacon Press, 1977), p. 117.

16. These points will be discussed further in chapter 10.

17. See Anne Wilson Schaef, *Women's Reality: An Emerging Female System in White Male Society* (New York: Harper & Row, 1986).

18. See Augustus Y. Napier, Ph.D. and Carl A. Whitaker, M.D., *The Family Crucible* (New York: Bantam Books, 1978).

7. LURING TO SHALOM

1. Daniel Day Williams, *The Spirit and the Forms of Love* (New York: Harper & Row, 1968), pp. 244-45.

2. D. Preman Niles, *Resisting the Threats to Life* (Geneva, Switzerland: WCC Publications, 1989), p. 62.

3. Perry B. Yoder, *Shalom: The Bible's Word for Salvation, Justice and Peace* (Newton, Kans.: Faith and Life Press, 1987), p. 18.

4. Ibid., p. 15.

5. Ibid., p. 16.

6. Ibid.

7. Williams, *The Spirit and the Forms*, pp. 245-46.

8. Niles, *Resisting the Threats*, p. 63.

9. Yoder, *Shalom*, p. 45.

10. Williams, *The Spirit and the Forms*, pp. 244-45.

11. Cited in Niles, *Resisting the Threats*, p. 60.

12. Williams, *The Spirit and the Forms*, pp. 114-22.

13. See Paul Tillich, *Love, Power, and Justice: Ontological Analyses and Ethical Applications* (New York: Oxford University Press, 1954).

14. See Murray Bowen, *Family Therapy in Clinical Practice* (New York: Jason Aronson, 1978).

15. See James Nelson, *Embodiment: An Approach to Sexuality and Christian Theology* (Minneapolis: Augsburg, 1978).

16. See Phyllis Chesler, *Women and Madness* (Garden City, N.Y.: Doubleday, 1972).

17. See Frantz Fanon, *The Wretched of the Earth,* trans. Constance Farrington (New York: Grove Press, 1968).

18. One of the clearest examples of the way double standards put persons in an extremely difficult double bind at the core of their selfhood, is found in studies on what therapists determined to be mentally healthy qualities for males and females. The healthy adult was defined in terms of masculine qualities. To be healthy, women had to become like men. But to become like men is to violate what they are expected to be as women. If they remain as they are, they are unhealthy; if they become healthy, they are no longer valued as women. Such a double standard, and the double bind it engenders, not only illustrates a reprehensible expression of lovelessness, but the systemic and cultural character of personal identity and identity development. Thus, as Phyllis Chesler makes so clear, disturbed and underfunctioning women are merely fulfilling the expectations that the culture has for them (see Chesler, *Women and Madness*). See also I. D. Broverman et al., "Sex Role Stereotypes and Clinical Judgments of Mental Health," *Journal of Consulting and Clinical Psychology* 34 (1970): 1-7.

19. Williams, *The Spirit and the Forms,* p. 272.

20. See Merle Jordan, *Taking on the Gods: The Task of the Pastoral Counselor* (Nashville: Abingdon Press, 1986).

21. See Ana Maria Rizutto, *The Birth of the Living God: A Psychoanalytic Study* (Chicago: University of Chicago Press, 1979).

22. See Don S. Browning, *Atonement and Psychotherapy* (Philadelphia: Westminster, 1966). See also, Jordan, *Taking on the Gods.*

23. See John Patton and Brian H. Childs, *Christian Marriage and Family: Caring for Our Generations* (Nashville: Abingdon Press, 1988); John H. Patton, *Is Human Forgiveness Possible?: A Pastoral Care Perspective* (Nashville: Abingdon Press, 1985).

24. See Marie Fortune, *Sexual Violence: The Unmentionable Sin* (New York: The Pilgrim Press, 1983).

25. John Patton's book on forgiveness seems to perpetuate this approach, in spite of his very insightful discussion of shame as central to forgiveness. He does not discuss the need for accountability on the part of the perpetrator; in fact, he seems to think that healing takes place in discovering that one is also a perpetrator of injustice. His overemphasis upon the perspective of the victim minimizes or neglects the role of accountability of the perpetrator in the healing process. His failure to recognize the larger systemic reality of domination/subordination results in his incorrect assumption of equality between the offender and offended. This raises very difficult questions about the relation of justice, mercy, and forgiveness. See Patton, *Is Human Forgiveness Possible?*

26. See chapter 3, pp. 79ff.

27. See Mark Pilisuk and Susan Hillier Parks, *The Healing Web: Social Networks and Human Survival* (Hanover and London: University Press of New England, 1986).

28. See Edward P. Wimberly, *Pastoral Care in the Black Church* (Nashville: Abingdon Press, 1986).

29. See *The Ecumenical Review* 41, no. 4 (October 1989).

30. Charlene Spretnak, "Diversity in Ecofeminism," *The Nation* 246 (April 2, 1988): 475.

31. Alexander Cochburn, "Amazon Symbioses: Social Justice and Environmental Protection," *The Wall Street Journal,* December 29, 1988, A7.

32. Sally Thane Christensen, "Is a Tree Worth a Life?" *Newsweek,* August 5, 1991, pp. 10-11.

33. Ibid.

34. Ibid.

35. See *The Denver Post,* August 5, 1991.

8. RELEASING THE CAPTIVE

1. Natalie Sleeth, *Adventures of the Soul* (Carol Stream, Ill.: Hope Publishing, 1987), p. 18.

2. I am indebted to my colleague Delwin Brown for his interpretation of freedom as

contextual creativity (see Brown, *To Set At Liberty: Christian Faith and Human Freedom* (New York: Maryknoll, 1981), pp. 34ff). According to Brown, "creativity and context are the polar elements of freedom. . . . In process philosophy there is no context that is not creatively appropriated, however small the margin of creativity. Likewise, there is no creativity that escapes the profound weight of the past, its context, as the source and lure for its present becoming." I have expanded his concept of contextual creativity and applied it specifically in relation to the ministry of care and family systems.

3. See above, pp. 18ff.

4. See Lily Pincus, *Death in the Family: The Importance of Mourning* (New York: Pantheon, 1975).

5. See Anne Wilson Schaef, *Women's Reality: An Emerging Female System in White Male Society* (New York: Harper & Row, 1986).

6. See William H. Grier and Price M. Cobbs, *Black Rage* (New York: Bantam Books, 1968).

7. I am indebted to the Rev. Bill Reid-Allen, a Ph.D. candidate in the University of Denver and Iliff School of Theology Pastoral Counseling Program, for helping me connect the prophetic tradition to the experience of grief. The discussion that follows is based upon his insights and research in the writings of Walter Brueggemann.

8. Walter Brueggemann, *The Prophetic Imagination* (Philadelphia: Fortress Press, 1978), p. 51.

9. Walter Brueggemann, "Covenanting as Human Vocation," *Interpretation: A Journal of Bible and Theology* 33 (1979): 115-29.

10. See Kenneth R. Mitchell and Herbert Anderson, *All Our Losses, All Our Griefs: Resources for Pastoral Care* (Philadelphia: The Westminster Press, 1983).

11. See Joanna Rogers Macy, *Despair and Personal Power in the Nuclear Age* (Philadelphia: New Society Publishing, 1983).

12. Ibid., p. 27.

13. These steps are summarized on page 37 of Macy.

14. See Schaef, *Women's Reality*.

15. See Gay Hendricks and Russell Wills, *The Centering Book: Awareness Activities for Children, Parents, and Teachers* (Englewood Cliffs, N.J.: Prentice-Hall, 1975).

16. See Paul Pruyser, *The Minister as Diagnostician: Personal Problems in Pastoral Perspective* (Philadelphia: Westminster, 1976).

17. I am indebted to Sharon Thornton for the summary of the history of this movement. See Sharon Thornton, "Pastoral Care and the Reality of Suffering: Pastoral Theology from the Perspective of Theology and the Cross" (Ph.D. diss., Graduate Theological Union, 1991).

18. Ibid., p. 10.

19. Ibid., p. 11.

20. Ibid.

21. Ibid., p. 12.

22. Ibid.

23. Ibid., pp. 13-14. See also the back page of *The Network Journal*, a publication of the San Francisco Network Ministries, 942 Market St., No. 612, San Francisco, CA 94102. See especially the February 1990 edition.

24. Thornton, "Pastoral Care and the Reality of Suffering," p. 14.

25. Ibid. A further profile of the San Francisco Network Ministries is found under the title "Image Report," *San Francisco Examiner*, April 1, 1990.

26. Thornton, "Pastoral Care and the Reality of Suffering," p. 14.

27. Ibid.

28. Daniel Day Williams, *The Spirit and the Forms of Love* (New York: Harper & Row, 1968), p. 4.

9. REBUILDING THE COVENANTAL FRAME

1. Jane Carey Peck and Jeanne Gallo, "JPIC: A Critique from a Feminist Perspective," *The Ecumenical Review* 41, no. 4 (October 1989): 574.

2. Perry B. Yoder, *Shalom: The Bible's Word for Salvation, Justice and Peace* (Newton, Kans.: Faith and Life Press, 1987), pp. 29-30.

3. Ibid.

4. S. Dean McBride, Jr., "Polity of the Covenant Peoples: The Book of Deuteronomy," *Interpretation* 41 (1987): 229-44.

5. Peck and Gallo, "JPIC: A Critique," 574.

6. Ibid.

7. Ibid.

8. Walter Brueggemann, "A Shape for Old Testament Theology, II: Embrace of Pain," *Catholic Biblical Quarterly* 47 (1985): 398.

9. See Salvador Minuchin, *Families and Family Therapy* (Cambridge, Mass.: Harvard University Press, 1974).

10. See Alice Miller, *Thou Shalt Not Be Aware: Society's Betrayal of the Child* (New York: Farrar, Straus and Giroux, 1984). Miller writes searingly on these dynamics.

11. See Anne Wilson Schaef, *Women's Reality: An Emerging Female System in White Male Society* (New York: Harper & Row, 1986).

12. Report of the American Psychological Association's Task Force on Women and Depression, reported in *The Denver Post*, December 6, 1990. See also, Hope Landrine, "Depression and Stereotypes of Women: Preliminary Empirical Analyses of the Gender-Role Hypothesis," *Sex Roles* 19, no. 7/8 (October 1, 1988): 7.

13. See James Nelson, *The Intimate Connection: Masculine Spirituality* (Philadelphia: Westminster, 1988).

14. This discussion is based upon Lynn Hoffman, *Foundations of Family Therapy* (New York: Basic Books, 1981).

15. See chapter 4, p. 99.

16. Jay Haley and Lynn Hoffman, *Techniques of Family* (New York: Basic Books, 1967), p. 170.

17. See chapter 4, pp. 194ff, chapter 6, pp. 149-54.

18. Pastors have a moral, if not a legal, obligation to report knowledge of abuse of minors and the intention of homicide or suicide, even if received in confidence. Parishioners should know this at the outset, and congregational policies established to support this approach.

19. Edwin H. Friedman, *Generation to Generation: Family Process in Church and Synagogue* (New York: Guilford Press, 1985), pp. 52-54.

20. See Pamela Couture, "The Context of Congregations: Pastoral Care in an Individualistic Society," *Journal of Pastoral Theology* 2 (1992); paper presented to the Society for Pastoral Theology, Denver, Colorado, June 1991. She details a variety of macrosystemic realities that constitute the "social ecology" of pastoral care in our time. She writes, "This changing context of care is being produced by macroeconomic shifts which are pushing the middle-class upward or downward in the social structure; in addition, these processes are so destabilizing to poor communities that they cannot provide the stable social fabric which supports secure life development and social opportunities for poor young men and women of color. In our poorest communities, joblessness, underground economy, alcoholism, drug abuse, the early death of young men and the early pregnancy of young women have become the norm. While the numbers of the permanently and temporarily poor are increasing, supports for struggling persons, such as welfare, educational loans and grants, medical insurance, low income housing, and subsidized food have diminished."

21. See Evan Imber-Black, *Families and Larger Systems: A Family Therapist's Guide Through the Labyrinth* (New York: Guilford Press, 1988).

22. This case is described in ibid., pp. 36-43.

23. Ibid., p. 39.

24. Ibid., p. 42.

25. Ibid.

26. Ibid., p. 43.

27. The literature on pastoral care of homosexuals is sparse, but beginning to grow. Don Browning has written on this in *Religious Ethics and Pastoral Care* (Philadelphia: Fortress Press, 1983) and Paul Mickey has recently published *Of Sacred Worth* (Nashville: Abingdon Press, 1991). A helpful overview of the ethical options related to homosexuality can be found in James Nelson, *Embodiment: An Approach to Sexuality and Christian Theology* (Minneapolis:

Augsburg, 1978). Virginia Ramey Mollenkott and Letha Scanzoni offer an instructive analysis of homophobia and heterosexism in *Is the Homosexual My Neighbor: Another Christian View* (San Francisco: Harper & Row, 1978).

28. James Nelson identifies four orientations to homosexuality: rejective-punitive, rejecting non-punitive, qualified acceptance, and full acceptance. It is clear that the view that I espouse is full acceptance. That also was the view of the pastoral psychotherapist and his supervisor in this case. The parents' values related to homosexuality conflicted with their pastoral psychotherapist's. They were somewhere between rejecting non-punitive and qualified acceptance. It is clear that all parties were able to harmonize their conflicting values in this case.

10. RESTORATIVE AND LIBERATING CARE

1. John B. Cobb, Jr., "The Political Implications of Whitehead's Philosophy," in *Process Philosophy and Social Thought*, ed. J. B. Cobb, Jr. and W. W. Schroeder (Chicago: Center for the Scientific Study of Religion, 1981), p. 22.

2. The framework for my study of the congregation was a grant by the Lilly Foundation to explore various aspects of congregational care and discipline in contemporary North American church life. This write-up parallels an article prepared for publication under the editorship of K. Brynhof Lyon entitled, "Healing the Congregation: The Dynamics of a Congregation's Process of Recovery from Its Minister's Sexual Boundary Crossing with Parishioners." (In press.) It also appeared in condensed form under the title, "Healing the Congregation," in *Conciliation Quarterly Newsletter* 19, no. 2 (Spring 1991): 2-4, 15.

3. The congregation is disguised, though it has made its identity known in other public settings.

4. It must be stated that I did not interview the former minister or anyone from the Conference office. Anything attributed to them is by hearsay from the interviews I had. I have not written anything concerning the former minister and the Conference that was not independently reported to me by at least two people. Most of what I have shared is regarded as common knowledge by the congregation.

5. It is unclear to this day whether he was asked to resign because of his unethical behavior or whether the resignation he submitted (on the grounds that it was time to move on) was merely accepted by the congregation. The lack of clarity on this point was at the time, and remains today, a source of conflict in the minds of many about whether the congregation did too much or too little to hold him accountable.

6. David Augsburger, *Caring Enough to Forgive: Caring Enough Not to Forgive* (Scottsdale, Pa.: Herald Press, 1981).

7. See Marie M. Fortune, *Sexual Violence: The Unmentionable Sin* (New York: The Pilgrim Press, 1983). Fortune also provided a study paper on the sexual abuse of power by clergy.

8. Christine Hamilton-Pennell, "Pastoral Sexual Abuse: One Congregation's Ordeal." *Daughters of Sarah* (July/August, 1987): 1-4.

9. Speed B. Leas provides some important criteria for discerning when a congregation has resolved the trauma of losing a pastor under conflictual situations. These criteria are useful in my assessment of the congregation in this study, but space does not permit a fuller discussion of them. See Speed B. Leas, *Moving Your Church Through Conflict* (Washington, D.C.: The Alban Institute, 1985).

10. On the relationship of power and shame, see John Patton, *Is Human Forgiveness Possible?: A Pastoral Care Perspective* (Nashville: Abingdon Press, 1985); and R. Randall, *Pastor and Parish: The Psychological Core of Ecclesiastical Conflicts* (New York: Human Science Press, 1988).

11. For a compelling example of the difficulty of assessing proper accountabilities in these cases, see Marie M. Fortune, *Is Nothing Sacred? When Sex Invades the Pastoral Relationship* (New York: Harper & Row, 1989).

12. I did not disclose my own view until the second feedback session in which I was invited by the church to provide interpretation and guidance. At that time, I shared my conviction that the main ethical issue here was that the minister violated the integrity of the pastoral office and abused the unequal power differential between the professional minister and vulnerable

parishioners by inappropriately sexualizing the pastoral relationship without the presence of genuine mutual consent. In my view, which is heavily influenced by Marie Fortune, it was the minister's role to keep such events from occurring, and that he must accept the full responsibility for his behaviors and for setting the subsequent dynamics into motion.

13. Cobb, *Process Philosophy*, p. 22.

Actual entity: The basic energy event or the smallest "droplet of experience" in the universe, according to process philosophy.

Adventure, Principle of: The pastoral recognition that God is present as an ally on the side of transformation and liberative change.

Advocacy, Principle of: Lending the pastoral caretaker's voice, and the voice of the caretaking community, to shaping public policies that promote a positive environment for the careseeker.

Agential power: The dimension of power that influences the world and resists undue influences from the environment.

Beauty: The term in process philosophy for a satisfactory outcome of the creative process. Beauty is characterized by an optimal combination of intensity and harmony of experience. It contrasts with evil, which is viewed as disharmony and triviality of experience.

Bi-polar power: The concept that refers to the ability of any entity simultaneously to be an agent and receptor of influence.

Dissonance: The uneasy state between homeostasis and change within the psychosystemic matrix; a precursor to symptom formation and change within the system.

Collusion: The often hidden or unrecognized collaboration of persons or entities in maintaining symptomatic behaviors.

Concrescense: The term for the coming together of the past and present into something novel which affects the future.

Conscientization, Principle of: The pastoral responsibility to expand awareness of how the careseeker's difficulties derive from one's location in an unjust social order, and to assist with strategic responses to change the injurious social order.

Consciousness: The combination of accountable intentionality and knowledge-able awareness.

Contending values: A concept which delineates how conflict between values is at the heart of reality, requiring decisions about the manner in which power, transactions, contexts, and creativity will be arranged.

Contextual creativity: The pervasive capacity for change which is built into reality, however limited it may be in particular cases. The locus of the appetitive and intentional dimensions of life.

Contextual impairment: A rupture of the boundaries, accountabilities, and dynamic processes which maintain stability in the psychosystemic matrix.

Contextual integrity: The state in which the structures comprising the system are intact and endure in a manner that protects it from internal and external threat.

Contextual organization: The identifiable continuity of the system as a whole, and of each subsystem or entity comprising the system. Also referred to as structural organization, or homeostasis.

Covert: Hidden interchanges between elements within the system.

Culture: The means by which humans collectively receive, synthesize, and transform the influences of their world.

Demonic: The "principalities and powers," or the dominant social and cultural conventions, which distort life by elevating some partial good or truth into a dominant position from which all other goods or truths are evaluated.

Differential organization: The relative degree of power or influence each element and subsystem has in relation to each other in the receiving, synthesizing, and transforming processes of the psychosystemic matrix.

Differentiating accountabilities: Clarifying proper responsibility, and working to make persons and systems more responsive and flexible.

Discounting: Attitudes, messages, and behaviors which keep the needs, aspirations, and perspectives of one person or group in a disadvantaged relation to some other individual or group.

Disordered hierarchies: Inappropriate differentiation of power and influence.

Dominance: Unjust power and value arrangements whereby one or more persons or groups subordinate other persons and groups for the advantage of the dominant group.

Double bind: Being required to respond to two opposite commands, without the ability to acknowledge the contradiction or to avoid the negative consequences of how one responds.

Double standard: Holding one person or group accountable for values or behaviors from which another is exempted.

Ecological partnership: Personal and collective alliances between nature and humans for the purposes of preserving and fulfilling each.

Enculturation: The processes by which humans learn language, sex roles, religious perspectives, and loyalty to race, tribe, and nation.

Ethical egoism: The ethical orientation which measures good and evil in terms of the impact upon the integrity and fulfillment of individual selves. Synonymous with expressive individualism.

Evil: Characterized as the combination of triviality and disharmony. It is the opposite of Beauty, which is the optimal combination of harmony and intensity of experience.

Expressive individualism: Understanding good and evil in terms of the degree to which something enhances or impedes the needs of the self. Synonymous with ethical egoism.

Faith work: Refers to explicit attention to persons' religious beliefs, practices, and experiences; looking at what individuals regard as the spiritual centers of their lives, and how these are thematized in their religious vocabulary, symbol systems, and life-styles.

False self: Designates that the psyche has substituted a partial or distorted synthesis of experience for more complete and congruent syntheses.

Family: The structured ongoing kinship system which consists of two or more persons who by blood, choice, and/or law are bound together in a primary life-long relationship with one another, and with those to whom each is also similarly related.

Harmony: Balance and synergy among elements within a system or subsystem.

Historicism: A broad intellectual movement which seeks to understand individual and collective human experience in terms of its historical function and development.

Humanocentrism: Understanding the natural order primarily as a resource for human welfare.

Individuation: The awareness and ownership of what is actually happening in the consciousness and behaviors of the individuals in a pastoral situation.

Intensity: The process theological concept that refers to intrinsic good, and is experienced as excitement, challenge, and vital stimulation. It is the opposite of triviality.

Interpathy: The intentional cognitive and affective understanding of the thoughts and feelings of persons from other cultures, world views, and epistemologies.

Intrapsychic: The psychological dynamics and processes, both conscious and unconscious, indigenous to human individuals.

Justice: Right relations between persons and the various components of their worlds.

Liberation: Freedom from domination or subordination in individual and collective social life. Liberation refers to the capacity for a combination of agential and receptive power on the part of all elements in the psychosystemic matrix in the building of a loving, just, and ecologically responsible universe.

Liberation theology: A cluster of theological positions which begin their interpretation of religious faith from the perspective of marginalized and oppressed groups of persons. They promote freedom from the injustice of oppression and a transformed social order in which all participants share both the responsibilities and the benefits in a mutually accountable manner.

Love: Divine and human activity which seeks to restore that which is estranged to new harmony and cooperation and to promote communion of selfhood among free and equal partners. It also refers to the generous embodied giving and receiving by God and persons on behalf of the welfare of individuals and the larger social communities comprising them.

Nature: All entities making up the universe which are capable of endurance, generativity, and change apart from human influence.

Network: The activity of linking elements within the system into constructive coalitions of mutual partnerships.

Ontological: Pertaining to the basic elements of reality; the categories or principles which are necessary for anything to have reality, or being.

Oppression: The unjust domination of one individual or group by another individual or group in the social, economic, political, cultural, racial, and gender dimensions of life.

Organicity, Principle of: Delineates the pastoral task of assisting symptomatic persons to discern and respond to the patterns of interconnectedness accounting for their difficulties.

Overt: Hidden or unacknowledged activity between elements in a system or subsystem.

Parallel process: The term used to describe the phenomenon which occurs when either symptomatic or beneficial patterns in one subsystem appear in another subsystem to which one is emotionally connected. Sometimes used interchangeably with the terms transference and countertransference and isomorphic process.

Participation: Indicates strategic relatedness to a system or subsystem. It involves conscientization as well as a variety of activities such as boundary setting, alliance building, and rule changing.

Pastoral theology: A branch of theology which develops theoretical understandings of and practical guidelines for the ministry of care. It attempts conceptually to relate specific acts of pastoral caretaking to selected aspects of the religious heritage in which the caretaking occurs and to relevant secular theories about the nature and care of persons.

Person: The term for the unique human individual who emerges as a synthesizing and creating center of experience which reflects and at least partially reshapes the other systems in which he or she is embedded. Synonymous with self.

Power: The capacity to influence and to be influenced by the environment.

Privatism: Characterized by focused interest upon the intrapsychic and interpersonal dynamics of persons apart from attention to the larger public social order.

Process theology: The theological vision derived from the process philosophy of Alfred North Whitehead and Charles Hartshorne. It emphasizes that all reality, including God's, is characterized by dynamic relationality and novel emergence rather than as fixed and static substances.

Projective bonding: More commonly known as projective identification, it refers to the largely unconscious identification with a power center outside oneself. This identification has an ongoing, usually hidden, influence upon one's attitudes, belief systems, feelings, and behaviors.

Psyche/soul: The activity by which human individuals synthesize and create experience, and the outcome of the process of this synthesis and creation.

Psychosystemic matrix: The totality of the network of actual entities, persons, families, societies, cultures, nature, and God as these are contextually organized consciously and unconsciously by contending values, bi-polar power arrangements, reciprocal transactions, and creative potentialities.

Psychosystemic: The reciprocal interplay between the psyche of individuals and the social, cultural, and natural order.

Receptive power: The capacity to be influenced by the environment. It is the polar opposite of agential power.

Reciprocal transactions: The conceptual element in psychosystemic theory which accounts for the exchange of influence between the elements in a system or subsystem.

Reframing: The activity of changing the meaning of events by modifying the emotional and/or conceptual framework through which they are interpreted.

Religious ministry: The totality of strategic activities engaged in by the religious community and its individual members to increase the love of self, God, and neighbor, and to promote a just social order and a livable environment.

Runaway system: A cybernetic term used in family systems to indicate that the normal processes of maintaining order and regulating communication are no longer intact and that the system is out of control.

Scapegoat: Identifying one person or group as the agent(s) responsible for what is wrong in a system, and responding to them according to what is deemed an appropriate negative consequence.

Self: The qualitative and unique expression of the psyche which emerges from reciprocal transactional processes within individuals and between individuals and their environments.

Shalom: The religious reality from the biblical and theological heritage which joins love and justice for the sake of greater community and harmony.

Simultaneity, Principle of: The pastoral guideline by which change is promoted by recognizing and strategically responding to the intersystemic consequences of and resistances to efforts to assist persons in crisis.

Strategic love, God's: The divine activity by which God selects the most positive option to assist in the next moment of becoming for each entity in the universe.

Symptom: An escalating condition of dissonance and disharmony at one or more points in the system which indicates the need for a strategic response by which the system may be maintained or advanced.

Synaptic: The ongoing interplay between elements in the psychosystemic matrix characterized by mutual reception, rejection, struggle, and creative accomplishment.

Synchronicity: The harmonious coming together of contending values to create new patterns of positive experience.

Synergistic power arrangements: The configuration of bi-polar power in such a manner that agency and receptivity are blended to promote mutual partnerships rather than hierarchies of domination and subordination.

Synergy: Refers to a non-coercive and non-exploitive positive interplay between the entities making up the system. It is marked by cooperation, creativity, and novel accomplishment.

Systems thought (systemic): A manner of interpreting reality which emphasizes togetherness, ongoing processes and transactions, and cooperation and reciprocal influence rather than autonomy and separateness.

Transactional effectiveness: The quality of the reciprocal transactions which exist when any entity or system is stimulating and creative.

Transactional impasse: The state of being which occurs when systems are impervious to change or when contexts resist creative potentialities.

Transformation: The emergence of dramatic new patterns of relatedness, value, and structural organization within the system.

Transgenerational family dynamics: The cross-generational persistence of overt or covert influences which define family limits, channel family energies, and shape family destiny over time.

Triangle: A stabilizing arrangement which reduces tension and moderates the exchange of power and contending values between two persons, or two subsystems, by involving a third person or subsystem.

Triviality: An occasion or entity being less than it could otherwise be; characterized by boredom, underdevelopment, and inertia. It is the opposite of intensity, and a form of evil in process theology.

True self: The state of being which occurs when the synthesis of experience comprising individual personhood is comprehensive and congruent with the energies, values, and creative potentials of the psyche.

Unbalancing: The pastoral strategy of upsetting a given homeostatic balance in order to create more positive patterns of relationship.

Victimizing: The power arrangement whereby one individual or group stands primarily as a dominant agent over another. The victimized individual or group is in a power relationship of nearly exclusive receptivity vis-à-vis the agent, without genuine consent or the present capacity to change his or her subordinated status.

Index